# RACETRACK BETTING:
# THE PROFESSORS' GUIDE
# TO STRATEGIES

# RACETRACK BETTING: THE PROFESSORS' GUIDE TO STRATEGIES

PETER ASCH
*Rutgers University*

RICHARD E. QUANDT
*Princeton University*

New York
Westport, Connecticut
London

**Library of Congress Cataloging-in-Publication Data**

Asch, Peter.
   Racetrack betting : the professors' guide to strategies / Peter
Asch and Richard E. Quandt.—Paperback ed.
      p.   cm.
   Reprint. Originally published: Dover, Mass. : Auburn House, c1986.
   Includes bibliographical references and index.
   ISBN 0-275-94103-5 (pbk. : alk. paper)
   1. Horse race betting.   I. Quandt, Richard E.   II. Title.
[SF331.A73   1991]
   798.401—dc20        91-13947

British Library Cataloguing in Publication Data is available.

A hardcover edition of *Racetrack Betting* is available from the
Auburn House imprint of Greenwood Publishing Group, Inc.
(ISBN 0-86569-147-9).

Library of Congress Catalog Card Number: 91-13947
ISBN: 0-275-94103-5

First published in 1986
Paperback edition 1991

Praeger Publishers, One Madison Avenue, New York, NY 10010
An imprint of Greenwood Publishing Group, Inc.

Printed in the United States of America

The paper used in this book complies with the
Permanent Paper Standard issued by the National
Information Standards Organization (Z39.48-1984).

10 9 8 7 6 5 4 3 2 1

*To our wives and sons*

# PREFACE

We are going to tell you how to bet at the racetrack. This book is in part the outgrowth of some serious academic research conducted during the late 1970s and early 1980s. People are sometimes surprised to hear that "real" academics would spend time on such things. There is, however, a fairly substantial literature in economics (our field), statistics, and even psychology that deals with the behavior of gambling markets.

Many "how to bet" books, pamphlets, and even computer programs have been written over the years. A few of them are very well done— indeed, they are extremely clever; many are mediocre; a few are considerably worse. Our effort is different from most in two ways. First, we do not offer you any simple or sure-fire ways to make money. The reason is that such methods do not exist. Anyone who says (or even hints) that they do shouldn't be trusted.

The second way in which this book differs from most of the existing literature is in its scope. Our intention is not simply to present you with winning formulas for betting but to show you how the "market" in horse race bets functions, and how relevant market data can be analyzed (as you will see, racetrack betting has important similarities to stock markets and other financial arenas). Why do this? As educators, the answer is that we believe in the old cliche, knowledge is power. The great success stories in virtually every area of human endeavor—from medical research to gambling—have not been written by people applying magic formulas given to them by others; rather, these stories are written by people who understand the basic principles that govern the problems they are addressing.

In examining these principles, we discuss a good deal of academic research on racetrack betting, including our own. We regard this as useful—essential, in fact. It does raise a problem, however. Some of the most relevant research is pretty complicated; writing and reading about it can be tough going, and the use of some mathematical and statistical concepts cannot really be avoided. We have tried to simplify things up to a point — the point beyond which further simplification would hide important parts of the story from you. Should you feel at some places that things are getting too involved, we provide an alternative: Chapters 2 through 7 contain preambles that convey the gist of what we have been saying in purely nontechnical language.

We encourage you to read through the full presentations, which can be done a piece at a time; at least skim what we're saying. If you are really averse to technical material, much of it can be skipped. This will not seriously hamper your ability to apply the basic principles and methods we discuss. It may well, however, prove a hindrance to those of you who wish to get down to work and develop your own racetrack betting methods. To do this successfully is hard, and the job doesn't really permit shortcuts.

In writing this book, we have been helped by a number of people who have offered us highly competent assistance as well as advice and encouragement but who bear no responsibility for the final product. They include David Asch, Rita Z. Asch, Barbara M. Grindle, Elvira Krespach, Denise J. Kronyak, Laurie A. McGinnis, and William T. Ziemba (sometimes known as "Dr. Z"). We owe a special debt to our friend and colleague, Burton G. Malkiel, a gentleman, a scholar, and a keen judge of both horses and risk taking.

Finally, we are grateful to the Alfred P. Sloan Foundation and to the Rutgers Bureau of Economic Research for financial support of some of the research that underlies this book.

Peter Asch
Richard E. Quandt

# CONTENTS

*Chapter 1*

# An Introduction: Horse Racing and the Betting Scene

## What We're Doing

As in many other countries, betting on horse races has long been a popular activity in the United States. To our way of thinking, this is easy to understand. A day or evening at the track is great fun—in fact, a sheer delight. It is, first of all, a colorful and varied scene. At our favorite New Jersey retreat, Monmouth Park, the grounds are spacious, green, and well kept. The horses are in most instances truly magnificent animals, and the riders (jockeys) are exceptional athletes.

The typical racetrack crowd is also interesting. You will rub elbows with janitors, production workers, stockbrokers, artists, musicians, students, physicians, and on occasion, the dean of a prestigious school of management. Within the confines of the track, however, your station in life doesn't carry any weight. All that matters is your ability to pick the winner of the next race, and in this task everyone starts out—in a sense—with the same chance. A democratic place indeed! (Many of us like to think of the United States as a classless, or at least a mobile, society; but how often do accountants, garbage collectors, and pianists gather in common endeavor?)

As college professors, we find a day at the races to be a complete change of pace. The atmosphere is utterly different from that of the classrooms, libraries, and computer centers where we spend most of our working lives. A visit to Monmouth Park or the Meadowlands is a real, if brief, holiday for us, and quite obviously for many others as well.

When you add to this the intellectual challenge of trying to predict which of several large animals is going to run fastest around a prescribed course, the excitement of a wager on that event, and the

1

bragging rights that are acquired if one's predictions prove out, the attraction is strong indeed! Like most good things, however, visits to racetracks are costly, and the costs are potentially large ones.

In this book, we will show you how to keep these costs down (you could, of course, stay home or go to the track and not bet, but then you would miss all the fun as well!). We do not promise to make you a winner. Horse race betting, as we shall see, is a hard game to beat; and anyone who promises riches must be suspected of being a charlatan or a fool or both. But we will give you the best possible shot at winning, based on the latest scientific evidence.

In the process, we also will show you a number of things you should know about examining and analyzing data (and data are truly abundant in horse racing). If you are willing to put up with a little bit of mathematical notation and a few statistical concepts, you actually will learn some of the most basic and important measurement techniques in the social sciences. Finally, we shall try to demonstrate some interesting characteristics about the economics of human behavior under conditions of risk—which is to say, something about the way we all anticipate and react to the vicissitudes of life.

## Fundamental and Technical Analysis

The terms "fundamental" and "technical analysis" are borrowed from the stock market and can be applied quite directly to racetrack betting. A fundamental analyst, in Wall Street jargon, is someone who studies the real underlying factors that are likely to determine the future success or failure of prospective investments—for example, the quality of a company's management, the growth potential of its major markets, and the abilities of its corporate rivals. The purpose of such study is to determine whether the company in question is a "good" investment.

In contrast, the technical analyst (sometimes known as a "chartist") tends to ignore the fundamentals, focusing instead on the behavior of the prices of prospective investments. The technician does not necessarily claim that fundamentals don't matter. Rather, the argument goes, one need not study the fundamentals, because they tend already to be reflected in the prices of the investment possibilities. In other words, information about the investment prospects can be gleaned simply from studying the recent history of their market prices; and certain patterns of price behavior point to propitious investments.

The analogy with horse racing is reasonably close, if not precise.

Certain fundamental factors, such as the speed and condition of rival horses, determine their winning probabilities. The study of such factors may therefore reveal which horse is most likely to win a particular race; this analysis in turn may suggest which is a "good" bet.

Technical analysis of horse racing, in contrast, focuses on the "price" — that is, the betting odds — of the various horses. Is a particular horse a very fast runner? "Fine," the technician will say, "this information no doubt has been recognized by bettors, and is already 'in' this horse's price in the form of relatively low betting odds on the animal." As in the stock market case, certain movements in odds (prices) may suggest a "good" bet.

In the chapters that follow, we will describe the kinds of fundamental analysis of horse racing that have been suggested by writers on the subject and show you how to approach this task if it appeals to you. The truth is, however, it is possible to be a relatively successful racetrack gambler without knowing a great deal about horses or racing. (Not terribly surprising when you consider that after all, you may be a very good driver without understanding the internal combustion engine or a competent user of standard computer programs without really knowing how computers work.) In fact, ultimately we will argue that the most effective verifiable betting strategies do not require a great deal of expertise about the horses themselves.

Studying the fundamental characteristics of horses, however, has major virtues, and we recommend it, at least up to some point. In the first place, it may at times give you some useful — that is, profitable — insights. Technical betting strategies need not rule out all conceivable judgments based on fundamentals. Second, analyzing the horses and races is a significant part of the fun of the track. Take away the fun, and you might as well throw your money into other forms of legally sanctioned gambling: casino games in Nevada or Atlantic City; stock, bond, and commodity markets; or (heaven forbid!) state lotteries, which offer some of the poorest bets yet devised by humankind.

## Some Basics

As in virtually any field of study, one must start by defining key terms — if you are a veteran of the racing wars, you may want to skip to the next section or chapter. We provide a glossary at the end of the book for easy reference, but here are a few things that you absolutely must know right now.

**Table 1-1    Approximate Payoffs to Successful Win Bets of Various Sizes
at Various Odds**

| | Size of Bet | | | | |
| --- | --- | --- | --- | --- | --- |
| Odds | $2.00 | $5.00 | $10.00 | $20.00 | $50.00 |
| 1–2 | $ 3.00 | $ 7.50 | $ 15 | $ 30 | $ 75 |
| 3–5 | $ 3.20 | $ 8.00 | $ 16 | $ 32 | $ 80 |
| 4–5 | $ 3.60 | $ 9.00 | $ 18 | $ 36 | $ 90 |
| 1–1 | $ 4.00 | $ 10.00 | $ 20 | $ 40 | $ 100 |
| 6–5 | $ 4.40 | $ 11.00 | $ 22 | $ 44 | $ 110 |
| 7–5 | $ 4.80 | $ 12.00 | $ 24 | $ 48 | $ 120 |
| 3–2 | $ 5.00 | $ 12.50 | $ 25 | $ 50 | $ 125 |
| 8–5 | $ 5.20 | $ 13.00 | $ 26 | $ 52 | $ 130 |
| 9–5 | $ 5.60 | $ 14.00 | $ 28 | $ 56 | $ 140 |
| 2–1 | $ 6 | $ 15.00 | $ 30 | $ 60 | $ 150 |
| 5–2 | $ 7 | $ 17.50 | $ 35 | $ 70 | $ 175 |
| 3–1 | $ 8 | $ 20.00 | $ 40 | $ 80 | $ 200 |
| 7–2 | $ 9 | $ 22.50 | $ 45 | $ 90 | $ 225 |
| 4–1 | $ 10 | $ 25.00 | $ 50 | $ 100 | $ 250 |
| 9–2 | $ 11 | $ 27.50 | $ 55 | $ 110 | $ 275 |
| 5–1 | $ 12 | $ 30 | $ 60 | $ 120 | $ 300 |
| 6–1 | $ 14 | $ 35 | $ 70 | $ 140 | $ 350 |
| 7–1 | $ 16 | $ 40 | $ 80 | $ 160 | $ 400 |
| 8–1 | $ 18 | $ 45 | $ 90 | $ 180 | $ 450 |
| 9–1 | $ 20 | $ 50 | $100 | $ 200 | $ 500 |
| 10–1 | $ 22 | $ 55 | $110 | $ 220 | $ 550 |
| 11–1 | $ 24 | $ 60 | $120 | $ 240 | $ 600 |
| 12–1 | $ 26 | $ 65 | $130 | $ 260 | $ 650 |
| 13–1 | $ 28 | $ 70 | $140 | $ 280 | $ 700 |
| 14–1 | $ 30 | $ 75 | $150 | $ 300 | $ 750 |
| 15–1 | $ 32 | $ 80 | $160 | $ 320 | $ 800 |
| 16–1 | $ 34 | $ 85 | $170 | $ 340 | $ 850 |
| 17–1 | $ 36 | $ 90 | $180 | $ 360 | $ 900 |
| 18–1 | $ 38 | $ 95 | $190 | $ 380 | $ 950 |
| 19–1 | $ 40 | $100 | $200 | $ 400 | $1000 |
| 20–1 | $ 42 | $105 | $210 | $ 420 | $1050 |
| 21–1 | $ 44 | $110 | $220 | $ 440 | $1100 |
| 22–1 | $ 46 | $115 | $230 | $ 460 | $1150 |
| 23–1 | $ 48 | $120 | $240 | $ 480 | $1200 |
| 24–1 | $ 50 | $125 | $250 | $ 500 | $1250 |
| 25–1 | $ 52 | $130 | $260 | $ 520 | $1300 |
| 30–1 | $ 62 | $155 | $310 | $ 620 | $1550 |
| 35–1 | $ 72 | $180 | $360 | $ 720 | $1800 |
| 40–1 | $ 82 | $205 | $410 | $ 820 | $2050 |
| 45–1 | $ 92 | $230 | $460 | $ 920 | $2300 |
| 50–1 | $102 | $255 | $510 | $1020 | $2550 |

*Note:* Payoffs assume "dime breakage"—the track rounds payoffs downward to the nearest 10¢
per dollar bet (20¢ on a $2 bet). This is now the common practice at U.S. racetracks. Under
"nickel breakage," as practiced at Canadian tracks, payoffs are somewhat higher.

## Betting Odds

As we have said, betting odds are, in effect, the prices of the horses running in a race. The odds tell you how much you will be paid if you bet on a particular horse to win a race and that horse does win. For example, say the odds on Fast Runner are 3 to 1 (usually shown simply as "3" on the racetrack displays, known as "toteboards"). This means that every dollar you bet on Fast Runner will return you $3 (in addition to the $1 you bet in the first place) if he wins the race. A $2 bet on a first-place winning horse will give you a payoff of $8: the $6 return indicated by the 3 to 1 odds, plus your initial $2 "investment." Table 1–1 shows the approximate payoffs to bets of various sizes at various odds. Just one word of caution at this point. The racetrack offers a wide variety of bets, which we are about to describe. But the odds are usually displayed for only one type: win bets. If you engage in other types of wagering, your prospective payoff will not always be so clear — in fact, it will at times prove quite difficult to estimate.

## Types of Bets

Betting on a race is an easy thing to do. You simply walk up to the window and say, "Two dollars to win on number four." However, there are various types of bets to choose from, and deciding which is right for you may not be so easy.

*Win-Place-Show Bets.*   These are the oldest, and undoubtedly the best-known, racetrack bets. A *win bet* is just what it sounds like. You bet that a particular horse will win a particular race; if it does, you receive a payoff; if not, you get nothing. Actually, that is not precisely true: You still have your ticket (which you would have to present for the payoff, had your horse won), and these make excellent bookmarks.

A *place bet* pays off if your horse finishes first or second; otherwise it does not pay off. Whether the horse is first *or* second does not affect the size of your payoff. The good news about this type of bet is obvious: It pays off more frequently than does a win bet (this is because your horse — indeed, any horse — has a better chance of finishing first or second than of finishing first!). The bad news is that the payoffs to place bets tend to be lower. The reason is again obvious: The sum total bet on all horses to place (called the *place pool*) must be shared by backers of the first two finishers, not merely the backers of the first horse. The more people you share with, the less you yourself receive.

Note, however, that your contingent payoff on a place bet — the amount you will collect *if* your horse runs first or second — cannot be precisely inferred from the odds on your horse. There are two reasons why not. First, the payoffs to place bets depend solely on patterns of betting *in the place pool*. These patterns may or may not approximate closely the odds on win bets, which is what the track displays on its "toteboards."[1] The second reason why the place payoff is unpredictable is that it depends on the amounts bet both on your horse *and on the other top finisher*. It therefore matters which horse "comes in" with yours; but this is something that cannot be known until the race is over. How the place pool is divided among bettors on the first two horses is clearly a matter of interest and importance, but we shall defer the precise arithmetic to Chapter 6. Suffice it to say for the moment that you are best off sharing the pool with as few others as possible.

A *show bet* is similar to a place bet, but it covers the first *three* finishers. You get a payoff if your horse comes in first, second, or third; otherwise you get nothing. The order of finish within the top three doesn't affect the payoff. As a rule, you will collect more frequent payoffs betting to show than to win or place, but not surprisingly, they will usually be smaller. There is also somewhat more uncertainty about the size of these payoffs: Racetracks do not display show odds, and your prospective payoff now depends on *two* other finishers whose identity is unknown until the race is over. We again defer the arithmetic of show-pool division to Chapter 6.

You will sometimes hear references to *combination* or *across-the-board* bets. These refer to a bet on a particular horse to win, place, and show, with equal sums on each possibility. Thus, a "$6 combination on number seven" is a bet of $2 to win, $2 to place, and $2 to show on horse number seven.

The payoffs in a race are typically reported in the following form:

| Horse | Win | Place | Show |
|-------|-----|-------|------|
| Gallant Dan | 8.80 | 5.20 | 3.60 |
| Proud Rebel | | 9.20 | 5.00 |
| Enmity | | | 2.80 |

Let's translate. Gallant Dan won this race and paid $8.80 to a $2 win ticket — payoffs are always stated in terms of a $2 bet, the minimum that the tracks permit. A $2 place ticket on Gallant Dan would retrieve $5.20, and a show ticket, $3.60 (it is not logically impossible for a horse to pay more to show than to place, or more to place than to win, since each payoff depends on the pattern of betting in a completely separate pool; you will observe the first of these events occasionally, but the second is exceedingly rare). Proud Rebel, the second-place finisher, paid $9.20 to place and $5.00 to show; and the number three finisher, Enmity, paid $2.80 to show. Notice, as we pointed out, that the order of finish does not determine the size of the payoff within the top group; the payoffs depend solely on how much money has been bet on each of the horses in the pertinent betting pool.

*Exotic Bets.* These refer to a variety of "compound" bets on two or more horses. The exotics are low-probability wagers—you are relatively unlikely to win them, but if you do, the payoffs can be hefty.[2] The most common, not all of which are offered at all tracks, include the following:

- *Exacta* (sometimes called "perfecta"). You select the number one and number two finishers in a given race, specifying the order. If your horses finish 1-2 in the specified order, you win; otherwise you lose. Should the animals you pick 1-2 finish 2-1, that's a loser and a heartbreaker; exacta players frequently bet a pair both ways. They are also prone to "wheel" a horse. Wheeling means that you couple your horse in a series of exacta bets with all other entrants— if, for example, you are convinced that Old Ben is going to run away from the field in today's race, you buy exacta tickets that pick Old Ben number one, and *each rival horse* number two on one of your tickets. Wheels obviously can become quite expensive, especially if you wheel "both ways"—in our example, adding to the tickets above a second set in which Old Ben is picked to run second, and each rival is picked first in turn.
- *Quinella.* You select the first two finishers in a race. The bet is won if the horses you pick are the first two, *regardless of the order.* Any other result, and you lose your bet.
- *Trifecta.* This is like the exacta, but you select the first *three* finishers *in order.* You win if, and only if, the horses you pick 1-2-3 come in 1-2-3. You may of course wheel here as well, but this can run into truly big money. Quite obviously, the trifecta is a low-probability (or long-odds) bet in most instances, and the payoffs, accordingly, can be extremely large.
- *Daily Double.* This is a bet in which you pick the winners of two consecutive races. You win your bet if both picks come in first; otherwise you lose. The daily double is very similar to what is known as a *parlay*—that is, betting on a horse in the first race, and, *if you win*, betting your entire *payoff* on a horse in the next race. Traditionally, the tracks offer daily double bets on the first two

races of the day. This type of betting is now so popular, however, that you may also be offered a "late double" involving two consecutive races toward the end of the day.

- *Big Q.* This is, in effect, a parlay of two quinellas in consecutive races. You pick the first two finishers, regardless of order, in the first race; if you win, your winning ticket entitles you to a similar choice (rather than a cash payoff) in the second race.
- *Pick Four* (or Pick Six, etc.). These bets (sometimes called Super Four, etc.) are structurally like the daily double except that you must pick winners in four (or six) consecutive races. Your chances of winning such bets are slim, but the payoff if you do hit it is likely to be mighty fine.

You will encounter other kinds of exotic betting at some racetracks, but all are variations on the same theme. In each instance, you must pick two or more horses to finish in specified positions (with some flexibility only in the quinella). In an actuarial sense, the exotics are poorer bets than "straight" win, place, or show; this is because most states allow the tracks to take a larger share out of exotic betting pools, thereby lowering the expected dollar value of your bets. But if you like to gamble on improbable, but big, prizes — as many people do — this is where the action is. Beware, however. Numerous agonies are likely to accompany your occasional jackpots.

## At the Racetrack: The Available Information

Once you arrive at the track and pay your admission fee, you should purchase two items: a track program and the *Daily Racing Form.* Your total expenditure prior to the start of the races is now about $5 plus transportation. (Of course, you may choose to spend some money during the course of the day on such delicacies as the track's hotdogs, pizza, and beer — all of which are consumed by some patrons in remarkable quantities. Strictly speaking, these items should be counted in the costs of your racing day.) If you are truly frugal — that is, cheap! — you could do without the program and *Racing Form*, but they will enhance your enjoyment (just like the hotdogs and beer), and perhaps improve your winning chances (unlike the hotdogs and beer), at a very low cost.

### The Program

A sample program page from the Meadowlands Racetrack is reproduced in Figure 1–1. All track programs look much the same. At the top of the page are various bits of information about the race, in this instance the fourth of the day. There is trifecta wagering on this race should you be interested. The name of the race is the Brick Kiwanis Memorial. This information is of no conceivable use to your betting strategy, but remember, you are here to enjoy the atmosphere as well. You may well object that the Brick Kiwanis Memorial is not very atmospheric, unless perhaps one is a Brick Kiwanian. Right you are! On occasion, however, you will encounter some genuinely amusing race titles—for example, the Englebert Humperdinck Claiming Race, which we viewed with delight at Monmouth Park a number of years ago.

The race in Figure 1–1 is a 6-furlong race (a *furlong* = ⅛ mile) for *maidens*—that is, horses who have never before won a race. *Maiden races* usually involve young horses (in this race they are 2-year-olds), often with little racing experience. One of the things this means is that relatively little data about these horses will be available—they do not have extensive track records. The race is for New Jersey Breds (a matter of not much significance to you as a bettor), and the specified weight to be carried by the entrants is 118 pounds (more on this shortly).

The *purse* in this race, or the sum of money that will be paid to the owners of the top finishers, is $8,750 (ordinarily the purse is shared, in unequal proportions, by the first four). Whereas this bit of information is not very useful taken alone, it does say something about the "class" or quality of the horses running; as a rule, higher-priced races attract better entrants. One may, therefore, use the "price" of a race to determine, very roughly, whether any of the horses are moving "up" or "down" in class—that is, running in "faster" or "slower" company than they have in previous races. Quite obviously, this *is* a potentially useful type of information.

Notice that this is a *claiming race*. This means that every horse running is offered for sale. Each may be bought, or claimed, by a trainer prior to the race, at the stipulated price. In this case the claiming price is $16,000. (The offer to buy must be entered prior to the race; the actual claim and exchange of title occurs afterward.)

Look now at all ten of the listed horses. Each horse has a number next to its name; for example, Happy Hoot is number 8. This is actually very useful information: When you go up to the betting window, you must give the number of the horse you want to bet on—the name of the animal will get you nowhere! These numbers also are displayed on the flanks of the horses, which makes it easier to follow the fortunes of your "investment" as the race progresses.

The *owner and trainer* of each horse are listed. The latter could be a

# TRIFECTA WAGERING THIS RACE

**6 FURLONGS**

**4**

| WIN | PLACE | SHOW |
|-----|-------|------|
| | | |

TRIFECTA

**MAIDEN/CLAIMING
PURSE $8,750**

## BRICK KIWANIS MEMORIAL

(Purse Reflects $1,750 New Jersey Bred Enchancement)
MAIDENS, TWO YEARS OLD, Registered New Jersey Breds, 118 lbs. Claiming Price $16,000

TRACK RECORD-1:08 2-5 FOG a BALLA, 117 lbs., 9-6-83; EILLO, 114 lbs., 9-27-83

### MAKE SELECTION BY NUMBER

| | OWNER | TRAINER | Jockey/Morn.Line |
|---|---|---|---|

**1**
JOHN PATITUCCI — OWNER
Red, Gold Sash, Red Bars on White Sleeves, Red Cap
**REGAL JEWELS** ☉ **118**
Ch.c.'82, Regal Rout-Stolen Jewels-Vertex
**15** JUAN MONTENEZ

**2**
LORRAINE & CINDY STABLE — R. McELIHINEY
Black, Yellow Cross and "LC", Yellow Band on Sleeves, Yellow Cap
**SPINDIE** ☉ **118**
Dk.b. or br.c.'82, Wig Out-Sharp Cindy-Sharp Vote
**10** RAPHAEL ESTRELLA

**3**
DAL CON STABLE — J. ROSEN
Green, White Triangle, Green Cap
**DAL CON'S BOY** ☉ **118**
Ch.c.'82, Miteas Well Laff-Di Ed's de Lite-Czar Alexander
**4** JOSEPH ROCCO

**4**
JAMES W. SCHOEPFLIN — S. SCHOEPFLIN
Red and White Hoops, Red "JWS", Red and White Stripes on Sleeves, Red Cap
**PONTOREUS** ☉ **118**
B.c.'82, Pontifex-Aureaus-North Flight
**6** MIKE A. GONZALEZ

**5**
FRED ELLER — R. ALABRUDZINSKI
Black, Red Circled "E", Black Cap
**COLOR ME TEA** ☉ **118**
Ch.g.'82, Tea Tray-Herby Costa-Hansom Harve
**7-2** NICK BOLLENTINO

**6**
S.P.S. STABLE — CHARLES CARLESEMO, JR.
Yellow, Blue "M", Blue Sleeves, Yellow Cap
**SUBSIDIZED** ☉ **118**
B.c.'82, Capital Idea-Super Courier-Diplomat Way
**20** MIKE GOMEZ

**7**
FRANK SALVO — H. HINE
Gold, Black Collar, Gold Band on Black Sleeves, Black Cap
**ENTREPEAU** ☉ **118**
B.c.'82, Miteas Well Laff-Melody in Bay-Tom's Music
**10** HERBERT MCCAULEY

**8**
IDYLL ACRES FARM — D. HEIMER
Red, White Panel, White Stripes on Sleeves, Red Cap
**HAPPY HOOT** ☉ ***113**
B.c.'82, Over Arranged-Whodee Hoot-David 2nd
**8** BRANDON SIMPSON

**9**
BRIARDALE STABLE — J. IMBESI
White, Red "B" on Green Cross Sashes, Red Sleeves, Red and Green Cap
**DEVILISH MAJOR** ☉ **118**
Ch.c.'82, Ad Majora-Devilish Angel-Maribeau
**5-2** INOCENCIO AYARZA

**10**
SONS OF VAL STABLE — C.L. DICKEY
Black, Black "V" on Red Ball, Black Blocks on Red Sleeves, Black Cap
**DROP THE CHARGES** ☉ ****111**
B.g.'82, No Robbery-Malic Toward None-Malicious
**20** KEN BLACKSTUN

Change of Equipment—SUBSIDIZE, Blinkers Off.
Scratched—HI IDEAL.

## Selections: 9-5-3-4

**NOTE:** ALL WINNING TICKETS ARE REDEEMABLE FOR SIX (6) MONTHS FROM DATE OF ISSUE.

**Figure 1-1   A Sample Track Program Page.**
*(Source: Meadowlands Race Track Program, New Jersey Sports and Exposition Authority. Reprinted by permission.)*

useful item to know. Elsewhere in the program you will find a list of leading trainers for the current meet (racing session). You can thus determine whether a horse you are considering backing has been prepared by someone who is enjoying much current success. Bear in mind, however, that every other track patron can make this determination as well.

*Weight carried* is listed next to each horse. Notice that Happy Hoot carries 113 pounds, five less than most other entrants (and five less than specified at the top of the program page). This refers to the weight of the jockey plus whatever additional weight is added according to the rules of the race and/or the judgment of the track handicapper. As you may surmise, jockeys are necessarily small, thin people—whether by natural endowment, strenuous dieting, or some combination thereof. Enjoyment of food has led some talented riders to seek other occupations.

Weights are frequently assigned so that, in principle, all horses will have similar winning probabilities—the weaker animals are aided by carrying less weight, the stronger are literally handicapped by carrying more. The asterisk (*) next to the number indicates that Happy Hoot is receiving what's called an *apprentice allowance*. His jockey is inexperienced (an apprentice), and this presumed *disadvantage* is being compensated for by a weight "break."

The *jockey* for each horse is shown at the right of the program. Brandon Simpson, our apprentice, is riding Happy Hoot. This may or may not be useful information, depending on whether you know or can find out anything about the riding abilities of Brandon or the other jocks. You can check the leading riders of the current meet, listed elsewhere in the program. Perhaps Brandon, despite his inexperience, is a "hot" rider. If he is, however, the crowd may well back Happy Hoot strongly, thus *depressing* his betting odds and the payoff should he win.[3] Here we have an example of a basic paradox in horse racing: Apparent good news about a horse, if the crowd sees it, can be bad news for a bet on that horse. It is therefore hard to know whether the good news is, on balance, good—a problem we will have more to say about.

The *morning line odds* (or simply the *morning line*) are shown for each horse at the extreme right of the program, just after the jockey's name. These are the "starting" odds that you and other track patrons see before the betting on a race begins. These odds will be displayed on various toteboards, and perhaps on tv screens, around the track. The morning line represents the best guess of the track's expert (sometimes called a "handicapper") about the horses' relative chances of winning. The morning line on Happy Hoot is 8—that is, 8 to 1. The expert is stating that this animal has only a one in nine chance to win the race—better than some (Drop the Charges is the morning line longshot at 20 to 1), but not as good as others (Devilish Major, at 5 to 2, is the morning line favorite; the expert believes he has the best chance to win in this group of entrants).

A couple of salient points about the morning line odds are worth bearing in mind. First, these odds simply represent the racetrack handicapper's best guess about the winning probabilities of the entrants. As we shall see below, these estimates do contain real information, but only one piece among many. One cannot make money using these data alone. Second, the morning line odds do *not* tell you how much you actually will win by making a successful bet on any horse. Once the betting begins, it is the pattern of the bets that determines the actual odds, which the track will display conveniently at various locations, with updates every 60 to 90 seconds. The payoffs to winning bets are determined by the *final odds*, when the betting ends and the race begins. (Typically, the betting period lasts 20 to 25 minutes.)

Consider an example. Let's suppose that Happy Hoot, who is 8 to 1 in the morning line, is not favored by the betting crowd. Few track patrons believe that he has a real chance to win, and by the time the betting ends, his odds are 22 to 1. This means, in effect, that the "market's" opinion of the horse is a good deal worse than that of the track handicapper. It also means that if you bet $2 on Happy Hoot to win, and he *does* win, your payoff will be quite healthy—roughly $46 (the $44 suggested by the 22 to 1 odds plus the refund of your original $2 investment). We say "roughly" because the reported odds are rounded; the true odds are unlikely to be precisely 22.000 to 1.

This aspect of odds and betting is worth dwelling on for a moment. What we observe at the racetrack is something quite unlike a bet in roulette, blackjack, or craps. In those games the "odds" and payoffs are fixed (at different levels for different types of bets). If you put down $5 on number 17 in roulette and number 17 comes up, your payoff is the same ($180), regardless of how much money others have (or have not) bet on that number. In contrast, the payoff to a winning bet on a horse is determined by the proportion of the handle that is bet on that horse (the handle is the sum total of bets on all entrants). This is what is frequently referred to as a parimutuel betting system: The payoffs are determined (or "driven") by the pattern of the bets.[4]

## The Daily Racing Form

The current (1986) price of the *Daily Racing Form* is $2. It's a bargain. Each issue of this "bible" of horseplayers contains enough data to keep a statistician happy for at least a couple of days. You may not want to do extensive analyses of the horses' records (in fact, we are going to suggest below that such efforts are not especially helpful to profits); however, it is interesting, and also fun, to see what factors in an animal's background may predict success. Furthermore, as educators, we firmly believe that people should have *some* familiarity with the systems or devices they use. True, one needn't understand the internal combustion engine in order to drive well, but it is nice to know something about the engine when the car sputters and stalls. Similarly, one can do many more things with a computer if one understands what the computer is than if it is simply regarded as a marvelous but mysterious box. The *Racing Form* will provide you—most of you, at any rate—with all the information you need or want to predict race outcomes.

Initially, you will observe that some of the information in the *Form* duplicates that of the program. In the reproduction in Figure 1–2, for example, we see that the first race at Gulfstream on January 31, 1985, is a 1 1/16 mile claiming race for fillies (a filly is a female horse not more than four years old). The general claiming price is $15,000.

Notice next the scheme for weights. The initial specification is 121 pounds for all horses, but those that have not won a race recently are given a break: minus 3 pounds for nonwinners of a race 1 mile or longer since December 31; minus 5 pounds for nonwinners of such a race since December 15. Furthermore, horses may also be entered at a claiming price of $14,000 or $13,000. Each $1,000 off the general claiming price ($15,000) yields a further weight allowance of 2 pounds.

Look now at Sexy Sixma, one of the entrants in this race. (The following lettered paragraphs match the letters in Figure 1–2.)

a. *Color, Sex, Age.* Sexy Sixma is a gray female 3-year-old. The horse's color is irrelevant to its winning prospects (unless one holds to a very weird theory!), but it is useful in following the animal's progress during the course of the race. Sex and age may in some circumstances make a difference, but as a rule they do not provide much useful information. A bit more on this later.

b. *Pedigree* (parentage). Sexy Sixma's sire (father) is High Echelon; her mother, Liliuo Kalani, is a daughter of Hawaii. Such information is not especially helpful to bettors. If you follow the horses seriously,

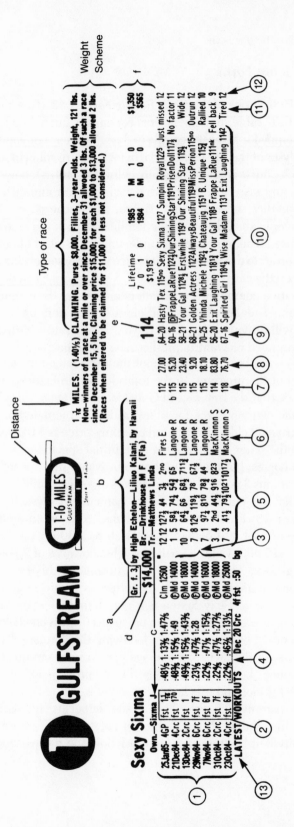

Figure 1-2   A Past Performance Chart from the Daily Racing Form.
(Source: Copyright ©1986 by Daily Racing Form, Inc. Reprinted with permission
of copyright owner.)

you may know something about the quality of certain ancestors of today's entrants; but even this information is not likely to weigh heavily in your calculations. It's what today's runners can do, not the glories of Mom and Pop, that will determine the race results.

c. *Owner, Breeder, Trainer.* As in the program.

d. *Claiming Price.* The claiming price for Sexy Sixma is $14,000. Again, this is the price at which the horse is offered for sale *prior* to the race. It is a signal of the horse's quality, as judged by its owner and trainer.

e. *Today's Weight.* Sexy Sixma weighs 114 pounds; this weight also will be listed in the program.

f. *Summary of Horse's Record.* This box shows the number of times Sexy Sixma has run, number of "in-the-money" finishes, and amounts of money earned—over the horse's lifetime, and for each of the past two years, 1984 and 1985. The letter *M* in 1985 means that Sexy Sixma is still a *maiden*—that is, she has never won a race. The filly has run once this year, finishing second. In 1984 she ran six times and did not finish first, second, or third on any occasion. The horse's lifetime record—in this instance simply the sum of the two years' experience—is seven starts, no wins, one place, no shows. Sexy Sixma has earned $1,350 thus far in 1985 (for her second-place finish). The $565 earned in 1984 was for a fourth-place finish. (Horses pay their backers only if they finish in the top 3; but, as noted above, the number 4 finisher also receives a share of the purse.) As we shall see, some handicappers believe that these summaries are a useful, if rather crude, basis for judging a horse's *consistency.* Consistency may be evaluated in various ways, for example, percentage of in-the-money finishes, or earnings per start.

Now let's examine the details of Sexy Sixma's past performance. (The numbered paragraphs match the numbers in Figure 1–2.)

1. *Date, Race Number, Location.* Sexy Sixma's last race took place on January 25, 1985, in the fourth at Gulfstream; her previous effort was on December 21, 1984, in the fourth race at Calder Race Course (there is a table elsewhere in the *Racing Form* that gives you the abbreviations for all North American racetracks—for example, Crc for Calder). This is useful information in at least two respects. First, one probably ought to be cautious about horses that have not run for a long time (not a problem with Sexy Sixma, who raced 6 days ago); long layoffs are an anathema to most handicappers, apparently for good reason. Second, it may be useful to know where an animal has been running. Performances at Calder, for example, may differ in some systematic way from those at Gulfstream and, if so, will require appro-

priate interpretation. Quite obviously, however, one must become some-thing of an afficionado before getting into such subtleties.

2. *Track Condition and Distance.*   Sexy Sixma's last race was on a fast track at a distance of 1 1/16 miles (same as today's). There are several categories of track condition: *Fast* refers to a dry, hard surface (on which horses usually run relatively fast). A *good* track is not quite as good as a fast one; there has been some rain, and the racing surface has not fully dried out — a bit spongier than ideal. *Muddy, slow, heavy,* and *sloppy* describe varying degrees of poorness in the condition of the racing surface. A *sloppy* track usually occurs while it is still raining or when a heavy downpour has just ended, leaving puddles on the racing surface.

Track condition is important for several reasons. The first is compara-bility: What a horse does under favorable conditions may not be a good indicator of performance on an "off" track. Certain horses may do well under adverse conditions (they are usually known as "mudders"); and it is conventional wisdom that a front-running horse — one that starts fast and frequently is the early leader in a race — has an advantage on a sloppy track. The front-runner kicks considerable slop back into the faces of the following animals, thereby discouraging their efforts.

Some handicappers regard a poor track as a kind of unpredictable element, a "wild card" in which "proven" methods of picking winners don't work. They advise, accordingly, that "all bets are off," both figuratively and literally, when the rain comes down. Other racetrack betting "experts" (the word is in quotation marks because, as you shall see, we are not convinced there is any such thing) believe that profits can be made on poor tracks. They warn, however, that terms such as "fast" and "good" must be viewed with great caution, for each category embraces a range of track conditions (fast may mean fast-fast or slow-fast), and different racetracks may define the categories differently.

The distance of past races is also important for purposes of compara-bility. Sexy Sixma's performance in a 6-furlong (¾ mile) race may tell us something about how she will run at 1 1/16 miles but is probably not as pertinent as her record in races of precisely the same distance.

3. *Type of Race.*   Sexy Sixma last ran in a $12,500 claiming race and previously in a $14,000 maiden race limited to females (desig-nated by Ⓕ ). As we have noted, this tells you something about the "class" or quality of opposition in the races described and makes it possible to judge, at least roughly, whether any horse is likely to face a stiffer or easier test today than in the recent past. It is not only the "price" of the race but its category that is meaningful. Maiden and

claiming races are most common and tend to draw entrants of relatively low quality. Higher in prestige are stakes and allowance races.

4. *Fractional and Final Running Times.* The first two numbers in this line (which are not included in all editions of the *Racing Form*) are the running times of the *leading* horse at the ¼- and ½-mile marks respectively. The last number is the "final" time — that is, the time in which the *winning horse* completed the race. In Sexy Sixma's last race, the winner ran the course of 1 1/16 miles in 1 minute, 47 and 2/5 seconds (1:47 2/5). This is interesting information. If the horse you are examining won the race, the winning time tells you how fast that horse ran. If the horse in question did not win, its running time may be estimated as follows: Add to the winning time 1/5 second for each length behind the winner that the horse finished (we are about to show you where this information appears). In either event, then, the running time of any horse in any race can be determined (the lengths-behind rule is an approximation, but a reasonably accurate one). Since one would expect faster runners to have higher winning probabilities, such calculations are clearly useful.

5. *Running Line.* The first number in this line is the horse's post (or starting) position; position number one is closest to the rail. This may have a significant influence on the winning chances of a horse. Many handicappers believe, however, that the importance of a particular post position in thoroughbred racing depends on the idiosyncracies ("biases") of the racetrack in question — an inside position (one close to the rail) might be good at, say, Pimlico but bad at Gulfstream. In harness racing, where the horse pulls a rider in a two-wheeled cart ("sulky"), there is a general consensus about the importance of post position: The closer an entrant is to the rail, the better the winning chances.

The next four numbers show the horse's position at different "calls," or points of progress, in the race: the start, the one-quarter mark, the one-half mark, and the stretch (usually about 1 furlong from the end, or finish, line). The fifth number is the final position — that is, the horse's outcome in the race. In her last race, Sexy Sixma was in post position 12 and was running twelfth at the start and the one-quarter point. At the one-half mark, she had moved up to fourth. In the stretch, Sexy Sixma was third, and she finished second (quite a nice-looking effort). Notice the superscripts on these running positions, for example, $4^4$ at the one-half mark in Sexy Sixma's last race. This superscript indicates that the horse was running 4 lengths (horse's body lengths) behind the leader at that point; at the next call (the stretch), Sexy Sixma was running third, only half a length behind the leader; and she finished second by a nose ("no"). (For a horse that is leading the race, the superscript indicates the number of lengths this horse is ahead of the number two runner.)

It is the number of lengths behind at the finish that permits calculation of the horse's running time. In this example, Sexy Sixma finished so close to the leader (a nose means precisely that) that her running time is effectively the same as that of the winner, 1:47 2/5. Had Sexy Sixma finished 8 lengths behind, we would add 8/5 of a second to the winner's time, and conclude that the horse had run the race in 1:49.

6. *Past Jockeys.* The track program shows what jockey is riding each entrant today. If today's jockey is different from the past, one may speculate why. The reasons for a jockey change are varied and ordinarily obscure; the speculation, therefore, tends to be idle.

7. *Weight Carried.* Sexy Sixma carried 112 pounds in her last race and carries 114 today. This does not seem an important difference, although an economist may suggest that, at the margin, everything can be important. The comparison between current and past weights may be interesting, however. The animal that is carrying considerably more (less) today could be hindered (helped) somewhat.

8. *Final Odds.* These are the betting odds on the horse in previous races. Sexy Sixma, we note, went off at 27 to 1 in her last race, probably providing nice payoffs to place and show bettors. As we shall discuss in great detail later, it is interesting to see whether the betting odds, which represent the public's estimate of a horse's prospects, do a generally good job of predicting race outcomes. Knowing specifically the odds at which a particular animal has run in the past, however, is not usually helpful in formulating today's bets.

9. *Speed Rating and Track Variant.* These are indexes of the horse's running speed, about which we will have more to say later on. Roughly, the speed rating indicates how fast/slow a particular horse ran in comparison with the record time for the distance of the race at the track where the race was run. A speed rating of 100 would indicate that the horse matched the track record—a rare event; a rating of 99 would mean that the animal ran just 1/5 of a second slower than the record time; 98 would indicate that the horse ran 2/5 off the record, and so forth.

The track variant indicates the average speed of *winning times* at the track on the day a race was run, also in comparison with the track record. Higher numbers imply slower winning times. Thus a track variant of zero would tell us that winning times were, on average, equal to the track records; whereas a variant of 5 would mean that the winning times were 1 full second (5/5 of a second) slower than the track records, again on average.

10. *First Three Finishers, Weights, and Margins.*  These items are best described *via* a quick description of Sexy Sixma's last race. The winner of the race was a horse named Hasty Tex; the horse carried 115 pounds and won by a nose. Sexy Sixma, carrying 112 pounds, finished second, and was 7 lengths in front of the number three horse, Sumpin Royal. Sumpin Royal carried 122 pounds and was 5 lengths ahead of the fourth finisher, whose identity is not given. This set of data adds little to what we know from the other items available. Occasionally, it will point to an interesting comparison if past rivals are also competing in today's race.

11. *Comment.*  Sexy Sixma "just missed"—that is, almost won— her last race. We knew that already. The comments are often amusing to glance at but not very informative. On occasion, however, they may tell you something you want to know. For example, a horse that ran a miserable race may have been "bumped" or "boxed in" by the other entrants. Such comments suggest that the animal suffered a misfortune that probably will not recur; thus you may not want to weight its poor performance too heavily.

12. *Number of Starters.*  If the horse you are looking at finished, say, ninth in the last race, this number will tell you whether or not he beat anyone! Not a highly informative item.

13. *Latest Workouts.*  This is a report of what are, in effect, the horse's practice runs. What's shown are the date, track, distance, and running time. Sexy Sixma did 4 furlongs in 50 seconds at Calder last December 20. The letters "bg" indicate first that the animal was "breezing," or not being pushed very hard by its rider (b), and that the workout was run from a gate (g) of the type that is used in actual races. Workout information is interesting if it suggests that a horse is capable of bettering its past racing performance. These reports, however, are subject to a great deal of "noise" or statistical uncertainty, including the possibility that deliberately misleading information is being reported.

The *Racing Form* contains some other interesting information—for example, the selections of the "expert" handicappers shown in Figure 1–3. Notice that while no one picks Sexy Sixma to win the first race, enough of the handicappers pick her second or third so that she is, overall, the number two consensus choice.

This kind of information is very intriguing to those of us interested in market analysis generally. Here, after all, are several presumed specialists telling us which horse they believe will win each race. These people

# Gulfstream

Consensus Totals Based on 5 points for First (7 for Best Bet), 2 for 2nd, 1 for 3rd. Best Bet in Bold Type. Reigh Count selections not included in Consensus.

| | TRACKMAN | HANDICAP | ANALYST | HERMIS | SWEEP | REIGH COUNT | CONSENSUS | |
|---|---|---|---|---|---|---|---|---|
| 1 | Zindian / Sexy Sixma / Phenomenal Girl | Frappe La Rue / Sexy Sixma / Dark Rumor | Screen Princess / Dark Rumor / Sexy Sixma | Dark Rumor / Our Billie C. / Peter Duck | Princess Ali / Our Billie C. / Lady Lillie B. | Our Billie C. / Crimson Dolly / Frappe La Rue | Dark Rumor / Sexy Sixma / Frappe La Rue | 8 5 5 |
| 2 | Restless Buck / Sudden Switch / Old Baldy | Able To / Lizzidear / Ole Man Fred | Angel Light / Pierre / Restless Buck | Ole Man Fred / Pierre / Restless Buck | Angel Light / Pierre / Able To | Olde Blue Boy / Question Quilla / Subsidary | Angel Light / Restless Buck / Ole Man Fred | 10 7 6 |
| 3 | Ice And Fire / Amagallant / Bold Signature | Varick / Florida Recluse / Place In The Sun | Florida Recluse / Ice And Fire / Place In The Sun | Aswan High / Varick / Ice And Fire | Varick / Aswan High / One Gold | Easy And Fast / Damas Sham / One Gold | Varick / Ice And Fire / Florida Recluse | 12 8 7 |
| 4 | Alcatraz / Lucky Belief / Play Cap | Dowry Dan / Attribute / Lafayette Park | Dowry Dan / Attribute / Lucky Belief | Dowry Dan / Victory For Sure / Nice Touch | Victory For Sure / Dowry Dan / Pragmatist | Lafayette Park / Dowry Dan / Vannelli | Dowry Dan / Victory For Sure / Alcatraz | 17 7 5 |
| 5 | The Train's Comin / Cute Appeal / Cannonball Miss | The Train's Comin / Cannonball Miss / Cherokee Dee | Or De France / The Train's Comin / Cannonball Miss | The Train's Comin / Cannonball Miss / Proudest Babe | The Train's Comin / Cherokee Dee / Island Victory | Cherokee Dee / The Train's Comin / Cute Appeal | **The Train's Comin** / Cannonball Miss / Or De France | 22 6 5 |
| 6 | General Buck / Le Wild / Villa | Prince Batita / Crusher / Unfold | Apuron / Unfold / Crusher | Crusher / Racing Ransom / Le Wild | Unfold / Faultless One / Racing Ransom | **Muffies Diver** / Crusher / Le Wild | Crusher / Unfold / General Buck | 8 8 5 |
| 7 | Exuberant Attitude / Aveen / Wigwam's Are Out | Rozzi's Flyer / Malcolm's Lady / Debutant Dancer | **Exuberant Attitude** / Debutant Dancer / Touch Not | Wigwam's Are Out / One Fine Lady / Aveen | **Debutant Dancer** / Aveen / Malcolm's Lady | Bitterbite / Exuberant Attitude / Rozzi's Flyer | Exuberant Attitude / Debutant Dancer / Wigwam's Are Out | 12 10 6 |
| 8 | **Falkland** / Silver Rich / Magic North | Stack / Trout Stream / Silver Rich | Regal Brek / Record Turnout / Lautaro | Trout Stream / Stack / Verification | Stack / Old Main / Trout Stream | Popops Choice / Qld Main / Regal Brek | Stack / Trout Stream / Falkland | 12 8 7 |
| 9 | I Wanna Talktopapa / Good Economics / Warglo | **Good Economics** / Warglo / Lantana Lady | Permissive / Good Economics / Pull The Wool | **Good Economics** / Warglo / Permissive | Lantana Lady / Good Economics / Warglo | Nadias Charm / Wishing Coin / I Wanna Talktopapa | Good Economics / Warglo / Lantana Lady | 20 6 6 |
| 10 | **Golden Mermaid** / Snappy Verdict / Too Coy | Tisane / Courageous Heart / Too Coy | Tony's Jig / Autumn Changes / Red Holly | Courageous Heart / Too Coy / Autumn Changes | Frau Caricia / Golden Mermaid / Iron Skillet | White Linen / Autumn Changes / Tony's Jig | Golden Mermaid / Courageous Heart / Tisane | 7 7 5 |

Figure 1-3   Selections of Expert Handicappers in the Daily Racing Form.
(*Source: Copyright ©1986 by Daily Racing Form, Inc. Reprinted with permission of copyright owner.*)

have probably spent far more time analyzing the horses' records than we have. Should we follow their (almost "free") advice or ignore it on the ground that advice is usually worth what you pay for it? And does this advice in fact influence the betting behavior of the crowd?[5]

Without getting too far ahead of ourselves, we inject a quick note of caution: Some reasonably careful examinations have shown that following the recommendations of these experts—either an individual handicapper or the consensus—is a money-losing strategy. It is both interesting and important to consider why this is so.

Does this mean that the experts know not whereof they speak? The answer is, not necessarily. It is more likely that the disappointing bottom line reflects two distinctive elements. First, the experts—any experts—*are wrong* a large part of the time. They may know whereof they speak as well as anyone, yet still predict incorrectly in two-thirds or more of the races. This is a little bit like baseball. The batter who hits safely once in three times at bat is considered superior simply because the task is so difficult. Indeed, if he does this in the major leagues, he is unquestionably a multimillionaire. The racetrack handicapper who picks one winner in three may, by similar token, be doing a first-rate job.

There are further reasons why we should not be surprised that following expert predictions is not a way to make money. If the person called Trackman, for example, could pick winners in a mere 50 percent of all races, he (she?) could, with some judicious wagering, amass a substantial fortune over a period of years. Trackman may or may not be paid a nice sum for his (or her) daily selections in the *Racing Form*, but it is inconceivable that a fortune is being built up with this activity alone. In a properly functioning market, alas, we *do* tend to get just about what we pay for. This is not to say that bargains do not exist, but don't expect someone to point you in the direction of riches for pennies a day!

A further reason why following the experts does not work is something we have already alluded to and will continue to note with (perhaps distressing) frequency. It is the good-news-may-be-bad-news paradox, which, while perhaps less obvious, is of absolutely fundamental importance. This paradox arises in various forms, but the underlying principle is constant: In racetrack betting any popular system must lose money. Conversely, a profitable betting system cannot be popular— that is, it must be used by relatively few people. The essential reason is the parimutuel betting system, which we have described above.

What is very likely happening to some extent is that racetrack bettors *are following* the selections of Trackman and the other handicappers. This drives down the odds on the selected horses and the payoffs on those that actually win. Consensus favorites, for example, just don't pay very much on average; and since they fail to win the majority of their races, the low payoffs that they provide cannot make up for the more frequent lost bets. Trackman may be an extremely good predictor of horse race winners in some objective sense. But if bettors recognize this expertise and follow Trackman's picks with their own money, they may be caught up in a terrible betting strategy. Good news—that an expert considers a particular horse to be the best in a race—becomes bad news for bettors on that horse.

## The Racing Industry: Trouble in Paradise?

Horse racing may be known as the sport of kings, but a racetrack is a business, just like IBM, the Ford Motor Company, or your local pizzeria. The track owners and managers sell a service—betting on races—to their customers. Building and maintaining the racetracks require investment, and someone must therefore be induced to invest. Horse owners require some compensation (*via* purses) as well, although thoroughbred racing appears to be a distinctly unprofitable activity for many of them. Jockeys, trainers, grooms, ticket sellers, and electricity bills must all be paid. Thus, the racetracks must earn sufficient revenues to cover expenses, including, presumably, some rate of return to investors. In fact, the closest business analogue to racetracks are public utility companies that are regulated by state or regional commissions. The various states not only oversee racing with a view toward maintaining "integrity," but also regulate the prices and quantities of the services the tracks provide. In this respect, the analogy to gas, electricity, and water suppliers is really quite close.

The notion of the *price* that racetracks charge their customers is of basic importance. It is a somewhat unusual price that we shall refer to frequently, and thus it bears brief description now. When you go to make a $2 (or $5 or $100) bet, you simply buy a $2 (or $5 or $100) ticket that conveys to you a simple right: Should the event that you bet will happen actually occur, you are entitled to a payoff. The size of the payoff is determined by the betting odds and the amount that you bet. What do you pay for your $2 (or $5 or $100) ticket? Precisely $2 (or $5 or $100). What, then, is the "price" of the ticket? The fine folks at the track don't seem to be charging you any premium for your bet.

The answer, of course, is that the price appears, a bit indirectly, in the payoffs that successful bettors receive. The track *takes out* some proportion of the moneys bet in order to cover expenses. This percentage, which is regulated by the state, shows up in the form of reduced payoffs and comprises the "price" of betting. On average, the price or *track take* in the United States is about 18 to 20 percent. We'll return to the significance of this price very shortly.

The recent history of American racetrack betting looks superficially rosy, at least until 1985. As Table 1-2 shows, both total attendance and revenues (that is, handle, or amount bet) have risen significantly up to a point. But this picture is unfortunately quite misleading. The more meaningful statistics in Table 1-2 indicate clearly that average daily attendance has been declining over the same period. Whereas the per capita daily handle (amount bet per visit to the track) had been rising until 1985, after that the average daily attendance and the total handle have been falling. In fact, when stated in real terms—that is, adjusted for price inflation—the amount bet by the typical racegoer was on average lower in 1989 than in 1965. The sum wagered in 1989 was $151, about 2 times as great as the $73 wagered in 1965; but during this same period, the consumer price index, a broad measure of the nation's price level, increased more than four times.)

Racetrack revenues and attendance would be even more unfavorable if states had not been increasing the number of racing days per year. This strategy is clearly a mere Band-Aid that cannot go on for long. There are only 365 days in a year, and in many states climate further limits the potential for racing days. It's possible to

Table 1-2    Horse Racing in the United States: Attendance, Racing Days, Revenues[a]

|  | 1965 | 1975 | 1985 | 1988 | 1989 |
|---|---|---|---|---|---|
| Total attendance[b] | 62.8 | 70.7 | 73.3 | 68.9 | 59.9 |
| No. of racing days | 8,051 | 13,110 | 13,745 | 14,285 | 14,240 |
| Average daily attendance | 7,011 | 6,001 | 5,336 | 4,827 | 4,398 |
| Total handle[c] | $4.62 | $7.86 | $12.22 | $9.47 | $9.02 |
| Per capita daily handle | $73.38 | $111.27 | $166.61 | $137.34 | $150.65 |
| Revenue to states[b] | $370 | $675 | $625 | $596 | $585 |

[a] Includes all forms of horse racing. Thoroughbred and harness racing account for 85 to 90 percent of the totals.
[b] millions.
[c] billions.
Source: *Pari-Mutuel Racing*, A statistical summary prepared by the National Association of State Racing Commissioners (Lexington, Ky.: annual).

make customers comfortable in almost any weather by building enclosed grandstands, but horses simply cannot run safely in certain circumstances, primarily during the winter.

The true picture of the health of the racing industry thus provokes considerable and justifiable anxiety. Yet we have just finished telling you what great fun the racetrack is; furthermore, it is common knowledge that many people love to gamble. Where, then, does the problem lie? Observers have suggested various possibilities, among them the following:

1. *The energy crisis.* During the 1970s, the price of energy took some huge leaps, largely as the result of OPEC's machinations. Whereas the power of OPEC has now waned, this traumatic event had some lasting consequences. To the extent that it has instilled a conservation ethic, encouraging people to stay close to home, it may have reduced people's willingness to travel substantial distances to racetracks (one does not find a track around every corner). Even if this effect is not "large," its impact on the racetracks may be quite noticeable.

2. *Changing tastes.* Horse racing may be suffering from what economists call a "secular decline" in popularity. Perhaps younger generations simply don't like this particular leisure time activity as much as their parents' and grandparents' generations.

3. A *low-growth economy.* The real per capita income of Americans has not risen very rapidly over the past 20 years. If going to the racetrack is an income-sensitive (or elastic) activity, then slow-growing income may partially explain stagnant track expenditures. (Notice that the income sensitivity of demands for goods and services varies quite widely: It is presumably much higher for Chanel No. 5 than for emergency appendectomies.)

4. *Increasing competition.* Alternative forms of legalized gambling have expanded in recent years. Many states have introduced lotteries; a few now have off-track betting, and one (New Jersey) began to offer casino gambling. Any of these may siphon off some of the money that would otherwise have found its way into the racetracks' coffers.

It may well be that each of these factors has contributed to the rather dismal state of the racing industry. But we have another prime candidate for blame: *price.* The price of racetrack bets—that is, the track take—has gone up substantially in many states. Not only have the take percentages been on the rise, but breakage rules (which govern the extent to which the tracks may round payoffs downward) have been revised so as to reduce further the sums paid to winning bettors. And it is likely that this has made a big difference to the fortunes of the tracks. To see why, let's first consider the case of our friend Burt.

Burt loves the races but he has a responsible job and a family; he therefore goes to the track only 12 times per year. At each visit he bets $10 per race on 10 races for a handle of $100 per day (this is reasonably close to the actual per capita handle at many racetracks). Let us suppose that each year Burt has two "bad" days in which he picks no winners; two "good" days in which he picks four winners; and eight "mediocre" days of two winners. All these numbers are obviously artificial but they reasonably represent the experience of a typical bettor. Look now at how the price of betting affects Burt's fortunes.

*Case 1: Price (track take) = 0.* This is sheer fantasy. If the track that Burt attends did not take any money out of the betting pools, he would find that

| | | |
|---|---|---|
| On bad days: | Amount bet = | $100 |
| | Payoffs = | 0 |
| | Net result = | − 100 |
| On good days: | Amount bet = | $100 |
| | Payoffs = | 200* |
| | Net result = | + 100 |

*Payoffs assume average odds of 4 to 1. A $10 bet on a horse at 4 to 1 pays $50 (including the return of the initial $10). Four such payoffs = $200.

| | | |
|---|---|---|
| On mediocre days: | Amount bet = | $100 |
| | Payoffs = | 100** |
| | Net result = | 0 |

**Same assumption of 4 to 1 odds; two payoffs = $100.

Notice that over the entire year Burt would just break even, winning $200 on good days, losing $200 on bad days, and winning/losing nothing on mediocre days. This is precisely what the average experience of all bettors would be if the price of bets were zero — every dollar bet would be returned. We are probably being a bit unfair to Burt, who is a pretty good judge of horseflesh; but so be it.

*Case 2: Price (track take) = 10%.*

| | | |
|---|---|---|
| On bad days: | Amount bet = | $100 |
| | Payoffs = | 0 |
| | Net result = | − 100 |
| On good days: | Amount bet = | $100 |
| | Payoffs = | $180* |
| | Net result = | + 80 |

On mediocre days:    Amount bet  =   $100
                     Payoffs     =     90*
                     Net result  =   − 10
*Same assumption of 4 to 1 odds on all bets; but only 90 percent of total bets
are now returned to bettors in payoffs.

*Case 3: Price = 20%.*

On bad days:         Amount bet  =   $100
                     Payoffs     =      0
                     Net result  =   − 100
On good days:        Amount bet  =   $100
                     Payoffs     =   $160*
                     Net result  =   + 60
On mediocre days:    Amount bet  =   $100
                     Payoffs     =     80*
                     Net result  =   − 20
*Same assumption of 4 to 1 odds on all bets; track now returns 80 percent of
bets in payoffs.

Now compare cases 2 and 3. Burt still has the same proportions of
good, bad, and mediocre days (the track take does not affect his ability
to pick winners). Notice that a bad day does not become worse as the
price of betting increases; betting $100 still results in a $100 loss. But
the good days are not quite so good at a price of 20 percent as they were
at 10 percent; and the mediocre days—which are most frequent—are
much worse: losses of $20 rather than $10.

Indeed, at a price of 10 percent, it might well be that Burt could
delude himself into thinking he is breaking even (perhaps even winning a little) over the course of the year—he is, in fact, losing $120. At a
price of 20 percent, it's much harder to do that. Burt is a true fan who
will not stop going to the track at the higher price. But if he responds by
going just once or twice less per year, or by betting a bit less whenever
he goes—and if Burt is typical of many other patrons—the effect on the
track will be quite severe.

We suspect that this is precisely what has been happening to American horse racing. More general data tend to show that as track takes
rise, revenues and daily attendance fall.[6] This may not be the sole cause
of racing's current plight, but it is almost certainly a significant part of
the story. Why, then, do the tracks continue to raise their takes? It may
be that state regulators simply assume that an increase in price will
increase the revenues in which they are interested as a source of taxes.
This assumption may seem plausible because the price is "hidden" in
reduced payoffs that bettors might not notice. (But observe in Table 1–2

that track revenues paid to the states have actually declined somewhat since 1975, even as percentage takes have been rising; one would think that state regulators would pay some attention to this "paradox.") Further, there may be a tendency, even among relatively sophisticated business managers, to believe that higher prices are invariably helpful to revenue and profit positions.

All these beliefs, which are closely related, can be viewed as a failure by economists to educate people about the effects of price changes. There is an important economic measure known as price elasticity of demand that describes the sensitivity of buyers to changes in the price of a good or service. As a general rule, increases in price lead to decreases in amounts purchased. If the price elasticity (sensitivity) is high enough, an increased price will reduce not only the number of units purchased but the sum of money (revenues) that consumers spend on the item in question. Economists know this, but apparently haven't done a good job of explaining it to others. Clearly, racetrack regulators and managers aren't aware of the problem. *Nostra culpa.*

## Honesty and Dishonesty at the Racetrack

Are the races honest? Disgruntled bettors are at times prone to complain that "the fix was in." This usually occurs when their betting systems are yielding large losses. It is easier and more satisfying to blame one's failure on a crooked jockey or trainer than to blame oneself. But is it justified? No one can be completely sure—not us, not you, and not the railbird who assures you with absolute certainty that "his" jockey has just "thrown" the last race.

Based on our observation of betting behavior, our best guess is that horse racing in the United States is a predominantly honest game. There are, no doubt, some exceptions. Horses can be drugged, although this tends to be risky and is probably quite uncommon. Riders can—perhaps at the behest of owners or trainers—fail to make a serious effort to win a race. Such outright dishonesty, however, does not appear to be widespread. For one thing, state regulators do exert some influence in making it harder, riskier, and generally more costly to cheat. At least we think they do; it seems implausible to believe that no such effect exists.

For another thing, observed patterns of betting suggest a generally straight game. Cheating is possible, but when it occurs, it should leave some clues in the form of betting behavior. Example: Heavy money is bet on an apparently hopeless animal who then wins a race easily. Such oddities are seen, but not very often; and state regulators are on the lookout for precisely these kinds of "inconsistent" behavior. As we shall point out later, the crowd at the racetrack usually produces quite an accurate and orderly evaluation of the winning probabilities of the horses in any given race. This is, to us, strong evidence of the general honesty of racetrack operations.

There is, however, one phenomenon suggesting a type of dishonesty in which we have both a professional and personal interest. This is *inside information*, another term borrowed from the stock market. As applied to horse racing, it refers to situations in which those people close to a stable can more accurately estimate the winning probability of a horse than can the crowd in general. Perhaps Old Siwash has just recovered from a prolonged bout of equine dysentery and is really ready to go in the seventh at Belmont today. But only his owner, trainer, and handlers have any inkling of this fact. The average bettor, viewing Old Si's recent performances in the *Racing Form*, simply regards him as an inferior entrant with no chance of winning. This is a form of dishonesty—or perhaps unfairness—albeit not quite in the same category as fixing a race.

The possibility of inside information is one that we have attemped to verify, as you shall see in detail later, with rather mixed results. It appears that an "informed" class of racetrack bettors may exist; but, if so, they are not a consistently strong or verifiable presence. Whereas this is not in itself conclusive evidence, it tends to argue against most forms of gross dishonesty.

## Endnotes

1. Virtually all racetracks display win odds at numerous locations. The amounts bet to place and show on each horse—but not the odds implied by these bets—are typically displayed at only one location.
2. They are also actuarially worse bets than win, place, or show at most racetracks. This is because state regulators usually allow the track a larger "take" from the exotic betting pools. At some places, for example, the average take including breakage is around 18 percent on "straight" bets but as high as 25 percent on exotics.
3. The basic relationship between the odds on a horse and the amounts of money bet—on that horse and on all others—is as follows:

$$\text{Odds}_i = \frac{(1 - t)B}{B_i} - 1$$

Where: Odds$_i$ are the odds on horse $i$.

$t$ is the track "take" (including breakage), the percentage of moneys wagered that the racetrack retains to cover its expenses.

$B$ is the sum total of moneys bet on all horses in the race.

$B_i$ is the amount wagered on horse $i$.

We shall discuss this relationship more extensively later.

4. This sort of "bet-driven payoff" is similar to some state lottery bets in which the payoff to a winning number is shared equally by all holders of tickets on that number. Thus, the larger the number of ticket holders, the smaller the payoff— just as in horse racing.

5. Precisely the same question may be posed about other racetrack "advisory services," such as tout sheets that are commonly sold for $1 or $2.

6. Some examples are presented by Maury R. Wolff, "Revenue Handicaps Crimp a Day at the Races," *Wall Street Journal*, March 11, 1985. For more detailed studies that also indicate a high price elasticity of demand for racetrack gambling, see Gruen (1976) and Suits (1979). The implication of a high elasticity, or sensitivity, is that an increase in price (here the track take) produces a disproportionately large decline in the amount of wagering that occurs. If this is the case, a *decrease* in the track take, by stimulating a disproportionate *increase* in betting, should increase total handle (track revenues).

*Chapter 2*

# Why You Usually Lose
# at the Racetrack

## Preamble

This chapter explores an unhappy fact of racetrack gambling: Bettors are engaged in what decision theorists call a "negative-sum game." Put more prosaically: People who bet on the races must, as a group, lose money because the track returns only part of the wagers that are made. What the track retains — the "take" — averages about 18 to 20 percent of the gambling handle (amount bet), a take that is worse than most casino games from the gambler's standpoint, although better than most state lotteries.

The implication of this unhappy fact is pretty obvious. In order to make money from betting the races, you must not only do "well" in some subjective sense; you must also outperform the betting crowd as a whole — and by a substantial margin.

Is this possible? Of course. Almost anything is possible. Whether you are *likely* to succeed, however, depends very directly on whether the "market" in racetrack betting is "efficient." As we point out in some detail, racetrack betting is quite similar to stock or securities markets in important respects. Markets are termed efficient if the prices of traded items reflect all pertinent, attainable information about those items. In the case of the racetrack, the question is this: Do horses' betting odds (which are, in effect, the "prices" of their tickets or shares) accurately mirror their true winning chances? If so, the market in racing bets is indeed efficient, and the task of beating that market and turning a profit will be small indeed.

What we must try to discover are market *inefficiencies* that will enable us to do better than other racetrack patrons. This means that we

31

must find a way not simply to "pick winners"—after all, virtually every bettor picks winners, and some pick a pretty good proportion of them. Rather, we have to *pick winners that others don't pick*, and do this often enough to offset our inevitable failures. A difficult task? You bet it is!

## The Track Take: Far from the Best Game in Town

All gambling provided by professional "vendors"—be they racetracks, casinos, state off-track betting (OTB) offices, or lottery agencies—consists of unfair bets. This is necessarily so because the vendor must cover a variety of expenses: operating costs such as rent or mortgage payments, utilities, insurance, and employee payrolls; and in the case of private enterprises, taxes and sufficient profits to keep the business going. The supplier of gambling services therefore cannot return all the money wagered by the customers. Some must be retained—usually termed the house (or track) "take"—to pay these costs. And the inescapable implication is that gamblers *as a group* lose money. Our particular interest is whether and how *individuals* betting at racetracks might win even though the group as a whole cannot do so. In this chapter we explain why the task is an extremely difficult one.

The unhappy arithmetic for the racetrack bettor is this: In the 29 states that permit horse race wagering, the track take ranges from 15 to 20 percent on "straight" win, place, and show bets, and from 16 to 25 percent on exotic bets.[1] Actually, things are even a bit worse than that. These percentages do not include *breakage*, the practice of rounding payoffs downward. The fact that states permit the racetracks to do this further loads the odds against bettors, but the size of the extra disadvantage varies from race to race.[2] Estimates are that breakage generally takes an additional 1 percent of the "handle," or amount wagered by the betting public. Overall, then, horse race bettors may lose around 18.5 percent of their money on straight bets, and around 23 percent on the exotics.

This is not only a big chunk of money; it is, as shown in Table 2-1, a heavy burden *relative* to most other forms of legalized gambling. Most casino games are far more favorable; only some slot machines and state lotteries are clearly worse. To see just how bad the situation is, consider exactly what a track take of 18 percent—close to the average figure—does to your payoff.

Let us suppose that $100,000 is the sum total bet to win on all horses in a particular race; $10,000 of it is on your selection, Thunderfoot.

Table 2-1   The "Take" (or "House Advantage") on Various Forms of Legalized Gambling

| Gamble | Take |
|---|---|
| Baccarat | About 1%. |
| Craps | Ranges from about 1% to 11% on most bets; as high as 16.7% on certain bets. |
| Roulette | 5.3% to 7.9%. |
| Blackjack | Player advantage of 2.6% to house advantage of 5% to 10%, depending on house rules and players' skills.* |
| Racetrack | Average of 18.5% on straight bets, 23% on exotic bets. |
| Slot machines | Highly variable and somewhat uncertain. Probably about 2.5% to 25%. |
| State lotteries | Variable. Usually 50% or more. |

* Blackjack is the only form of legalized gambling in which a player may in principle hold a consistent advantage. Whether this occurs will depend upon the player's skill and sophistication in pursuing winning strategies, and the ability of the house to detect and defeat such strategies.

Thunderfoot wins the race (of course! You are no dummy!). Imagine, just to dream a bit, that the track had offered you a fair bet. The entire $100,000 would be paid to Thunderfoot's backers, and you would get back $10 for each $1 you had wagered, or $20 on a $2 ticket.

The track take is 18 percent, however. This means that only $82,000 of the $100,000 bet *in toto* will be paid back to Thunderfoot's investors. A $1 bet will retrieve $8.20, and your $2 ticket will pay $16.40 rather than $20. Pretty bad. And we have used an example in which there is no breakage whatever! The take has indeed "taken" $3.60 away from our $2 bettor (had $50,000 of the total $100,000 been bet on Thunderfoot, the fair payoff to a $2 bet would be $4, but the actual payoff would be $3.28, rounded down to $3.20—a smaller loss in dollars, but a slightly higher proportion of the bet because of the breakage).

This arithmetic is inexorable. It affects every payoff in every type of bet in every race. It matters not one wit how people bet or which horses win: At the end of every race, betting day, and racing season, the track will have 18 percent of its patrons' wagers. People are occasionally tempted to think that racetrack bets are a good deal. After all, a $2 bet still costs $2, just as it did 20 years ago. True enough. But we pay quite dearly for our action.

Consider just how tough this situation is for the individual bettor. Suppose you come up with an excellent method of picking winners. You are smarter than most of your fellow track goers, so much so in fact that you beat the average performance of the crowd consistently by 15 percent. In a world of fair bets you would get back $115 for every $100 you wager, a very nifty rate of return (in fact, you could make a nice living this way)! In reality, however, every $100 you bet will return $97 — a respectable loss, but a loss nonetheless.

This is why, initially, you should be somewhat skeptical about the racetrack as an "investment" vehicle (and about vague stories of consistently big winners). Many sensible and even superior methods of betting will fail to show a profit over the long term. It's not the approach that is flawed. Rather, the bettor's "handicap" is just too great.


## Racetracks and Stock Markets

It is very tempting to think of racetracks and of the betting that goes on at them as a kind of market (this is one reason why some economists and experts in finance have an avid interest in the track). The similarities between racetrack betting and stock or securities markets are especially pronounced. In both cases, large numbers of investors/gamblers (the terms may be synonymous!) can purchase "shares" of companies or horses. There is a good deal of information available about the investment possibilities, the returns to any given choice are uncertain, and investors' opinions affect share prices (either the price of a company's stock or the odds on a horse). Furthermore, investors in both markets encounter transactions costs in the form of a track take or a broker's commission.

In stock markets, individuals make offers to buy or sell companies' shares (in a horse race there is no precise analog to "selling" a share). This bidding process occurs in a highly organized environment in which "specialists," or perhaps computer programs, set prices to clear markets — that is, they make sure everyone's buy or sell order is filled. Individuals' desires to own a particular stock have an immediate impact on its price: If on a given day many more people want to buy than sell, the price rises.

Now, why do people buy stock in the first place? Presumably not because they want to wallpaper their living rooms with stock certificates, but rather because of the future return that the ownership share in the company promises. This return consists partly of dividends paid by the company, and partly of the expected appreciation of the stock itself.

This immediately raises two questions. First, why would a company's stock appreciate? And second, how do people decide when such appreciation is likely to occur? The answer to the first question rests on the company's productive activities. If it manufactures a better mousetrap, people can be expected to buy its product in large quantities. The company's earnings will rise, and these earnings allow the payment of large dividends. Other things being equal, this makes the company's stock a very desirable investment, and people will want to buy it; but that, as we have just seen, will drive up the price of the stock and thus cause appreciation.

As far as the second question is concerned, there is no easy answer. Some potential investors may form their opinions by taking inspiration from the stars and drawing up horoscopes for company presidents. Others read the newspapers and subscribe to investment advisory services. Clearly, in this area there is always a mass of professional or semiprofessional advice. Furthermore, an enormous amount of "information" about companies, products, markets, domestic and international economic conditions, and what have you is available.

What about racetrack betting? Notice first of all, that racetrack betting is a simpler, sparser, and much more stylized activity than investing in company stocks. In the stock market, one must make choices among thousands of companies, each of which may produce hundreds of products that are sold in scores of countries and marketplaces. If one were to start from scratch, the legwork necessary to "forecast" the financial futures of these enterprises would be staggering in magnitude. Even if one were to rely on an investment advisory service, the information processing demands on the individual are enormous—for example, one of the most prestigious services, The Value Line, sends its clients a weekly report of some 165 pages, containing information on about as many companies.

In contrast, the average race presents the "investor" with some eight or ten choices (multiply by eight or ten for the full racing day). The horses have relatively brief "track records" that can be summarized without great difficulty, and their only "product" is running. Nevertheless, the similarity to stock markets is striking. Horses *do* have track records, and the information is readily available. Individuals can buy "shares" in the horses, although these shares differ from company shares in two ways: First, the shares are sold at a fixed price (for example, $2); and second, they convey no rights beyond the current race (with the daily double a minor exception).

What does vary when you buy a share in a horse is the payoff, should it win. Under the parimutuel system of betting, all money wagered (minus the track take and breakage) is paid out to backers of the winning horse. This means, of course, that you do best by betting on a winning horse *that has a very small fraction of the total pool bet on it*, otherwise known as a longshot. But the return is uncertain. Even though the track displays the odds on each horse up to the end of the betting period, thus permitting us to calculate roughly how much we will gain if our animal wins, no one can know with certainty whether a particular horse *will* win or not. In precisely the same way, nobody can be certain that a company with an allegedly better mousetrap will or will not encounter some catastrophe (such as the development of a *still better mousetrap* by someone else).

In both instances we have a situation in which (1) the investor pays money in order to secure an expected but uncertain return, (2) a great deal of apparently relevant information is available, and (3) a lot of professional advice can be purchased. We would be remiss, however, not to point out a rather important way in which the stock market and the racetrack betting market differ.

The stock market is what decision theorists sometimes refer to as a *variable sum game*. The market may "go up" or "go down" over time, thereby altering the total value of all investors' assets. If the stock market has a good year (or a good five years!), even the subpar investor can make a good deal of money. This is not possible in the racetrack betting market, which is a *negative sum game for the bettors*. The "market" in betting cannot go up or down. As we have noted, sadly, "investors" at the track always lose a fixed proportion of their bets. The subpar gambler will lose his shirt over the long haul, and only the most superior bettor has any real possibility of emerging with a profit.

## Market Efficiency

It may appear, based on what we have said above, that the way to make money in a market for the shares of companies or horses is to obtain better information than other people have. After all, if Peter is the only person who knows that Universal Mousetrap Executioners, Inc., has just invented an automatic mouse zapper that never needs to be baited because it synthesizes cheese out of thin air, and moreover that this device costs only two cents to manufacture, he will gain enormous returns by buying the company's stock before the rest of the world wakes up to this epoch-making discovery. Similarly, if Richard knows that Slow Poke, a horse who has never run a decent race in his life, is for some reason ready to set the world on fire in the fourth at Aqueduct today—and if no one else realizes this—there is much money to be made by the appropriate investment action. In both these cases, one would be willing to pay a healthy premium for the relevant information, whether obtained sneakily or in a straightforward fashion.

Unfortunately, life is not usually so kind to us. The reason is that there are few secrets, few treasure troves of information that can be exploited. Both horse "prices" (odds) and stock prices clearly reflect the information that people have. If everybody genuinely believed that IBM was going to go broke tomorrow, IBM's shares would not be selling for $150 today. The only way that IBM's shares can be priced "not right" is if Peter knows something about the company that is true and that nobody else knows. Market prices, however, by and large reflect all the information that is conceivably attainable, and one cannot systematically exploit better information for consistently above-average market profits. This is what is meant by the economist's term "efficient market."

But, you may object, this cannot be true because three times in the last three years I bought some company's stock on a "hot tip," and in each instance I tripled my money in three months! Congratulations, we would say, you were very lucky. Enjoy your profits. (Don't forget to pay Uncle Sam.) But, we would add, this is not really very surprising, and is not incompatible with the view that markets are efficient. Some stocks go up and others go down as the underlying information about companies changes. But *on the average*, prices reflect all the pertinent information. Sometimes this information turns out to have been wrong. When the investing public realizes this, stock prices are adjusted (up or down) so that the price again correctly reflects the currently available information. But, you may say, I knew to begin with that the original information was wrong, that the company's prospects were much brighter than people thought. But, if you knew that, *that knowledge in itself is information.* Unless you are willing to believe that you are the only one blessed with that insight, the current price of the company's stock will already reflect this more favorable outlook.

Here is one last thought on the efficiency of the stock market. We have just argued that market profits that are substantially above the average are unlikely to be obtainable in the long run. This is because as soon as information is widely available that a company's future is rosy, individuals' actions in buying the stock drive its price up to the point at which, if you buy it, no above-average profits can accrue. There is one reasonable qualification to this: What is meant by the average profit must be adjusted to reflect the different degrees of *risk* that buyers of various stocks are exposed to.

There are several ways in which one can measure risk. One reasonable way is what statisticians call the *variance*, which is a measure of the variability of outcomes around the expected value. Consider a stock that sells today for $50, and assume that everyone firmly believes that its price at some later date will either rise to $80 or fall to $40; and further, that each of these two outcomes has a probability of occurring of one-half. The *expected price* of this stock is then: (0.5) ($80) + (0.5) ($40) = $60.

Now consider another stock, also selling for $50 today, that has a future price of either $100 or $20, each again with a probability of one-half. This second stock obviously also has an expected future price of $60, but in a very real sense it is riskier than the first since the outcome that will materialize is further removed from the expected value or price ($100, for example, is further from $60 than is $80). The second stock is said to have higher variance than the first.

If stock market investors are risk averse—that is, they do not like uncertainty (and the second stock clearly has more uncertainty about it than the first)—they would not want to buy any of the second stock. It provides the same expected return as the first stock but carries more of the disagreeable attribute, uncertainty. For this reason, the second stock must provide a somewhat greater average return than the first one if it is to be willingly owned by some investors; holders of the stock must be compensated for assuming the larger risk. At a current price of $50, more people would want to sell the stock than to buy it; therefore, its current price would decline, say to $45. But this will assure stockholders of an average return of $(60 - 45)/45 = 33.33$ percent, greater than the average return on the first stock, which is $(60 - 50)/50 = 20$ percent.[3]

The greater return on the second stock is not a violation of market efficiency. Rather, it is a consequence of the greater equilibrium return that investors require on a riskier stock. The concept of market efficiency may thus be rephrased as follows: Stock markets are efficient if prices reflect all possible information so that no above-average profits can be made, once differences in risk are taken into account.

Similar considerations apply to racetrack betting, and we may ask whether the betting market is or is not efficient. Can one make consistently above-average profits in racetrack betting? We must first define the universe of investment opportunities over which we will examine this hypothetical average profit. Should we include all conventional investment instruments such as stocks, bonds, mutual funds, and so forth? The answer is probably not, partly because people go to the track for reasons other than profit, and partly because institutional restrictions prevent bank presidents from investing the funds at their disposal in horse races. The reasonable universe, then, is probably just the various horses that run at the track.

Now we already know that in the aggregate, racetrack betting is a losing proposition: Since the track takes out about 18 percent of all moneys bet, bettors as a whole experience a substantial negative return. But can one make profits much above this average by betting on particular horses? Since the average profit is $-18$ percent, even breaking even in the long run would seem to be a substantial achievement. (This is not the case in the stock market, where the long-run rate of return is in the neighborhood of $+10$ percent.) How can one accomplish this—or do even better?

As in the stock market, the name of the game is *information*. If you happen to know what nobody else knows, namely that Slow Poke, who has never won a race in his life, has shown remarkable recent improvement in tryouts and has been running 6 furlongs in 1:08(!), you should bet a large sum of money on him. Since everyone else thinks that Slow Poke is a dog, the proportion of the pool bet on him will be miniscule, and therefore the odds and the payoff if he wins will be enormous.

*But what makes you think that you are the only person who is privy to such information?* The horse's owners, trainer, riders, and probably many others all know this as well. Why should they not act on it? Alas, if they do, this will automatically depress the odds and the payout on Slow Poke. If the market is efficient, betting on Slow Poke will go on until the odds and the prospective payout on the horse are pushed down to the point at which there is no differential advantage to betting Slow Poke rather than some other entrant.

Within broad limits, the betting market is likely to be efficient in this sense—after all, few people are really *known* to earn consistently above-normal profits at the track. But the returns on different horses need not be equal if people who bet at the track are at all sensitive to the differential risk involved in betting on one horse rather than another.

In discussing the stock market, we argued that holders of riskier stocks must earn a higher rate of return on the average than holders of less risky stocks: If they did not receive this higher return, risk-averse investors simply would not hold the riskier stocks. In racetrack betting, however, we seem to be dealing with *risk lovers*, people whose utility or satisfaction actually diminishes when risk is lower.[4] In this circumstance, the returns on less risky horses must be higher, or less negative, on average; otherwise, no one would bet on these horses. This may seem counterintuitive, but it is a direct consequence of the fact that horse race bettors love risk.

In an environment in which risk matters to people, it should be no surprise that some horses exhibit higher average returns than others. The question of efficiency then comes down to this: Can above-average returns be earned by betting "cleverly," once the risk of various horses is accounted for?

## The Ability to Pick Winners: It's Not Quite Enough

You know by now that the racetrack odds are heavily against you. How, then, might you proceed to bet cleverly and make some money? Let us suppose that you are not privy to any "inside" information. You are, however, an intelligent person, and in reading the past performance charts you may notice some things that you suspect are not obvious to the average guy (or gal). Perhaps you will observe, for example, that recently claimed horses dropping down in class of race and carrying less weight than before win a very high proportion of their races, say 40 percent over a prolonged period. "Voilà!" you exclaim, "It's time to make a little money."

Can you actually do so? The answer: not if the betting market is efficient. Your relevant piece of information, the product of your intellect, will not be confined to you. Some others will also notice that these horses do very well, and they will act on this observation, just as you do. The odds on the horses you bet will be driven down to the point at which you will (1) cash 40 percent of your win tickets, and (2) lose money.

Whether racetrack betting really *is* this efficient, we cannot initially be sure. This is an essentially empirical question that we shall discuss in detail later. But there is an important lesson even at this point. You may be able to tell that a particular horse has a "good" chance of winning a race (what is "good" is up to you to define). This does not necessarily mean that the horse is a good *bet*, however. In fact, a good bet — one that an actuary will tell you has "positive expected value" — is a horse whose winning chances, whether "high" or "low," are *substantially underestimated* by bettors as a whole.

Consider the simple arithmetic. Your system picks winners 40 percent of the time (the horses you select may be said to have a 40 percent chance of winning their races). Pretty impressive, we'd say. To know whether they are good bets, however, we must know what the winning payoffs are. If your winners return, on average, $5 to a $2 bet, then your system just breaks even. But if the crowd likes these animals, convinced as you are that their chances are good, they may bet these horses down to the point at which the average payoff is, say, only $4.60. Your impressive system will continue to pick 40 percent winners, but you will consistently lose about 8 percent of the money you bet.

The implication of all this is not a terrifically happy one. Picking winners, by itself, isn't good enough. Indeed, you might do it very well and go broke in the process. To make money — that is, net profits — you must pick winners that *very few others can spot*. But this cannot be done consistently if the racetrack betting market is efficient. In a real sense, the search for systems that will "beat the races" is a search for inefficiencies in the market. Do they exist? Read on.

## Endnotes

1. An exotic bet is a bet on two or more horses, such as a daily double, exacta, trifecta, or pick four. Most states permit the highest take on bets that include more than two horses.
2. Breakage works in somewhat different ways depending on state law, but a simple example will show why the amount of breakage in any given race cannot be known in advance. Suppose that the betting odds imply that the correct payoff to a $2 bet on Old Pokey is $2.97, but that the state in which the race is run permits the track to round downward to the next payoff evenly divisible by 20. The actual payoff will then be $2.80, a reduction equal to 8.5 percent of a $2 bet. Alternatively, if Young Siwash had won, the correct payoff to a $2 ticket would have been $45.21. All that the track can do is round down to $45.20, a loss to bettors of a penny, a mere one-half percent of the $2 bet.
3. There is a special case we must mention briefly. Consider again a risk-averse investor who contemplates two investment opportunities: Stock A provides outcomes of 80 and 120 with 50:50 probabilities and Stock B provides, *for the same initial investment*, outcomes of 30 and 40 with 50:50 probabilities. Stock A has higher mean return and higher variance than Stock B. Thus, depending on the individual's precise tradeoff between mean return and variance of return, some people might prefer A to B and some B to A. But in this case, that does not seem reasonable *since every conceivable outcome of B is worse than the worst conceivable outcome of A*; hence everybody will prefer A.
4. This is not idle speculation. See the discussion in Chapter 6 of the evidence on racetrack betting patterns presented in the academic literature.

*Chapter 3*

# Betting Strategies: The Popular Literature

## Preamble

This chapter surveys the popular literature on how to beat the races. The discussion is not at all technical. Although we are quite skeptical about the value of much of this "investment advice," we have not set out to debunk it. A fair bit of the advice, in fact, is pretty sensible, and some of it actually is useful. To employ the popular literature in your own approach to betting, however, you must be aware of its three major weaknesses:

1. Most handicapping advice is very general, even vague; the real decisions are left to your judgment. You may have good judgment, but you are playing an awfully unfair game in which good judgment may not be good enough.
2. Most popular handicappers tell you a lot about the factors that influence horses' winning chances but not much about what constitutes a good or a bad bet. The very real possibility that a horse with a good chance of winning may be a very unwise bet (or, less frequently, that a horse with small winning chances is a good bet) is largely ignored by all but a small elite of handicapping writers.
3. Any handicapping method or betting system has the property that if it becomes widely known, it cannot yield profits. The very notion of a method that is *both* successful *and* popular is therefore suspect.

For all these reasons, we believe that following the popular literature in racetrack betting is unlikely to prove profitable. The best of the

43

handicapping writers will provide you with some interesting and potentially worthwhile ideas, but to follow their suggestions usually requires a good bit of your time and effort. At that point, the question is not merely whether their advice works, but whether it will compensate you adequately for the "investment" you must make to use it. The literature just might contain an excellent approach to racetrack handicapping that will enable you to make $15,000 per year if you devote every waking hour to it. That would be awfully impressive, but if you must give up your $25,000 per year job to do this, it is not much of a deal.

We remain frankly skeptical, but there is no reason why you should passively accept our skepticism. Exploring the handicapping literature is fun, and perhaps you will find something of value that we have missed. If so, more power to you! Remember, though: To maximize your gain, don't let others in on your successful betting methods. To share racetrack information may be noble, but it cannot be profitable.

## An Evaluation of the Popular Literature

Thus far we have discussed why we should expect racetrack bettors to lose, on average, a substantial portion of the money they wager, although it is conceivable that a clever individual bettor might turn a profit. We come now to a question that all scientists must pose about their field of inquiry: What is the evidence? Or, in our specific case: Are there demonstrable methods or systems of selecting and betting on horses that "work"—that is, that yield a net profit (or positive rate of return)?

Notice our emphasis on the word *demonstrable*. The "fact" that Richard has a friend whose father-in-law's dentist is said to win $40,000 at the racetrack every year doesn't really count. In the first place, even assuming everyone's honesty and good faith, we cannot be sure that the fact *is* a fact. Exaggeration is not confined to fishermen; it is human nature to recall every detail of one's successes and to forget one's failures. Perhaps the dentist wins $40 a year. Or possibly he was overheard to say that he *would love to win* $40,000 but hasn't been able to do so.

Indeed, to be scientifically interesting, it is not enough to believe that a particular individual has "beaten the races," even if we are completely convinced that this has occurred. We must also subject the "winner's" gambling method to empirical tests—that is, to actual observation— and reproduce the results!

We have divided the existing body of evidence on racetrack betting into two categories: popular and academic literature. By the former we mean "how to win" books (or calculators or computer programs) offered for sale to the general public, frequently at rather fancy prices. The latter category refers to more technical analyses, usually appearing as articles in professional journals and unknown to the public at large.[1] In a few instances, our distinction may be blurred. "Popular" books or programs are occasionally quite technical, and ideas in technical articles may (on rare occasion) become widely known or "popular." For the most part, however, the line between the categories is clearcut.

The most impressive thing about the popular literature on racetrack betting is its size and "staying power." There are quite a few books on how to pick and bet the horses (and, of late, a fair number of electronic calculators and computer programs). Moreover, many of the books have been around for 10 to 20 years, going through repeated printings and revisions. What this suggests is that, as in the stock market, there is considerable demand for "professional advice." Whether this advice is worth what we pay for it is (as in the stock market) an open question.[2]

## Some Consistencies and Inconsistencies

Much of the advice you will find in the popular literature is quite sensible; some of it, however, is so preposterous as to be almost funny. Much of what is said by various authors is also consistent, and widely believed by racetrack afficionados; there are, however, some big contradictions in the advice available at your local bookstore. Let's look at some of the high spots.

## Can the Races Be Beaten?

It will not surprise you to learn that most of the people who want to sell you advice on racetrack betting believe that it is possible to bet profitably. They *must* believe it, or at least they must *say* they believe it, and that they do in various ways. Consider, for example, the statement of Al Illich in his book, *Al Illich's How to Pick Winners* (1983, p. 45):

> *That many do win is attested to by the fact that approximately 85 percent of every dollar wagered at the tracks is paid back to the holders of winning tickets and by the number of tax returns based upon profit from playing the races.*

Most betting advisers are somewhat more restrained. Tom Ainslie (1979, p. 20), one of the very best writers on horseracing, puts it this way:

> ... *some players beat the races and most do not. For those who do not,*
> *the chief problem is lack of knowhow.*

Indeed, we have come across only an occasional pessimist on the topic, such as the well-known gambling expert the late John Scarne (1974, p. 81), who observed:

> *It should be obvious ... that "beating the horses" or rather "beating the*
> *state and track percentage deductions" is an impossibility in the long*
> *run.*

John Scarne, it should be noted, made this statement in a book on all forms of gambling, not just the racetrack. Scarne's wisdom, however, should not be underestimated!

## Some Major Points of Agreement

There is wide agreement on a number of general principles about selecting and betting horses. These include the following:

1. Spot betting is preferable to betting on every race.
2. Speed is an extremely important determinant of a horse's winning chances (this is not, of course, a big shock).
3. The distance of a race is an important consideration in determining which horse is likely to win.
4. A horse's condition is an important determinant of winning chances.
5. A horse's age can be an important influence on winning probabilities.
6. A horse's "class" is of major importance to winning; unfortunately, there is not much agreement about how class is to be defined and measured!
7. "Pace" can be an important factor in the winning or losing of a race. Some horses, for example, do best if they break fast and get an early lead; others enjoy more success by holding back in the early going and conserving their energies for a late "stretch run." Measurement of pace is not entirely straightforward, however.
8. The quality of the jockey and of the horse's stable can be quite important.
9. "Systems," meaning completely specific formulas for betting,

do not work well. Nate Perlmutter (1964) puts the point con-
cisely when he states: "The concept of a winning system is pure
meadow bull pie." [p. 72]

10. Exotic bets tend not to work well.
11. Horses coming off long layoffs are poor—or at least very
    risky—bets.
12. The consistency of a horse's past performance is important;
    frequency of finishes in the money may signal consistency.

The majority of handicapping authors agree on the points above.
Whether they are correct in their agreement is quite a different
question, however.

## Some Major Disagreements

The following are a few of the handicapping points on which popular
writers cannot agree at all:

1. Win betting is or is not better than place and show betting.
   Actually, most of the popular literature comes down strongly on
   the side of the win bet (only the late John Scarne disagreed). But
   the systematic evidence gathered by academic investigators argues the other way (see Chapter 6), and we suspect that this
   point of view will find its way into more popular references
   before too long.
2. A horse's earnings—either total or average per race—are or are
   not a good indicator of that horse's consistency and winning
   chances.
3. The weight carried by a horse either is or isn't important. If it is
   important, high weight is either a good or a bad sign.
4. Betting recently claimed horses is or isn't a good idea.
5. Horses "dropping down"—that is, running in a lower priced and
   presumably lower quality race than previously—are or are not
   good bets.
6. The odds on a horse either tell us something or tell us nothing
   about winning probability. (Here, incidentally, the academic
   evidence is strong and clear: Odds convey a great deal of
   information.)
7. Horses whose odds rise from the morning line are either good or
   bad bets. Similarly, horses whose odds fall are either bad or good
   bets.
8. A horse's post position either is or isn't important.

By this point, the idea should be clear. There is a core of agreed-upon principles in the popular betting literature, but also a fair amount of divergence. We now get back to the central question: What is the evidence? After all, many of the preceding suggestions would seem to be testable. Let's try to look at the facts.

## Handicapping

Most of the popular horse betting books tell you how to "handicap." We put the word handicap in quotes because its meaning in horse racing has come to differ somewhat from its more general usage. In common parlance, a handicap is a disadvantage or hindrance—as in a physical or mental handicap. Traditionally, the racetrack handicapper is the person who assigns weights—which are disadvantages—to horses in order to narrow the differences in their winning probabilities. Better animals carry heavier weight; the chances of the weaker entrants are thus improved, and more exciting races are expected to follow.

The term "handicapping" has also taken on a broader meaning in racing and in sports betting generally. It refers to the art of evaluating contestants (horses in a particular race) and then proceeding to select winners (or at least "good" bets). An expert handicapper thus refers not to the fellow who assigns weights to horses but to any bettor who studies the horses and produces a successful gambling record.

It would be difficult and not very rewarding to try to reproduce everything that popular handicapping advisers choose to tell us (if you really want to know, you will have to spend at least a couple of hundred dollars on the currently available books and several weeks of your time!). Here, however, is a selective sampling, again with an eye toward the *evidence*, which is unfortunately rather sparse.

The majority of writers tell us that there are at least three (and perhaps as many as 10) "critical" factors in handicapping. Most frequently mentioned are the *speed* of the entered horses, their *class*, and the *conditions of the race* in question (including distance, condition of the track surface, and the purse or "price" of the race). Let's look at these in turn.

### Speed

It is not a big shock to learn that faster horses do better, other things being equal! The trick, however, is to utilize information about the *past* performance of the entrants in a race (what we might term *ex post* data) to forecast the *future*. How, in other words, can one predict which horse will run fastest in the *next* race?

The *Daily Racing Form*, the handicapper's bible, provides much useful information. One can determine from the past performance records the approximate time in which every entrant has run each of his (her) past races. Further, the *Form* prints a measure called the *speed rating* for every horse in every previous race. This index expresses the horse's running time in a race relative to the record (fastest) time in which a race of the same distance was run at the same track. For example, a horse named Sworn Statement raced 6 furlongs at Aqueduct on February 11, 1982, with a speed rating of 90. This means that the horse ran ten-fifths of a second (or two whole seconds) slower than the record time for 6 furlongs at Aqueduct. (The record time is assigned a speed rating = 100; each fifth of a second slower than the record results in a speed rating of one less than 100.)

Since speed is such an obviously critical determinant of a horse's winning chances, why shouldn't we simply compare the running times (and speed ratings) of the contestants in a race and bet on the fastest animal? In a sense this is just what some writers suggest, but for several reasons it is not such a simple task.

The most obvious complication is that the past records of virtually all horses show a lot of variation in speeds. Sworn Statement had a speed rating of 90 at Aqueduct in November 1982; but his speed rating at Gulfstream in February 1983, also at 6 furlongs, was a far less impressive 70—a full six seconds (30-fifths of a second) off the track record. Few horses run all of their races in impressive times, and comparisons among entrants are thus not entirely simple or straightforward.

Other factors also compound the comparison task. There are unquestionably differences among tracks such that a particular running time or speed rating at, say, Aqueduct or Saratoga is not precisely equivalent to the same time at Gulfstream or Pimlico.[3] Moreover, a horse's speed on any given day will be influenced by such factors as weight carried and the condition of the racing surface—considerations that are variable and potentially important, yet may tell us rather little about the "inherent" capabilities of the animal.

How, then, should we make use of information on speed in our handicapping and betting? The popular literature at this point provides a few broadly consistent bits of advice. For example:

1. Draw comparisons among different tracks in order to adjust for

variations in running times and ratings that are attributable to
the tracks themselves rather than to the quality of the horses.

2. Pay more attention to more recent performances.
3. Modify speed information in light of other relevant information
   (weight carried, track condition, and so forth). Then pick your
   winner!

Note the initial difficulty here. The advice, though it may be perfectly sensible, is not very specific. Different handicappers using
these "criteria" may well select different horses a good part of the
time. And as for evidence about this method of handicapping: There
isn't any. An approach to choosing horses that is nonspecific cannot be
tested, precisely because we cannot specify its selections.

To see more closely what the problems are, let us consider a
randomly chosen race: the sixth race at the Meadowlands on October
30, 1984. This is a 6-furlong, $12,000 claiming race. Suppose that we
wish to "speed handicap" the race—that is, choose a likely winner on
the basis of available speed information.

If we simply look at the best race each horse has run at this
distance, as measured by the speed rating,[4] we would find the following ranking:

|   |   |   |
|---|---|---|
| 1. | Oil City | 98 (Oaklawn Park) |
| 1. | Snowgun | 98 (Rockingham) |
| 3. | Propaganda | 94 (Monmouth) |
| 4. | Set Forth | 94 (Monmouth) |

If instead we rank the entrants by the best speed rating in their *most
recent* 6-furlong race, we would find:

|   |   |   |
|---|---|---|
| 1. | Snowgun | 82 (Aqueduct) |
| 2. | What Mommy | 79 (Medford) |
| 3. | Set Forth | 76 (Monmouth) |

Alternatively, if we look at the best *average* speed rating for all
entrants in their past 6-furlong races, we have:

|   |   |   |
|---|---|---|
| 1. | Oil City | 93 |
| 2. | Propaganda | 87 |
| 3. | Snowgun | 85 |

The nature of the problem should now be evident. Simply to know
that speed is important—which is what every handicapping adviser
tells us—is not very helpful. A simple examination of entrants' speed
ratings does not point to a best selection; at most, it identifies three or

four possibilities.[5] Furthermore, there is no reason to suspect that complicating the analysis—for example, adjusting the ratings to reflect differences among tracks, and assigning a system of weights to ratings in "old" and "recent" races—would point to a clearer choice. Conceivably, it would alter somewhat the list of leading candidates for a win bet but not shorten that list.

There is a second major difficulty with the type of analysis we have just described. This concerns a fundamental shortcoming, not only in the speed rating but in any simple measure of a horse's running time. These statistics ignore such "external" factors as track conditions and the quality of opposing horses in the races being examined. For example, Quest Star's unimpressive speed rating of 63 at Laurel Race Course on December 3, 1984, may be partially attributable to the fact that the racing surface was sloppy or to the fact that the race was run by a bunch of slow horses (both facts are accurate). If so, this speed rating may be a misleading guide to Quest Star's chances at another time and place.

The track condition factor can be dealt with roughly in a relatively simple way. If you are handicapping races that are about to be run on a "fast" track, confine your analysis to the records of races on fast tracks—ignore those run on sloppy, muddy, or even "good" surfaces. This is not a completely satisfactory procedure, however, for even the meaning of a "fast" track will vary, perhaps significantly, among tracks and at the same track over time.

Quality of the opposition (and other external influences that may be significant on occasion) are also tricky to deal with. The eastern edition of the *Daily Racing Form* publishes another statistic—the *track variant*— that is relevant to this problem. The track variant measures the average winning times of races on a given day at a particular track relative to the record times. The track variant for the day of Quest Star's race was 24. This means that at Laurel on December 3, 1984, the average winning time of all races was 4.8 seconds (24-fifths of a second) off the track record times—not very good. This suggests that, other things being equal, we probably should not place a great deal of emphasis on Quest Star's poor speed rating in this race. The fact is that for one reason or another no horses were running very well at Laurel on that particular day.

Whereas it is a relevant piece of information, however, the track variant is not enormously helpful to speed handicapping. It tells you whether horses ran well (fast) on a given day at a given track, but not *why*. For example, last Wednesday may have been a "good" day at

Monmouth Park because there were several expensive races that
attracted some fast entrants. Winning times were close to the track
records, and the track variants were accordingly low. In contrast, the
previous Monday may have been a mediocre day: no big purses, few
fast horses, thus a much higher track variant. If we are handicapping
a race in which some entrants ran at Monmouth on Monday and others
on Wednesday, the track variant will probably be a misleading piece
of information. It suggests that the Monday runners were better for a
reason that, in reality, has nothing to do with their winning chances
today.

What, then, can be done? In principle, the answer is that we need a
different piece of information: the average winning times for various
qualities (classes) of races at various tracks. Quirin (1979) provides
some useful data along these lines, and Beyer (1975) describes clearly,
and in detail, a method for deriving such "ideal" ratings. Putting
together such indexes may well improve your predictive ability, but
there are two significant drawbacks to consider. In the first place,
even an ideal set of ratings, if such a thing exists, will not *consistently*
point you in the direction of winning bets. Most races will continue to
yield a mixed bag of ratings, as in our example above, so that you will
have identified only the three or four horses that look best according
to the speed criterion. On occasion, the procedure may work well,
identifying a clear best choice in a particular race. But these occasions
may be few, and it cannot be known whether the betting odds on such
clear picks will be consistently favorable.

The second problem with serious speed handicapping is that it
requires a great deal of time. Putting together an appropriate and
adequate set of ratings—one that will enable you to evaluate horses
whose records have been established at many tracks in a variety of
race classes—is a very big job (and, as Beyer frankly points out, a
boring one as well). The results may give you some good bets, perhaps
even an occasional juicy payoff. But the question now is not only
whether your handicapping activities "work" in the sense of producing some profits, but whether your profits compensate you adequately
for the time and effort spent.

## Class

Expert handicappers seem universally to agree that a horse's class is
an extremely important determinant of winning probability. Unfor-

tunately, there is little agreement about how class should be defined or measured. Nate Perlmutter (1964) observes that class "has been variously defined by players as truth has by poets." [p. 64]

Some writers attempt to be a bit more specific, suggesting, for example, that the term denotes some combination of physical abilities (speed, stamina, and so on) and competitive spirit. Fine, you may say, but so what? How does this notion help to identify the winner of the next race?

This is a very reasonable question, and it is one on which our handicapping advisers do a good deal of waffling. There is, once again, no specific formula that will tell us "how much class" an animal possesses. Indeed, the term is so vaguely defined that virtually any favorable element in a horse's past record might be considered a signal of "class."

There is, however, one recurrent and potentially useful suggestion in most popular discussions of the class factor. The quality of a race should be reflected in a fairly accurate fashion by its "price," meaning the size of its purse (or the claiming prices attached to its entrants). Something about the quality—or class—of a horse, then, may be inferred from the quality of the races in which it runs. Of course, a particular horse may be *outclassed* in any given race, and thus do very poorly against the opposition. But an animal that is consistently entered in high-quality races is presumably well regarded by its trainer and owners, who are expert judges and whose own money and reputations are on the line.

No handicapper is likely to suggest a betting strategy based simply on the quality of races in which horses run, but two plausible propositions emerge from this discussion. First, a horse's *earnings*—either *in toto* or the average per race entered—may be a meaningful reflection of what most writers have in mind when they discuss "class." Earnings, after all, depend directly on two factors: (1) how frequently the horse finishes in the money, thereby receiving some share of the total race purse and (2) how large the purses are. A horse's racing income is thus an indicator both of how well it has done in the races it has run and of the quality of those races.

The second plausible proposition, to which most handicappers subscribe, is that a horse's winning chances in a given race must be viewed in terms of the quality of the race relative to the quality of races the horse has entered previously. An animal "moving up" in race quality (class) faces stiffer opposition and will thus have a harder time of it, other things being equal. Similarly, the horse who is "dropping down" may fare better than in previous efforts against superior rivals. Despite the perfectly reasonable sound of these propositions, there is, once again, very little hard evidence of their actual value to the bettor. Quirin (1979), one of the very few popular writers to undertake a systematic analysis of racing data, reports that betting on horses with highest average earnings is a consistently losing strategy. So too is betting on horses that drop down in class of race immediately following a "good" race (good is defined by Quirin as finishing in the money, or close to the winner, or both); in this instance, however, losses do seem to be substantially smaller than those of the average bettor.

The popular handicapping literature, however, does not ordinarily recommend such specific betting strategies. Rather, the bettor is advised to take the "class factor" into account — indeed, to consider it very seriously — in making selections. It is difficult to argue with such obviously sensible advice. But it is virtually impossible to determine whether the advice is of the slightest practical value.

## Conditions of the Race

It is a truism that the conditions of a race — its distance, the state of the racing surface, the weights carried by the various entrants, and so forth — will affect the outcome. Moreover, the ways in which such conditions bear on the prospects of any particular horse are frequently obvious. A horse that has been running well early but tiring at the end of "routes" (that is, races of a mile or more) may have good prospects when entered in a shorter ("sprint") race, and one who gains at the end (but fails to win) in sprints may be well suited to a route.

Similarly, the horse who is a "good mudder" will have good chances, almost by definition, on a muddy or sloppy track. And the animal who is entered against heavier (or lighter) weighted rivals may have an advantage (or disadvantage). Interestingly, however, the weight factor can be argued both ways. A low weight, *everything else being equal*, helps a horse. But the very fact that a horse is assigned a low weight indicates that other things may not be equal. It may signal that the racing secretary or track handicapper who assigns the weights has a low opinion of the animal, or, in the case of an apprentice's allowance, that the horse is ridden by an inexperienced jockey.

What is the evidence? we ask again. Once again, there just isn't much of it. It is highly probable that the obvious hints to a horse's success or failure "work" in the sense that they do have something to do with winning probabilities. A good mudder, for example, *must run well in the mud*; if he didn't, the folks at the *Daily Racing Form* and at the various tracks would not term him a good mudder! They are smarter than that. But this circuitous statement tells us nothing about whether good mudders running in mud are also *good bets*. That most important question is one that is not systematically addressed in the popular literature.

## Trip Handicapping

Andrew Beyer has recently (*The Winning Horseplayer*, 1983) expounded an advanced approach to handicapping that has attracted a good deal of attention in the racing world. (Beyer, incidentally, developed this approach in response to dwindling returns to the speed handicapping methods he had previously popularized — another example, perhaps, of the reasonably efficient market catching up with a good idea.)

The essence of Beyer's new approach, "trip handicapping," is to examine the trips that horses have experienced in their previous races. Suppose, for example, that Old Ben ran an apparently unimpressive race his last time out: He finished fourth, 8 lengths behind the leader in a relatively slow time, and never mounted a serious challenge. In fact, however, Old Ben had a rough trip in that race. He was boxed in early by several other horses, and forced to "go wide" — run on the outside of the track, a long and inefficient route — in an effort to overtake the leaders. Beyer's argument is that in a case such as this, Old Ben's performance was much better than it appears superficially. He might, in fact, be a good bet the next time out, especially if the crowd, viewing his previous "poor" performance, does not back him heavily.

This is a sensible suggestion, and Beyer may be correct in arguing that attention to both speed and trips can form the basis for useful betting strategies. There are drawbacks to this approach, however. First, the definition of a good or bad trip is somewhat subjective; there are really no precise guidelines. Second, and more important, trip handicapping requires a great deal of information — more than can be gleaned in most instances from reading the *Daily Racing Form*. To follow Beyer's advice, you will need to study the races, both "live" and in the televised replays that the tracks provide, in order to evaluate the trips of the horses that interest you. This not only implies a substantial investment of time; it effectively puts the method beyond the reach of the casual or occasional track goer.

## Systems

As we have noted, most authors of racetrack books view "systems" with something close to contempt. And they may have a point. After all, if a completely mechanical "formula" that removes all vestiges of judgment from the task of selecting and betting on horses could work, why wouldn't everyone realize that and make use of it?[6] (There are further reasons why most of us might not *want* to believe in systems. If formula betting is as good as our best handicapping judgment, doesn't that indicate that our judgment and intellectual prowess generally are not worth very much?) Despite such doubts, systems have one great virtue from a scientific point of view: Because they are completely specific, we can test them. We can find out, in other words, whether any given system works. Much of the evidence about systems turns up (unsurprisingly) in the more technical academic literature, but there are a few popular books that provide some interesting tests.

Both Da Silva and Dorcus (1961) and Quirin (1979), for example, have found a pattern confirmed in numerous technical studies. Betting favorites doesn't work—that is, it is a money-losing strategy. Betting longshots on the other hand, is worse; you lose money at a faster rate. The following are some other negative findings with respect to very simple betting systems:

1. Betting horses at any given level or range of odds does not work (i.e., it does not produce a profit over a large number of trials).
2. Entries (i.e., two horses coupled in the sense that the "entry" wins if either horse wins) are poor bets, largely because bettors like them and drive down their odds.
3. No system based on weight alone yields profits; ditto for post position.
4. Horses whose last race was "good" (either in the money or close to the winner) are poor bets, again because they are favorites of the crowd.
5. Horses coming off a long layoff (30 or more days) are horrible bets.
6. Horses coming off a winning race are not especially good bets. They tend to do about as well (or poorly) as the average of all bets.
7. "Consensus" horses (those picked by the *Daily Racing Form* experts) are poor bets.

A few simple systems that are somewhat more promising, although not clearly profitable, include these:

1. Betting underlays (horses whose odds fall) that become favorites.
2. Betting horses that drop down following a good race.
3. Betting top-weighted horses in sprints (but not routes).
4. Betting horses that "bid, hung" in their last race. ("Bid, hung" means that the horse challenged for the lead [bid] but did not quite make it at the end [hung].)

Are there any simple systems that produce profits? We have our doubts, but here are a few (very few) suggestions:

1. Betting high-odds underlays (i.e., horses whose odds fall from the morning line but remain relative longshots).
2. Betting horses that have shown the best early speed in previous races (you must, however, know how to define and calculate "best early speed"!).
3. Betting recently claimed horses.

You may or may not regard these findings as surprising. Their virtue, however, is that they *are* indeed findings based on a systematic examination of the evidence. If you don't believe the results, invest in the *Daily Racing Form* for a few weeks, collect the data, and check out the systems that interest you.

What about more complex systems? There are many of them around, and their potential number is almost limitless. For example:

> *Identify all horses whose last race was at today's track. Take the three who had the highest speed ratings at today's distance. Bet the one that had the rating in the highest class race and/or when carrying more weight than today. Resolve ties in favor of the horse dropping the most weight.*

This beauty is one of 77 selected systems described by Tom Ainslie (1979). It doesn't strike him or us as very promising, but does have the virtue of being testable (the testing, needless to say, will be a little cumbersome).

Complex betting systems would seem to have one point in their favor. Precisely because they *are* complex, they are *not* obvious. It is therefore believable that such systems might work yet not be noticed by the vast majority of bettors. There is also a negative aspect, however. Truly complicated systems may be difficult to implement at the track; after all, you may have only 20 to 25 minutes between races, and it is clear that some betting formulas cannot be "solved" within this brief period. Of course, if your system depends solely on past performance data, you can buy the advance edition of the *Form* and spend a few hours the night before the races charting your selections. (Again, however, you should at this point ask whether even a system so fine that it yields you consistent profits is providing a reasonable rate of return to your time and effort.)

Perhaps complex betting systems can win. But do they? There is some evidence (see especially, Quirin, 1979) that winning systems can be devised, although the vast majority are clear losers. Any winning system presented in a form available to the general public should give you pause, however. At the very least, ask yourself:

1. If a fellow has a system that will return a 10 or 20 percent profit to his money consistently, why is he selling it to me for $20 or $50 or even $200?
2. If the system actually works, won't the word get around? If it does, as we keep pointing out, the system stops working.

## Some "State-of-the-Art" Evidence

"State of the art" is a slightly pretentious phrase that means roughly "on the frontiers of knowledge and technology." An obvious question that arises in considering popular racetrack advice is this: How well does the state of the art do? Suppose that we follow the suggestions of the most up-to-date people in the field. Can we make money by doing so?

We have chosen a few sources of advice: the experts whose opinions appear in the *Daily Racing Form*, two recently developed programs for use on personal computers, and one programmed calculator. Our procedure was as follows. We first chose, somewhat arbitrarily, a sample of about 100 races taken from several consecutive issues of the *Daily Racing Form* during the summer of 1985. This sample included races at Garden State, Pimlico, Belmont Park, Rockingham, Monmouth Park, and a few other tracks. We then applied the advice offered by each of our high-tech sources, making a hypothetical $2 bet on the horse recommended by each source in each race. For every race, we debited our hypothetical "account" by $2, the cost of our bet; if a particular bet was successful—that is, if the recommended horse

Table 3-1    Rates of Return to "State-of-the-Art" Betting Strategies

| Source of Advice | Betting Strategy | Sample Size (No. of Races) | Rate of Return (%) |
|---|---|---|---|
| *Racing Form* consensus | Bet top selection to win | 103 | − 27 |
| | Bet top selection to place | 103 | − 11 |
| | Bet top selection to show | 103 | − 7 |
| Reigh Count | Bet top selection to win | 79 | − 17 |
| | Bet top selection to place | 79 | − 20 |
| | Bet top selection to show | 79 | − 10 |
| *Handicapper* | Bet top selection to win | 103 | 41° |
| | Bet top selection to place | 93 | − 13 |
| | Bet top selection to show | 93 | − 23 |
| *Sports Judge* | Bet top selection to win | 103 | − 48 |
| | Bet top selection to place | 103 | − 23 |
| | Bet top selection to show | 103 | − 32 |
| *Horse Race Analyzer* | Bet top selection to win | 104 | 3 |
| | Bet top selection to place | 104 | − 14 |
| | Bet top selection to show | 104 | − 11 |

°Removal of one race lowers rate of return to − 25 percent.

"came in"—we credited our account with the actual track payoff (gleaned from the *Daily Racing Form* on the day following the race). At the end, we would see whether the sum of our payoffs was greater or less than our ($2 per bet) cost, and we calculated the rate of return to each "investment" strategy. (This type of experiment, incidentally, is known as a *simulation*; we will have more to say about such procedures when we discuss the academic evidence later.)

The results, which are based *on the same sample of races*, enable us to determine whether we can earn a profit following our state-of-the-art advice; they also allow us to rank the performances of the various advisers. The rates of return earned by following each adviser's top selection are shown in Table 3-1 (in some instances, we also followed the number two and number three selections of the advisers; we note the results of these efforts, but do not include them in Table 3-1).

## *The* Daily Racing Form *"Experts"*

As we have seen before, the *Daily Racing Form* presents a table of expert opinion for each racing day at each track. We have used these opinions to pursue several simulated betting strategies. First, we took the consensus of the experts and made bets on the top selection to win, to place, and to show (three separate strategies). We then did precisely the same thing for a particular expert, "Reigh Count." Who or what Reigh Count is, we do not know, but his (her? their?) selections are *not* included in the consensus and do not appear in the tables at every racetrack.

Notice that these betting simulations are extremely easy to perform (you can try them out yourself with a relatively small expenditure of time, money, and effort). No data about the horses need to be collected, entered, or analyzed; one simply identifies the chosen horses, checks to see if the hypothetical bet on each is successful, and if so, records the payoff. Adding up the gains and losses at the end, and calculating the rate of return to the betting strategy, is low-level arithmetic.

It is clear that betting the consensus choice to win is a very poor strategy (see Table 3–1); the rate of return to such bets is −27 percent, which is not only bad but considerably worse than the crowd as a whole does (recall that the average rate of return, which is equal to the track take, is around −18.5 percent). As we have noted before, this is not a surprising result, and it does not necessarily mean that the alleged experts are fools. The poor rate of return may instead indicate that quite a few bettors follow the consensus recommendations, thus depressing the odds and payoffs on those horses. Regardless of the reason, however, betting consensus selections to win appears to be a terrible investment strategy. Interestingly, betting these choices to place (rate of return = −11 percent) or to show (−7 percent) turns out to be a better procedure. Both choices lose money when applied to our sample, but the losses are smaller than those of the crowd as a whole.

The results of following Reigh Count's top selection in the 79 races in which he made a recommendation are also negative: a −17 percent rate of return to win bets, −20 percent to place bets (both of these are close to the average performance), and a slightly better −10 percent when betting the selections to show.

Some writers have observed that the experts labor under a (pardon the expression) handicap: the fact that they must pick a winner in every race rather than confining themselves to races that offer especially good choices. This may or may not be so; we are frankly skeptical that it makes much difference. The bottom line, however, is the same in any event: Following the experts appears to be a money-losing course.

## *The* Handicapper

The *Handicapper* is a personal computer program marketed by the Federal Hill Software Company. It sells for about $50. Of course, you will also need a computer, which may cost several hundred or several thousand dollars, to use this software. Once you have the program, a fair bit of work is required. You must enter into your computer some 12 items for each horse you analyze; these include such things as weight carried, change in class, time of last race, and quality of jockey. The program appears to pay particular attention to class, finishing position in the prior race, and time of prior race.

The *Handicapper* does a good deal of weeding out beforehand. For example, you don't consider, and therefore don't bother to analyze, any horse that has not run for more than two weeks or whose last race was not strong. Frequently, only three to six horses per race are eligible for analysis. Certain races are also eliminated from contention — for example, maiden events or races run on an off track. All of this tends to keep down the time required for computation, and it is usually possible to analyze a race in 10 to 15 minutes.

The evidence on the *Handicapper* is extremely interesting; in fact, our eyes popped when we first saw the results. Betting the program's top selection to win produced a spectacular rate of return of +41 percent! Bets on the top choice to place (−13 percent) or show (−23 percent) did not do as well. We also looked at the second and third picks provided by the *Handicapper* and found uninspiring outcomes: The rates of return ranged from −4 percent (betting the number three pick to place) to −65 percent (betting the number three pick to win), or a range of "not too bad" to "horrible."

What about that 41 percent rate of return, though? Do these people really know something, and if so, why are they selling it to us for a mere $50? Further examination revealed that this result was largely dependent on the outcome of a single race in which the winner paid $134. Remove that one race, and the rate of return plummets to about −25 percent. Of course, Federal Hill Software could contend, quite properly, that it is unfair to remove their big winner. Our conclusion about the *Handicapper* is therefore a bit problematic. The program did in fact perform quite well overall, but its success was so heavily determined by a single race (in a sample of 103) that we remain skeptical about its value. Perhaps another 100 races would tell a different story.

## *Thoroughbred Handicapping System by the* Sports Judge

We next tried a somewhat more expensive personal computer program, *Sports Judge*, distributed by PDS Sports for a price of $129. The computing requirements of this program are broadly similar to those of the *Handicapper*. One must enter 12 items for each horse to be analyzed, plus three variables for the race itself. These include such things as the distance of the race, size of the purse, and the horse's earnings and days since its last race. The program appears to attach major importance to the type of track on which the race is run, the horse's position at the first call in its previous race, and its current year's earnings. There is no prior weeding out of horses by *Sports Judge*, so analysis of a given race takes more time, typically about 20 minutes.

The results we obtained for our sample using the *Sports Judge* program were, with one quirk, pretty dismal. Betting the program's top selection to win produced a huge negative rate of return of −48 percent, far worse than we would expect from purely random choices. When we bet the top pick to place or show, the results improved somewhat (−23 percent and −32 percent, respectively) but remained worse than the average bettor's loss. The results obtained from following *Sports Judge*'s number two selections were also poor for win and place bets; show bets did better, losing only 4 percent over our sample.

The one quirk that we found using this program appeared in the number three selection: Betting number three to win yielded a positive rate of return, +18 percent; place and show bets yielded modest losses of −7 percent and −8 percent, respectively. This was a rather strange result, but our general conclusion regarding *Sports Judge* is clear: You can do at least as well, and probably better, without spending the time and money that this program requires.

## Horse Race Analyzer

The *Horse Race Analyzer* is a widely advertised programmed calculator sold for about $50 by Mattel Electronics. It is small and runs on a battery, so you can take it to the track. It is rather cumbersome to use, however, and there may not be enough time between races to analyze all the horses. The program requires that you enter 30 items for each horse, and one more for the race itself. These include such things as the horse's running position and lengths behind the leader at various points ("calls") in its previous race, and its current and past earnings. Earnings per race appear to receive heavy attention in the calculation of the *Analyzer* program.

Despite the rather clunky nature of this program, the results we got from the *Analyzer* are of some interest. Betting the top selection to win yielded a +3 percent rate of return, not significantly better than breaking even, but a good deal higher than the average return to all bettors. Place and show bets on the top selections produced losses of 14 percent and 11 percent, respectively. Bets on the number two and number three selections of the *Analyzer* proved to be unspectacular; some rates of return were above the crowd average of −18.5 percent, but all lost money.

## Summary

Can you win money by following the state of the art in racetrack betting? We cannot claim to have the definitive answer, but the results overall are discouraging. The experts are poor guides to investment, whereas the programmed systems are quite erratic. As noted, the *Handicapper* program produced a large positive rate of return to win bets. We suspect this was a fluke, but further testing may be in order. The *Horse Race Analyzer* provided, in effect, a break-even result (+3 percent); this is far enough above the average to be of some interest.

The general lesson, however, is pretty clear. If we follow what is presumably the best advice available, we will usually lose money; in some instances, we will lose considerably more than the average bettor. There may be a couple of exceptions, but even here caution is advised. If the systems used by the *Handicapper* and the *Horse Race Analyzer* were to perform consistently well—and that is a very big if—the word might get around. When and if it did, these programs would presumably continue to pick the same proportions of winners, but their rates of return would fall dramatically.

We are thus forced to conclude that following expert advice doesn't work; the state-of-the-art devices cost a good bit of money, require substantial investments by the user (both time and, in two cases, computer hardware), and do not provide auspicious results.

## Some Final Observations

How good or bad is the popular racetrack literature? The answer is, of course, that it varies! Much of what has been written is unlikely to help your profit and loss statement. The reason for this is usually obvious. Whereas many "investment advisers" provide abundant information— much of it quite sensible—about what factors may influence a horse's winning chances, relatively few tell you what may constitute a profitable betting strategy. Picking winners, as you know, is only part of the game. When added to the other major weakness of most handicapping advice—its lack of specificity—our conclusion about the bulk of the literature is, to put it mildly, skeptical.

There are, however, some important exceptions to this melancholy assessment. The very best handicapping advisers—such people as Quirin, Ziemba and Hausch, Fabricand, and Mitchell—recognize clearly the distinction between a "good horse" and a "good bet." Their suggestions are thus quite interesting and, for the most part, extremely clever. Even here, however, two important questions must be posed. First, is the time, effort, and money required to follow high-quality handicapping advice likely to be rewarded *adequately*? (If you can net $100 per week following someone's sophisticated system, but it takes you 30 hours per week to do so, you are "making money" but earning less than the minimum wage!) Second, if someone has a really excellent system and writes a book about it, won't the word get out? When and if it does, the system will no longer work. It will continue to pick the same proportion of winners as before but will not turn a profit.

We do, then, remain skeptical about the value of popular racetrack advice. As scientists, however, we do not ask you to take our views on faith. By all means, sample the popular literature and see if it enables you to win money consistently. We have our doubts but we could be wrong. If we are wrong, however, our advice is that you tell no one about it, and clean up just as quickly as you can.

## Endnotes

1. The relevant professions are most frequently economics and finance, statistics, mathematics, and psychology.
2. It will not remain open for long. We are about to discuss it.
3. Writers such as Beyer (1975) and Davidowitz (1983) also claim that some tracks have "biases," idiosyncrasies that work strongly for or against certain post positions.

4. Alternatively, we could examine actual racing times. The resulting menu probably would not look dramatically different.

5. In this particular race, Propaganda was the winner, paying $7.00, $3.60, and $2.60. Global Jet placed ($4.80, $3.20), and Snowgun showed ($2.60).

6. Recall our basic paradox, however: If "everyone" uses a betting system, the system *cannot produce profits* no matter how "good" it is intrinsically. Even a perfect system that yields winners in every race could not work—the ultimate result would be either that the racetracks would shut down, or that they would survive by returning about $1.60 to each $2 winning ticket!

# Chapter 4

# Why Do People Bet?

## Preamble

Racetrack betting is only one of innumerable examples of activities in which we do something without being certain of the outcome. Uncertainty is an intrinsic part of life, and we face it and cope with it daily. We buy products without assurance that they are not going to turn out to be defective. We cross streets without the certainty that a careless driver is not going to run us over. In the many situations in which uncertainty is present, how do we balance our desire for a particular object or outcome against the uncertainty of our quest for it?

First of all, casual observation suggests that we engage in quite a few activities that are designed precisely to reduce the uncertainty we face. For one thing, we buy insurance, and that has the direct effect of reducing uncertainty. Without a homeowner's policy, for example, we face two possible outcomes: either our house does not burn down and our wealth is unchanged or it does burn down and we are many thousands of dollars poorer. With insurance, either the house does not burn down, or in the event of a fire, the insured value of the house is paid back and our wealth is not reduced (by nearly as much).

In the area of consumption goods, many people spend time reading magazines such as *Consumer Reports*, buying products with "good" warranties, or even purchasing a separate service contract, which is a form of insurance. The purpose of all such activities is again to reduce uncertainty.

Racetrack betting seems to be the very opposite type of activity. Here we take something that is certain (the $2 in our pocket) and convert it to something highly uncertain: We might lose the $2 or we might end up winning a small pile of money. People who act like this seem to seek out risk rather than shun risk, and it may seem paradoxical that the same person might *simultaneously* seek some risks and avoid others!

A key element in understanding this type of situation is the manner in which the individual's satisfaction changes as his or her wealth level changes. As one has more and more wealth, one's satisfaction generally increases. Suppose that we start from some initial level of wealth and ask what happens if our wealth level increases by $100, then by another $100, and another $100, and so on. Does the satisfaction level increase by smaller and smaller amounts for each $100 increment in wealth? Or does it increase by ever-increasing amounts? If the former, the person will be a risk *averter*; this person will like to buy insurance and not like to gamble. If the latter is the case, the person will be a risk *lover*. Combining these two possibilities, if reductions in wealth are increasingly painful at the same time that increments in wealth are increasingly pleasurable, the individual can be both: an insurer who pays a modest fee to avoid a great loss that will occur with a small probability, *and* a gambler who pays a modest fee to obtain a great gain that also occurs with a small probability. It does not make sense to castigate gamblers by saying that they are irrational any more than it does to castigate people who buy insurance. Both types act because of the way in which they derive satisfaction from more or less wealth. What matters is the expected satisfaction from the risky situation compared with the satisfaction from a situation in which risk elements have been removed. If the former is greater than the latter, the individual will gamble and not otherwise.

Of course, we know that there are other reasons for gambling. People go to the racetrack, for example, because it is fun to watch horses; and betting for some people may represent only the ritual behavior expected of them at the track. But in the rest of this book we shall use as our working assumption the proposition that racetrack goers care about their wealth level and are risk lovers.

## Attitudes Toward Risk

Imagine an idealized world in which everybody had complete knowledge and foresight about everything. Such a world, of course, does not exist; if it did, we could provide a simple answer to the question, Why does Peter choose to eat a meal in Restaurant X and not in Restaurant Y? The answer has to be that, for whatever price he is prepared to pay, he knows he will get a more delectable meal in X than in Y.

Unfortunately, very little is certain in life. All restaurants have "off" days on which the chef is distracted and over- or underseasons the food, or days on which waiters are surly or forgetful. Most of these things are not within our (Peter's) control, and it is very difficult to forecast when these "off" days will occur, since they may depend on the chef's lovelife and similar unforeseeable circumstances. But experience may have taught us that, on the average and in the long run, off days occur in Restaurant X about 20 percent of the time and in Restaurant Y about 10 percent of the time.

Now we are in a quandary: Restaurant X serves intrinsically better meals (because the chef is more talented or has more experience or whatever) but has an appreciably greater hazard of producing a terrible meal. Which restaurant will Peter prefer and why? The answer has to depend not only on how much of a gourmet Peter is—that is, how much sensuous pleasure he derives from Gratin de queues d'écrevisses washed down with a bottle of Corton Charlemagne—but also on what his attitude toward risk and uncertainty is.

In the following sections we shall attempt to be a bit more precise about what we mean by "attitudes toward risk" and how this concept relates to racetrack betting.


## The Satisfaction from Having Money

Few people would argue with the proposition that having more wealth is preferable to having less. In a real sense we can say that having a wealth of $100,000 gives one more satisfaction than having only $50,000. Why this is so may well depend on the individual. If suddenly given a large sum of cash, some people would convert it into pretty things like paintings or tasty things like caviar; others would stuff it into the mattress because they really care about the dollar bills themselves. But in any event, for most people more is better than less.

It would be useful to devise a way of measuring the amount of satisfaction that a person derives from varying amounts of wealth. If one could do this, it would be easier to describe that person's state. This is somewhat analogous to the measurement of temperature. Having a Fahrenheit or centigrade scale for measuring temperature is not essential in everyday life, but it certainly is useful. If we had no temperature scale, the *New York Times* might report yesterday's temperature as, "Of the people interviewed, 78 percent were shivering uncontrollably and 16 percent had actually turned blue," or "It was sufficiently warm so that 92 percent of the people interviewed had a rosy glow on their cheeks, and a full 48 percent had some perspiration on their upper lip." It certainly makes life easier to be able to say that the temperature was 12 degrees Fahrenheit or 87 degrees Fahrenheit or what have you. Quite analogously, we could describe in more or less cumbersome prose how much sweeter it is to have a wealth of $100,000 than $50,000, but it might be more straightforward if we could derive a measure for it.

At first blush, such an undertaking seems doomed to failure. Satisfaction is subjective, and we would somehow have to get into the mind of a person to glean how much pleasure he is getting from this or that. But a ray of hope is provided by the following thought: If a person acts deliberately rather than haphazardly, the choices that he makes in life are likely to reveal what gives him more or less satisfaction! So, if we are clever enough to observe a person, we may devise a satisfaction scale for him, not unlike the way in which we could devise a temperature scale for him.

Now, how would one devise a temperature scale? First, we might note the kind of weather in which our subject turns blue and has icicles hanging from his nose, and arbitrarily decide that we shall call the temperature that produces this effect "zero degrees." Then we might observe what temperature makes him sweat profusely and call that 100 degrees. Of course, we shall have to fill in other points on the scale, but we have established so far the *origin* or *zero point* on the scale, and implicitly we have established the units in which our scale is measured (between turning blue and sweating profusely there are exactly 100 degrees). When we are done filling in other points on the scale, it might look like the scale on the opposite page.

Of course, once we have translated our subjective sensations into a temperature scale, we could use that scale quite effectively to make rather complex judgments such as, "When it is 25 degrees outside, I would be willing to step outside in my bathrobe for 30 seconds to pick up the milk that the milkman left by the door, but I would be unwilling to sit, even wearing a sweater, in 30-degree temperature for two hours."[1] Most simply, the temperature scale is just a numerical translation of the warmth we feel: The higher the temperature, the more the warmth. The scale is not like the scale we use to measure weights or distances in the following sense: It is very reasonable to say that 2 miles is twice as far as 1 mile, or 12 pounds is 4 times as heavy as 3 pounds. It makes no sense at all to say that 100 degrees is twice as warm as 50 degrees, which is five times as warm as 10 degrees,

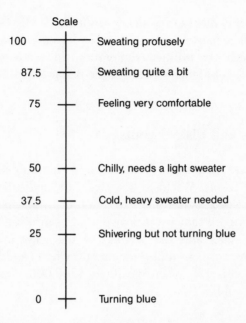

and so on. To convince yourself of the truth of this, imagine that we are using Fahrenheit rather than centigrade. One hundred degrees centigrade corresponds to 212 degrees Fahrenheit, and 50 degrees centigrade corresponds to 122 degrees Fahrenheit; yet 212 is certainly not equal to $2 \times 122$. The information in the temperature scale is relatively modest in that it gives us only an indication of "more" versus "less."

At least in the beginning, a satisfaction scale should have the same feature—that is, it should distinguish more from less. It is clear that the placing of the zero point on such a scale must be arbitrary (what is it that yields exactly zero satisfaction?) and that the units in which we measure the scale must be arbitrary (if $100,000 yields me 100 units of satisfaction and $200,000 yields me 150 units of satisfaction, I might with equal validity say that $100,000 gives 1,000 units, and $200,000 gives 1,500 units of satisfaction). So the first step in constructing a scale would be to arbitrarily pick an origin (zero point) and unit for the scale. The next step is to assign numbers from the scale to dollar amounts such that if I get more satisfaction from one dollar amount than from another, the satisfaction scale number assigned to the first will be greater than that assigned to the second.

To avoid using the awkward term "satisfaction scale number" over and over, we shall adopt the economists' term and refer to these

numbers as utility numbers or simply *utilities*. The first result we then
have is that, since most people get more satisfaction from more wealth
than less wealth, the utilities (remember, these are the satisfaction
scale numbers) get higher whenever the dollar amounts get higher.

## Probabilities and Risky Events

So far we have reached an obvious and, undoubtedly, somewhat
disappointing result. We have not given any indication of how we
would *in practice* assign utilities to different wealth positions (dollar
outcomes). Suppose that we pick two utilities arbitrarily (as we have
to, since the units and the original of the scale are intrinsically
arbitrary). Say we pick utility equals 100 when wealth is $100,000
and utility equals 150 when wealth is $200,000. A simple way of
writing this would be

$$U(100,000) = 100$$
$$U(200,000) = 150$$

and means exactly what the above sentence says: To $100,000 we
assign the utility number 100, and to $200,000 we assign the utility
number 150. This immediately suggests that we attach no importance
to views such as "$200,000 is twice as good as $100,000." In fact, in
the system of measurement we are describing, that statement would
be as meaningless as the statement that 90 degrees Fahrenheit is
twice as warm as 45 degrees.

But what about some intermediate dollar amount? What is the
utility number corresponding to, say, $125,000? We know that since
125,000 is greater than 100,000, its utility number must be greater
than 100 (which is the utility of $100,000): Since 125,000 is less than
200,000, its utility number must be less than 150. But just what
number should it be? Should it be 110? or 149? or 100.00001? In
principle, any of these numbers seems all right and what we have
discovered so far gives us no help in choosing the "right" number in
the 100 to 150 interval.

In order to go further, we must now start to talk about risky events
and probabilities. Risky events are those in which we do not know the
outcome with certainty. Games of chance are a simple illustration.
Flipping a coin can have two outcomes. It can come up heads or tails

(in principle, it could also stand up on its edge, but most would agree that this is so rare an event that we do not have to take it into account as a matter of practice). Roulette can come up any one of the numbers 0,1, ..., 36 (with American roulette having double-0 as well). But risky events are a much broader category than just games of chance. Going to a restaurant is a risky event because the chef may have prepared an excellent meal or she may have an "off-day" and serve us slop. Any situation in which the outcome can vary and in which we cannot know with certainty what will happen is a risky event.

Now, in flipping a coin, we would agree that for a geometrically and metallurgically perfect coin, the probability is 1/2—that is, 0.5 that it will land heads up, and 0.5 that is will land tails up. What this means is that if we tossed the coin a very large number of times (perhaps millions of times), the observed proportion of heads would be 50 percent or very close to it. If the roulette wheel is spun, a particular number will "come up" with probability 1/37—that is, if we spin the wheel many, many times, that number will come up about 2.7027 percent of the time.

There are two separate issues involved in dealing with probabilities. The first one is how we ever find out what the probability of some particular outcome is. In the case of the coin, we conclude that the probability $p = 0.5$ partly on the basis of experience and partly because some geometric considerations of symmetry in the coin make it implausible to argue that heads will come up, say, twice as often as tails. In other instances, the reasoning might be even more complicated and may draw on experience, analysis of physical or biological systems, complicated statistical procedures, and the like. Thus, the conclusion that Drug X is 75 percent effective against disease Y (that is, has a probability of 0.75 of curing the disease) is based on a host of complicated analyses, and we shall not go into further detail about how one might reach such a conclusion.

The second major issue is how individuals will act once they know (or *think* they know) the probabilities associated with the various outcomes. After all, most of the time we accept information provided by others as to what the relevant probabilities are: the probability that Drug X cures Disease Y, that a commercial airline flight will crash, that smoking causes heart disease and cancer, or that Lucky Guy will win the seventh race at Monmouth Park. Once we have this information and believe it to be true, we shall have to decide how to choose among the various risky prospects that face us.

## Expected Values and Expected Utilities

In order to return a little later to the construction of a utility scale, we must first define the concept of an expected value. Imagine that we are playing a simple game of chance. A coin will be tossed, and if it comes up heads, Peter will pay Richard $1, and if it comes up tails, Richard will pay Peter $1. If they play this game for a very long time, how much can Peter (or Richard) expect to win on the average (that is, how much are his winnings per toss in the long run)? Suppose they toss the coin 1,000,000 times. Half the time (approximately) Peter will win, and half the time he will lose. His net gain per toss is

$$\frac{\text{(Winnings of \$500,000)} - \text{(Losses of \$500,000)}}{1,000,000} = 0$$

More simply, we could take the payoff if he wins a toss ($1), his payoff if he loses (−$1), multiply these outcomes by the respective probabilities, and add them up. Thus, expected winnings are

$$(0.5)\,(1) + (0.5)\,(-1) = 0$$

If we now change the game so that Peter wins $1 if the coin comes up heads but loses $2 if it comes up tails, his average winnings become

$$(0.5)\,(1) + (0.5)\,(-2) = -0.5$$

and he loses 50¢ on the average. This calculation give us the *expected value* of the game: It is the *average outcome* of the game if it is played for a very long time. The general rule for calculating the expected value is simple: If $p_1$ represents the probability of "outcome 1" and $x_1$ represents the dollar value of outcome 1, and if $p_2$ and $x_2$ represent the probability and dollar value of outcome 2, the expected value of the game is

$$\text{expected value} = p_1 x_1 + p_2 x_2$$

that is, the probability of the first outcome times that first outcome plus the probability of the second outcome times the second outcome.

Since the probabilities of all conceivable outcomes must add up to 1.0, in a game with only two outcomes (heads or tails), we can write $p_2 = 1 - p_1$, and therefore

$$\text{expected value} = p_1 x_1 + (1 - p_1)\,x_2$$

We shall use the shorthand $E(x)$ to represent the expected value of $x$—that is, the expected or average outcome.

The notion seems to be a useful one for deciding whether Peter should or should not play the game. To illustrate this conjecture, we shall change the game once more. This time, if the coin comes up heads, Peter wins $2, but if it comes up tails, he loses only $1. Applying our expected value calculation shows that Peter has average (that is, per toss) winnings of 50¢, and it seems he would have to be crazy not to want to play the game. But suppose Richard says, "I will play this game with you only if, before each toss, you pay me an 'entrance fee' of 25¢ (that is, ante up) for the privilege of playing the game." Peter would obviously still be willing to play, since he wins 50¢ on each toss *on the average* but has to pay out only 25¢ per toss for playing the game. Thus, he is still comfortably ahead. Richard, of course, seems to have no incentive to play the game since he loses on the average! It would appear that both would be just indifferent between playing and not playing if the "entrance fee" charged by Richard were exactly equal to the 50¢ average winnings that Peter gets under the rules of this game.

Expected value calculations are important ingredients in assessing the characteristics of risky events, but they are not the whole story. First of all, Peter might well say, "I know that in the long run I shall have average per-toss-winnings of 50¢, but we will not play the game forever, and in any finite period of time, I might have a run of bad luck and lose much more often than win!" What Peter seems to be saying is that he cares not only what happens in the very, very long run, but also about the variability of the outcomes that one might reasonably expect. We shall come back to this issue later.

The other reason that expected value calculations are not likely to tell the whole story can best be illustrated with an example of another game. Imagine that Richard proposes a game to Peter that will have the following rules: (1) Peter will have to pay an "entrance fee" to Richard (as in the previous coin-tossing example), but we shall wait a bit before he specifies how much this entrance fee will be; (2) Richard will then start tossing a coin, one time after another, until "heads" comes up. If "heads" comes up right away, the game is over immediately. If "tails" comes up on the first toss, the coin is tossed a second time. If "heads" comes up on the second toss, the game is over; otherwise the coin is tossed a third time, and so on. Each extra toss required to produce a "heads" doubles the payoff (from what it would have been if the previous toss had produced "heads"). The payoffs that Richard has to pay to Peter are as follows (according to the rules of this game):

| "Heads" Comes Up | Payoff Richard Has to Pay Peter |
|------------------|--------------------------------|
| On the first toss | 2 |
| On the second toss | 4 |
| On the third toss | 8 |
| . | . |
| . | . |
| . | . |
| On the tenth toss | 1,024 |
| . | . |
| . | . |
| On the $n$th toss | $2^n$ |
| . | . |
| . | . |
| . | . |

The curious feature of this game is that the number of possible outcomes is infinitely large, since (in principle) the game might go on for a billion, billion tosses without producing "heads," or a billion, billion, billion tosses, and so on.

To compute the expected value of this game, we need to find out the probabilities of the outcomes. Thus, what is the probability that the game will end after one toss? two tosses? ten tosses? a million tosses? It is clear that the probability is 1/2 that the game will end after one toss. If the coin is tossed twice, the possibilities are

| First Toss Shows | Second Toss Shows | Outcome |
|------------------|-------------------|---------|
| H | H | game ends after first toss |
| H | T | game ends after first toss |
| T | H | game ends after second toss |
| T | T | game goes on |

If a coin is tossed twice, there are four possibilities, only one of which ends the game at that point; since the four possibilities are equally likely, the probability we need is ¼. (Consider this: you toss a coin twice and repeat the two-toss experiment a billion times. In roughly what fraction of your billion experiments do you expect each of the four possibilities to show up?) If a coin is tossed three times, the possibilities are:

| First Toss Shows | Second Toss Shows | Third Toss Shows | Outcomes |
|:---:|:---:|:---:|:---|
| H | H | H | game ends after toss 1 |
| H | H | T | "          "      "      "   " |
| H | T | H | "          "      "      "   " |
| H | T | T | "          "      "      "   " |
| T | H | H | game ends after toss 2 |
| T | H | T | "          "      "      "   " |
| T | T | H | game ends after toss 3 |
| T | T | T | game goes on |

Hence, only one out of eight possibilities terminates the game after three tosses, and the probability is ⅛. Proceeding in similar fashion, the probability of terminating the game after 10 tosses is 1/1024, after $n$ tosses $\frac{1}{2}^n$, etc.

Now we can calculate the expected value of the game. Remember that to calculate expected value, you must take each possible outcome, multiply it by the corresponding probability, and add up these products.

| Game Ends After Toss No. | Payoff | Probability | Payoff Times Probability |
|:---:|:---:|:---:|:---:|
| 1 | $2 | 1/2 | 1 |
| 2 | $4 | 1/4 | 1 |
| 3 | $8 | 1/8 | 1 |
| . | . | . | . |
| . | . | . | . |
| . | . | . | . |
| 10 | $1024 | 1/1024 | 1 |
| . | . | . | . |
| . | . | . | . |
| . | . | . | . |
| | | Total = | ? |

The expected value $E(x)$ is

$$E(x) = 2(\tfrac{1}{2}) + 4(\tfrac{1}{4}) + 8(\tfrac{1}{8}) + \ldots + 1024 \left( \frac{1}{1024} \right) + \ldots$$

and we keep adding up our infinitely long string of ones! The sum is clearly larger than any number you can name: All we have to do is to keep adding ones as we calculate the expected value. (In ordinary parlance you might say that the sum is infinitely large.)

Having made this calculation, and remembering the earlier game in which Peter would surely have an incentive to play if the entrance fee charged him were *less* than the expected value of the game, Richard modestly proposes that Peter pay him an entrance fee of a mere one trillion dollars. He assures Peter that in the long run he will surely do very well, since the expected value of the game is much, much larger than a trillion dollars; in fact, poor Richard will lose an incredible bundle in the long run!

Why might Peter be reluctant to agree to the terms of the game (including the entrance fee of one trillion dollars)? Possibly because he does not have a trillion dollars. But what if he did? Would he still refuse? Most likely, but why? Well, he might doubt Richard's ability to pay off. Suppose the game goes on for a zillion tosses. Richard would now have to pay off two raised to the zillionth power, and Peter may doubt whether Richard can pay this off (since two raised to the zillionth power is much larger than the entrance fee collected by Richard). This is a valid reason but still not the whole story. Peter would probably refuse to play, *even if he did not doubt Richard's ability to pay off.* What makes Peter refuse to play the game is this: Since the expected value of the game is greater than the entrance fee, Peter must be counting on some big wins. But he already had a lot of wealth to begin with, since he could afford to pay an entrance fee of a trillion dollars. Once you have a trillion, is a second, third, or tenth trillion as valuable to you as the first? If you had a trillion, would you stake a "double-or-nothing" game on a toss of a coin? In other words, would you risk losing your one trillion just to take a chance on getting your wealth up to two trillion or even to three or four trillion? Many people would answer this question firmly in the negative. The reason is that what matters to individuals is not the expected value of a game—that is, the expected dollars— but the expected satisfaction or *expected utility.* Since for most people the expected utility from having a wealth of two trillion dollars may be only very slightly greater than from having one trillion dollars (if you don't believe this, tell us what you would do with the second trillion), most people would refuse such a bet.

The main point of this discussion is that a sensible person will choose among risky alternatives (gambles, life choices, or what not) on the basis of expected utility and not on the basis of expected (monetary) value. But if this is the case, *we can use the choices a person makes to reveal his utility scale.* Here's how we do it. Let us return to an earlier example and imagine that our experimental subject, Peter, has a current wealth of $100,000. We have already argued that to fix the zero point and the units of the utility scale, we can pick scale values (utility numbers) arbitrarily for two wealth figures. Just for the sake of illustration we shall pick these as follows:

$$U(100,000) = 100$$
$$U(200,000) = 150$$

We are thus saying that, according to the units chosen, Peter gets 100 satisfaction units from $100,000 and 150 units from $200,000. Now let us present Peter with a choice. He can either keep his current wealth or he can buy a lottery ticket with his $100,000; this lottery ticket will pay him a prize of $200,000 or pay him nothing. Here is the situation:

|  | Peter's Action | |
| --- | --- | --- |
|  | Does Nothing | Buys Lottery Ticket |
| Peter's wealth | $100,000 | $200,000 if lottery ticket wins |
| after action |  | $0      if lottery ticket loses |

If Peter is sensible, he will refrain from deciding what to do until he obtains some information on the probability that the lottery ticket will win. If we assure him and he honestly believes that the winning probability is 0.99999999, he will most likely opt for the lottery. If this probability is, say, 0.1, he will probably not take the gamble. If he does take the gamble, its expected *utility* must have been greater than the utility of $100,000. In the other case, the expected utility of the gamble must have been less than the utility of $100,000. Now, how do we calculate the expected *utility* of the gamble (as opposed to its expected monetary value)? Expected anythings are always calculated by taking each of the possible "outcome values," multiplying them by the probability that that outcome will occur, and adding these up. In the calculation of expected monetary value, we take the *dollar payoffs*, multiply them by their respective probabilities and add these. To get *expected utility* we take the utility numbers corresponding to each outcome, multiply each by the corresponding probability, and add these up. Thus, the expected utility of the lottery ticket is

$$E(U) = p\ U(200,000) + (1 - p)U(0)$$

where $p$ is the probability that the lottery ticket wins—that is, the utility of the first outcome times the probability of the first outcome plus the utility of the second outcome times the probability of the second outcome.

We have seen that for large values of $p$, Peter will probably take the lottery ticket, and that for small values of $p$ he will almost certainly refuse it. Suppose that we keep asking him questions such as, "What would you do if the probability $p$ were 0.7, or if it were 0.8, or if it were 0.759862" until at some point he says that at that particular value of $p$ he cannot choose—that is, he is genuinely indifferent between just keeping his $100,000 wealth and buying the lottery ticket. For that value of $p$, the expected utility of the lottery ticket must be *exactly equal* to the utility of the stand-pat strategy! (If one were greater than the other, he would tell us which one he would choose.)

For the sake of illustration, imagine that Peter is indifferent when $p = 0.8$. Then the expected utility of the lottery ticket is

$$(0.8)U(200,000) + (0.2)U(0)$$

or, $(0.2)U(0) + 120$, since we earlier set $U(200,000)$ equal to 150 and 150 times 0.8 equals 120. Since this must equal the utility of $100,000 which we defined as 100, it must be that

$$(0.2)U(0) + 120 = 100$$

from which it follows that

$$U(0) = -100$$

We have just determined a new point on Peter's utility scale; so we now have

$$
\begin{aligned}
U(0) &= -100 \\
U(100,000) &= 100 \\
U(200,000) &= 150
\end{aligned}
$$

We could now proceed in similar fashion and present Peter with a variety of lottery tickets, each time varying the probability of winning until Peter reaches an indifference point between some sure alternative and the lottery ticket. Thus, if we now find that Peter would be indifferent between having a sure wealth of $150,000 on the one hand and a lottery ticket that gives him $200,000 with probability 0.95 and nothing with probability 0.05, the expected utility calculation gives

$$(0.95)U(200,000) + (0.05)U(0) = U(150,000)$$

or, substituting for $U(200,000)$ and $U(0)$ the values we already know,

$$137.50 = U(150,000)$$

In this fashion we can determine Peter's entire utility scale for wealth, and in practice we might actually approximate it quite well. We could even plot his utility scale in a diagram, with wealth being plotted on the horizontal axis and utilities on the vertical. The utilities we determined (shown by the dots) might form part of a utility curve as in Figure 4-1.

## Insurance and Gambling

Once we know a person's utility scale, we can determine from it whether that person is going to gamble or not.

Let us first consider a person whose utility scale we (partially) determined in the previous section. We would have to determine many more points on his utility scale to be able to undertake this analysis, but here we shall replace the hard work with a couple of

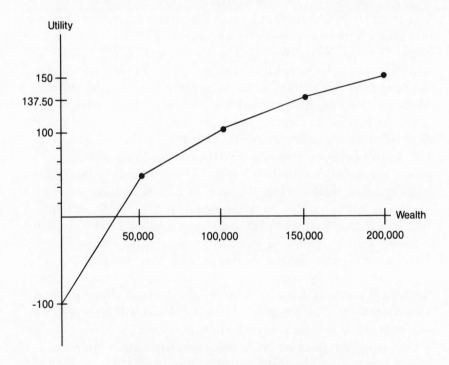

Figure 4-1   A Concave Utility Curve.

assumptions: (1) We shall assume that for this person $U(50,000) =$ 40; (2) between adjacent wealth levels for which we already have utility numbers (i.e., 0, 50,000, 100,000, 150,000, 200,000), the utility numbers fall on a straight line. The utility scale is shown in Figure 4–1. You can see that this scale as a whole is bowed forward or down; the economist calls this utility scale *concave*. It has the important feature that, as you have more and more wealth, the increments in the utilities due to having an extra dollar (or $1,000) get smaller. Now imagine that this person has current wealth of $150,000, consisting of a house valued at $100,000 and cash (or stocks and bonds) of $50,000. Life, however, is uncertain, and our friend knows that there is a probability of 1 in 100 that during the next year his house will burn down and be a total loss. So the expected utility he faces is

$$E(U) = (0.99)U(150,000) + (0.01)U(50,000) = 136.525$$

Now along comes an insurance company that says to him, "If you are willing to pay us a premium of $1,100, we shall insure your house."[2] To our friend this means that he can, if he wants to, trade an uncertain situation for one in which his wealth is $148,900 *for sure*: If the house does not burn down, he has his original wealth minus the $1,100 premium he has paid the company; if it does burn down, the company pays him $100,000 to replace the loss, and he still has $148,900 (since he has paid out the premium).[3] Now, what is the utility to him of $148,900, which he will have with certainty? Remembering our utility numbers, the utility scale increases from 100 to 150 between a wealth of $100,000 and one of $150,000; hence, *per dollar,* his utility increases in this range by 0.00075 for every dollar of wealth. Thus, the "cut" of $1,100 he takes when he decides to insure reduces his utility by $1,100 \times (0.00075) = 0.825$. Hence, his utility from $148,900 is $137.5 - 0.825 = 136.675$, *which is greater than the expected utility when he does not insure!* Therefore, he will insure his house. People with this characteristic are called *risk averse* by economists. What is crucial in understanding this type of person is that a risk-averse individual will always prefer a sure alternative to an actuarially fair gamble and will even prefer a sure alternative to some actuarially favorable gambles.

The opposite type of person, a *risk lover*, has a utility scale that is bowed upward (and is called *convex*). Figure 4–2 shows a possible configuration. The points on the scale correspond to

$$
\begin{aligned}
U(0) &= -10 \\
U(50{,}000) &= 0 \\
U(100{,}000) &= 20 \\
U(150{,}000) &= 50 \\
U(200{,}000) &= 100
\end{aligned}
$$

Suppose that this person has a current wealth of $100,000. He goes to the racetrack where he contemplates betting $1,000 on a horse that will pay off $51,000 if he wins his bet. What are the possibilities? If the horse wins, his wealth goes to $150,000. If the horse loses, his wealth is reduced by the amount bet to $99,000. What is the expected utility of the gamble? Let us assume that the horse (a real longshot) has only a 3 in 200 chance of winning. Then, expected utility from betting is

$$
\begin{aligned}
E(U) &= (0.985)U(99{,}000) + (0.015)U(150{,}000) \\
&= (0.985)(19.6) + (0.015)(50) = 20.056
\end{aligned}
$$

where we obtained the utility of $99,000 by assuming that the utility scale is a straight line between a wealth of $50,000 and a wealth of $100,000. The expected utility is *greater* than that of the *status quo*, and our friend will bet. The crucial thing is that the risk lover will want to bet even if (as in the case in racetrack betting) the bet is actuarially unfair. (Of course, if the bet is terribly unfair, even a risk lover may refuse it.)

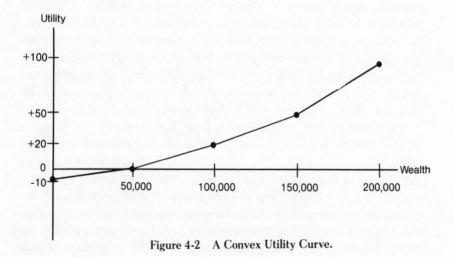

Figure 4-2   A Convex Utility Curve.

This means that, as a group, racetrack bettors—who continually take unfair gambles—must be risk lovers. Of course, some people go to the track because it is a pleasant way of spending the afternoon, eating hotdogs, drinking beer, and sitting in the sun. But as far as the betting activity is concerned, bettors must indeed love risk.[4] They don't all love risk to the same extent, however. This is why some bettors tend to bet on favorites, for which the expected monetary return is reasonably high and the expected risk is relatively low; whereas others prefer to bet on longshots, which tend to have much lower expected returns and much higher risk. These latter people love risk so much that they are actually willing to forego some financial return for the sake of a greater exposure to risk!

There is one remaining puzzle. The foregoing arguments about why people insure their houses while others gamble at the racetrack all hinge on the shape of their respective utility scales ("concave" for house insurers, "convex" for gamblers). Does this mean that insuring one's house *and* going to the racetrack are incompatible, and that none of the people one sees at the track on a sunny afternoon carry homeowners' policies on their houses?

The answer, of course, is no for a variety of reasons. We have already alluded to the first one—that spending time at a racetrack is an intrinsically pleasant activity, and the cost of a few bets is treated simply as part of the price of enjoying oneself. A second possibility is that the utility scale might well have a more complicated shape than we have suggested so far. It may consist of both concave and convex portions as in Figure 4–3. This person's present wealth is $100,000 and his utility scale is concave to the left of point A. He will thus want to insure against great losses that can be protected by paying a small premium. His utility scale is convex to the right of A, which means he will want to gamble if a small bet may return a large payoff. Thus betting and insuring are not incompatible for such a person at all. In fact, the utility scale may well be even more complicated looking for the average person; we tend to believe, for example, that when a person already has a huge wealth, further increments will no longer materially increase its utility. That suggests that somewhere to the right of point B in Figure 4–3 the utility scale may flatten out again and thus have a second concave portion. With such huge wealth the person would become a risk averter once again. Crudely speaking, this suggests that neither the very poor nor the very rich gamble at the racetrack; rather, mostly people with intermediate levels of wealth do so. While this is probably not wildly at variance with the facts, we

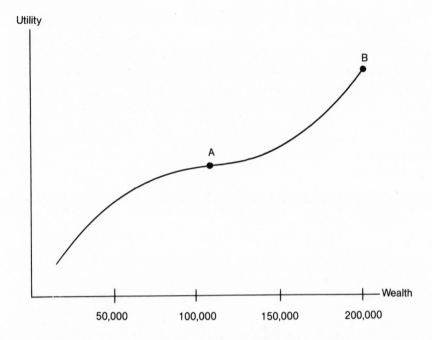

Figure 4-3   A Concave and Convex Utility Curve.

emphasize that we have concentrated in this discussion on the effect of risk attitudes toward betting; in real life, the situation is much more complicated because other motivations (such as watching pretty horses) also play a role.

## Final Observations

We have spent a good deal of time talking about why people gamble, even when the odds are heavily stacked against them. This discussion will not help you directly to earn profits at the racetrack (it may help indirectly, for reasons that we'll discuss later). Initially, you might have been tempted to answer the question, Why do people bet? by saying because they like to. Or because it's fun. What we have said does not contradict these statements, which are no doubt true for many people. Rather, we have tried to suggest that people's attitudes toward risk-taking activities—of which buying a ticket on a horse is only one—are complex and varied.

Some people are terribly uncomfortable with risk, whereas others thrive on it. Most of us hold different attitudes in different circumstances and times. It might thus turn out that when we look more closely at the risk-taking behavior of racetrack bettors, we will see nothing but a hodge-podge. Conceivably, however, patterns will emerge that may permit us to devise some useful betting strategies.

## Endnotes

1. It should be noted that the temperature analogy has one major defect. In reality, the temperature scale is established with respect to physical phenomena such as the freezing or boiling point of water.
2. Since one out of every 100 houses of such value burn down in a year on the average, the insurance company must charge at least $1,000 of premium; otherwise it would pay out more on the average than it takes in. We have assumed here that the extra $100 covers costs of operations and profit for the company.
3. It is clear that for simplicity we are abstracting from complications like partial losses of various magnitudes occurring with different probabilities, deductibility features in insurance policies, and so forth.
4. There is another possibility — that bettors love gambling as an activity (as distinct from the risk they take). Such people might prefer to accept ten very unfavorable gambles rather than one very favorable one! (We think this is weird behavior, but it cannot be ruled out completely.)

*Chapter 5*

# How Do We Assess Racetrack Betting Evidence?

## Preamble

The only potentially useful and interesting theories are those that make statements about factors or variables that are *observable*. Theories about how many angels can dance on the head of a pin may be amusing but certainly are not very useful. Theories about how to win at the racetrack tend to make assertions about facts; when they do, we ought to be able to *confront the theory with data* and see if it holds up.

This confrontation is not a trivial task. Even the data collection requires care, lest we introduce subtle or not-so-subtle biases by picking and choosing among the available information to suit our convenience. Once the data have been collected, we typically need to find out whether a relationship exists between two or perhaps more than two variables. We must specify not only the key variables between which the relationship is thought to exist (e.g., speed of a horse and gender of the jockey riding it) but also any other variables that might accidentally confound and confuse the relationship we are looking for and make us think there is a relationship when there really isn't one, or vice versa. In terms of the above example, the quality of the horse being ridden and the experience level of the jockey are extraneous variables that might obscure the relationship being investigated (between horses' speed and jockeys' sex). If, for example, male jockeys are on the whole more experienced than female jockeys, a higher success rate by men may erroneously be attributed to their "manhood" rather than to their greater experience.

After we have taken all these things into account, we must determine whether any relationships we find among the data are *statistical-*

*ly significant*—that is, "tight" rather than "loose." Finally, it is not enough to have a theory that predicts a "good" proportion of winners. If everybody could pick winners consistently, nobody would make any money because the odds would be depressed too low. To test whether our theory is a moneymaker, then, we must perform *simulations* in which we apply the theory and (hypothetically) bet on the horses it selects. We can then see whether we would have made money using our theory. Even here we must be very careful to avoid the biases that can creep in ever so quietly. If, for example, we "discover" our theory by staring at a set of data long enough, and then use this theory in a simulated betting exercise based on the *same* data, it should not surprise us that we are successful in proving that our betting strategy "works." A much more critical test of the theory is whether it generates profits when it is applied to a *new* set of data—a set that was *not* used in the process of "discovering" the theory. We show in the next few chapters various ways in which these general observations can be put to use.

## The Issues

Betting systems abound. Popular books recommend numerous ways to bet not only on horse races, but also on blackjack and other games of chance. And individual players often devise their own systems for craps, roulette, and of course racetrack betting. Go to the track or casino and you will see earnest people with hand-held calculators. Everybody seems to play a "system."

What is a "system"? In simplest terms, it is a set of rules that takes into account observable events and somehow transforms them into a prediction of what number will come up on the wheel or the dice, what number the dealer's cards will add up to, or which horse will win the race. The observable events may be nothing more than the outcomes of the last few plays of the game. Thus a roulette player may be thoroughly convinced (as we, of course, are not) that if the wheel has come up "evens" six times in a row, it is more likely to come up "odds" than "evens" on the next spin.

In racetrack betting, we might base our prediction of which horse will win the next race on the past records of each entrant (conveniently available in the *Daily Racing Form*), the records of the jockeys riding the entrants (presented in the day's racing program), the weather, the condition of the track, and the odds on the various horses, displayed a few minutes before the start of the race. In fact, as we have just seen, some information of this sort can be processed quite efficiently and quickly by special-purpose calculators developed precisely for racetrack bettors such as the *Horse Race Analyzer* by Mattel Electronics.

Some people will modify their prediction based on these objective factors, by other considerations. Thus, whenever Peter goes to the track, if there is a horse running named Aunt Louise, he bets on it because he has fond memories of his dear departed aunt and feels that his fondness for her will be promptly rewarded by the equine Aunt Louise. This sort of gambling, predicting, and plain guessing is by no means confined to the racetrack or casino. In picking stock market "winners," professional advisers and individual investors often use their own theories or "systems." As we have observed, some people predict on the basis of what are called *fundamental factors*: the company's products, the future strength of the markets for these products, the nature of the competition, and so forth. (A company that had been making the finest horse-drawn buggies might not have been the smartest investment at the beginning of the automobile era.) What such investors are trying to do is to predict the probable future courses of the company's sales and earnings.

The racetrack analog is "handicapping" on the basis of *fundamental factors* pertaining to horses: evaluations of past performance, weight carried, distance of the race, quality of the jockey, and so forth. As in the stock market, one is trying to predict the probable future success of one's prospective "investment."

Recall that others in the stock market rely on what is called *technical analysis*. They largely disregard the fundamental factors noted above and focus instead on the recent price history of the company's stock. The underlying belief here is that this history congeals in itself all there is to know about the future. Thus a "head-and-shoulder" pattern (a price sequence such as 50, 60, 55, 65, 55, 60, 50) might support one prediction for the future, while prices that break through a "resistance level" indicate something different, and so on.

The rough racetrack analog is a betting method that looks at the behavior of prices—that is, horses' *odds*—as opposed to the factors underlying those odds. One may believe, for example, that "smart money" dominates the betting at a particular track. If so, one looks for patterns in the odds that point to where (on what horse) the smart money is going. If you truly believe in such a system, there is no reason

to examine such "fundamentals" as running times, weights, and so
forth.

But how do we know whether a system or theory is true? How can
we tell that using one system will make us more money than another,
or more money than simply picking winners at random rather than
following any system?[1] Suppose somebody makes the following claim:
You should always bet on horses ridden by female jockeys for the
following reason. The public is generally distrustful of female jockeys,
perhaps because they are a relatively recent phenomenon or because
people do not think that female jockeys are as capable as male jockeys
(male chauvinist pigs are not unknown at the racetrack). As a result,
horses ridden by women will have relatively little bet on them, and
their odds will be relatively high. If these horses win, their payoffs will
be higher than if they had been ridden by males. Hence it is profitable
to bet on such horses.

But, now, wait a minute! What if bettors *are in fact right* in believing that female jockeys are less capable? Then, although the payoff on
a horse ridden by a woman will be higher if the horse wins, the
probability of its winning will be lower than if its jockey were a man!
Is it still profitable to bet on such horses? The answer must depend on
the decrease in the objective probability of the horse's winning (due to
being ridden by a female) *relative to* the increase in the payoff (due to
the fact that people's *perception* of female jockeys' abilities reduces
the amounts bet).

The upshot is that as simple as the system ("bet on horses ridden by
female jockeys") may sound, it rests on a very complicated theory. The
theory will stand or fall with the answers to the following questions,
*none of which is directly observable* in any given race:

1. Are female jockeys less able riders than male jockeys?
2. Do bettors perceive female jockeys as less able, and therefore bet
   less on their mounts than they would have if the horses had been
   ridden by males?
3. If both (1) and (2) are true, is the increase in odds and payoffs
   caused by (2) enough or more than enough to offset the decline in
   the objective winning probability caused by (1)?

You may have a gut feeling that you know the answer, but casual
observation will not do (this is precisely one of the weaknesses of the
popular racetrack betting literature). People may remember wins
more than losses. Feelings in one's guts are not very good guides to the
future, at least not when it comes to games of chance. Twice in his life
Peter had a chance to bet on a horse named Aunt Louise, and both

times he won; he obviously swears by his "system," conveniently forgetting that eight times he bet on a horse named after his equally beloved Uncle Harry and lost all eight bets. If we want to assess the validity of claims and counterclaims about betting systems, we must resort to more systematic procedures.

## Analyzing Data

At this point we must say a bit about the methodology of assessing betting systems. The broad question is, How do we decide that a particular theory or system is right or wrong? Only cold facts can reveal the answer. We could argue until we are blue in the face that according to aerodynamic theory it is impossible for a bumblebee to fly, and we would not settle the issue; however, as soon as we have seen a bumblebee fly, the argument is over. (You may ponder what it would mean if, over an extended period, you saw lots of bumblebees sit, walk, and crawl but never fly.) This means that we need facts and observations, otherwise known as *data*.

What data do we need? There is no easy answer to this question. Of course, the data should be relevant to the question to be investigated. Often one knows what the "ideal" data would be, but the pertinent information is either unavailable or too costly to obtain. (We recently obtained full computer printouts of the records of some 700 races at a well-known track. The printouts were rather indistinct carbon copies, so that we could not use an optical scanner to enter the numbers into a computer. The records contained over 2 million individual numbers. Think of the time and effort needed to enter these manually into the computer!)

Let us illustrate what we might do with the previous example in which the claim was made that it is profitable to bet on horses ridden by female jockeys. Suppose that we have tracked down and compiled the racing histories of 100 particular horses (including perhaps Aunt Louise and Uncle Harry). These histories include rides by both male and female jockeys. We can now investigate the claim in various ways.

First of all, we may ask, do horses win less often when ridden by females than by males? Suppose that the 100 horses in our sample each raced an average of 10 times, so that we are looking at 1,000 racing performances. Of these, female jockeys rode 200 times and males 800 times. Why don't we just count up the percentage of wins by females and compare it with the males?

An example will show that this comparison could be quite misleading. Suppose that our sample contains 40 awful horses ("Nags"), which were ridden five times each by females and five times by males. The women jockeys won 10 percent of the time they rode these horses (i.e., one out of every 10 races, or 20 out of the total of 200), whereas the males won 5 percent of the time (10 wins in 200 races). The other 60 horses in our sample were superior runners ("Secretariats") and were ridden exclusively by male jockeys.[2] The men won 50 percent of their races on these horses—300 wins in 600 tries (each of the 60 raced 10 times).

If we now compare the overall records, we see that women won 20 times in 200 races for a winning percentage of .10; the men won 310 races in 800 starts (10 winners out of 200 Nag races, 300 winners out of 600 Secretariat races) for a winning percentage of almost .39. The males thus appear to be much better jockeys. But this appearance is highly deceptive. It is due entirely to the fact that the men were riding better horses than the women. The women's performance when matched horse by horse against the men's was twice as good!

This suggests that we should look at the win percentages of women and men by individual horses. We could easily calculate these percentages from our historical record, numbering the horses 1, 2, 3, . . ., 99, 100. For each horse we then calculate the percentage of wins occurring in "female rides," and the percentage in "male rides." For horse number 1, the figures might be 0.05 for women and 0.10 for men; for horse number 2, perhaps the numbers would be 0.14 for women and 0.07 for men; and so forth. (Notice that in our sample we will have only 40 true points of comparison; 60 of the 100 horses had no female rides.)

The next step is to examine the *differences* in these percentages— that is, the women's winning percentage minus the men's winning percentage. For the first horse, this difference is −0.05; for the second it is 0.07, and so on. Now, if men are generally superior, these differences will tend to be negative figures by and large; if women are superior, they will tend to be positive on the whole. If men and women were equally able, we would expect to see these differences cluster very close to zero.

Of course, it is difficult to survey 40 or 100 numbers all at once and conclude that they are on the whole negative or positive or cluster close to zero. Statistical theory, the details of which we will spare you (!), tells us that a sensible procedure is to compute the arithmetic mean (or simple average) of these numbers and see whether it is "significantly" bigger or less than zero.

We put the word "significantly" in quotes because it is in itself a technical statistical term. The point is that even if men and women were exactly equal in riding ability, we could not reasonably expect the average difference in their winning percentages to be *exactly* zero, because there are always some random and unpredictable influences on the outcomes of races (and everything else!). Statistical theory allows us to judge "significance" by comparing the mean of the numbers we are examining with their *standard deviation*.[3] The standard deviation measures the dispersion or spread of the actual numbers around the mean, and statistical significance is judged by how large the mean is *relative to* the standard deviation. Thus, for example, if the mean difference between men's and women's winning percentages is 0.08, and the individual differences range from 0.07 to 0.09, the mean will more likely be considered "significantly different from zero" than if the individual numbers were spread out from $-0.05$ to $+0.21$.

Having determined whether horses win more or less often when ridden by women, we may investigate the next question: Does the public bet differently when it sees a female jockey? We could, for example, look at the final odds on each horse for each race in our sample, calculate the mean difference between "male rider odds" and "female rider odds," and repeat the sorts of calculations we have just discussed. Finally—since we are ultimately interested in profits—we could calculate the mean difference in winnings due to male and female riders if we had bet, say, $2 on each horse in our sample.

Procedures such as these yield tests of theories that are much more reliable than consulting tea leaves or the entrails of chickens. The results are not guaranteed since nothing of an empirical nature is dead certain (except for death and taxes, of course), but if the sample sizes are large, and the evidence has been carefully collected and analyzed, the numbers we come up with will be pretty convincing. As an example, consider the "theories"—or at least predictions—that many people made in 1981 when the government fired all striking air traffic controllers. It was widely asserted that the reduced number of qualified controllers in airport towers would create a sharply rising incidence of midair collisions. In fact, however, no such increase occurred. In light of this *fact*, it is difficult to maintain that there was a sizable increase in the probability of air accidents. Any such increase would have manifested itself in observable events in the huge sample of flights (many thousands per day) that take place.

Do we have an absolutely foolproof way of testing this theory? Of course not. There are many a pitfall to be avoided. We must, for example, be careful to avoid bias in collecting our sample (to test a theory about midair collisions, we would not want to look at a sample of flight *arrivals*, since, by definition, a flight that has arrived was not involved in a collision!). However, a much more subtle and pervasive problem must be considered: namely, the possibility that the *effect* we are analyzing has more than one *cause*. The frequency of airplane collisions, to cite the immediate case in point, is influenced by numerous events, of which the number of traffic controllers is just one.

Let us return to our previous example, the investigation of whether horses win more often when ridden by male or female jockeys. Suppose that we have carried out the suggested calculations and found, after comparing mean differences with standard deviation, the strong suggestion that male jockeys win more often. Along comes a skeptic, however, who says: "Aha! There is a problem here. In your sample, the male jockeys were generally much more experienced riders than the females, and experience counts for a lot in this business; so what you actually measured was not the effect of 'maleness' or 'femaleness' on winning percentages, but simply the effect of experience."

This is a potentially valid objection that seems to make everything much more complicated, but fortunately there are statistical techniques designed to cope with this sort of problem. We now turn to this issue.

## Regression Analysis

Let us begin by posing the problem a little bit differently. Suppose we have a sample of horses and wish to discover the effect of jockey experience on the speed with which each horse runs its races. Speed is measured in miles per hour and experience in numbers of years of competitive riding. We could tabulate these measures in a table (see Table 5–1), and then plot the pairs of numbers (speed and experience) in a diagram (see Figure 5–1, in which experience is measured on the horizontal axis and speed along the vertical axis). If we had a sample of 100 horses, each of which had run one race, there would be 100 dots on the diagram; to make it look less cluttered, we have put in just a few of the points, taken from the data of Table 5–1. The resulting picture certainly seems to suggest that there is a relationship between experience and speed.

Specifically, it appears that the more experience (abbreviated by $E$) a jockey has, the more speed ($S$) the jockey's horse has. It almost

**Table 5-1    Speeds and Experience Levels**

| Horse | Jockey's Experience (years) | Speed (miles/hr) |
|-------|------------------------------|------------------|
| 1 | 5 | 37.0 |
| 2 | 2 | 34.8 |
| 3 | 8 | 39.0 |
| 4 | 6 | 38.0 |
| 5 | 4 | 37.2 |
| . | . | . |
| . | . | . |
| . | . | . |
| 99 | 1 | 34.5 |
| 100 | 7 | 39.5 |

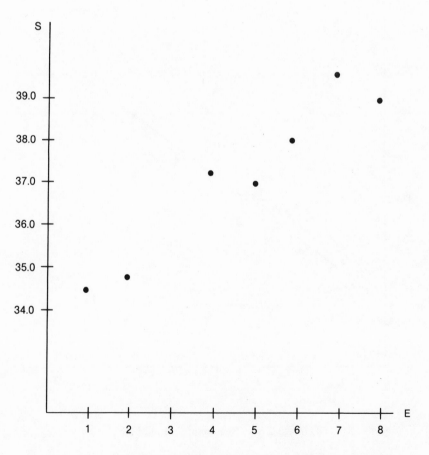

**Figure 5-1    Speed and Experience, Plotted from Data in Table 5-1.**

seems that the observed points may lie more or less along a straight line, the equation of which is $S = 33.50 + 0.753E$. With zero years of experience, speed is 33.50 miles/hour. With one year of experience, it is $33.50 + 0.753 \times 1.0 = 34.253$ miles/hour. With two years, it is $33.50 + 0.753 \times 2.0 = 35.006$ miles/hour.

This "reasonable" straight line is superimposed on our dots in Figure 5–2. The line seems to "fit" the observed dots fairly well. When that turns out to be the case, we say that experience *explains* speed and does so in a very specific sense: The experience level of the jockey can be used to *predict* the speed of the horse. Thus, for example, if a jockey had three years of experience, we would predict his horse's speed to be $33.50 + 3 \times (0.753) = 35.759$ miles/hour.

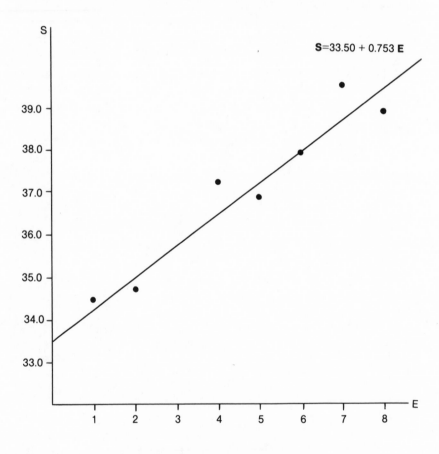

Figure 5-2   A "Reasonable" Fitted Line.

At this point, we must answer two questions. First, how do we "fit" a straight line to our observations? After all, the general formula for a straight line is $S = a + bE$, where $a$ and $b$ are general symbols that have to be replaced by specific numbers to give us a *particular* straight line. (You remember this, of course—your high school algebra class wasn't all *that* long ago!) How did we know that the "value of $a$" is 33.50 and the "value of $b$" is 0.753? The second question is, How can we decide whether the result is statistically significant? In other words, how do we know that the result we computed from the data, namely that $b = 0.753$, did not occur by chance, even though $b$ is in reality equal to 3 or 0 or whatnot?

With respect to the first question, we might suggest that one can fit the line easily using the naked eye and a ruler. Our line in Figure 5–2 has the equation $S = 33.50 + 0.753E$ and seems quite reasonable. Statisticians, however, frown on such freehand-eyeball procedures, believing that they are prone to individual bias and arbitrariness. What looks like the "best-fitting line" to Peter or Richard may not look like the best-fitting line to Midge, Richard's wife. In this case, our inclination is to trust Midge, but a more objective approach remains desirable.

To make any headway with this problem, we need a precise definition of "best fitting." Putting a straight line into Figure 5–2 always involves an approximation. For example, horse number 2 was ridden by a jockey with four years of experience, and the horse's speed was 37.2 miles/hour. Yet if we read off the fitted line, it predicts that this horse's speed would be about 36.5. The line thus makes an error of 0.7 in predicting the speed that corresponds to this level of jockey experience.

Statisticians have decided that the reasonable criterion for "best fitting" is that line (out of all conceivable lines) that makes the sum of the squares of these errors as small as possible. For this reason, we usually call this the *least squares criterion*, and the fitted line is called the *least squares regression line*. You may (or may not!) wonder how one determines what this line is. We shall skip the details and simply note that there are mathematical formulas that render the task not too arduous (boring, yes, but not intrinsically difficult). For your convenience, we present the relevant formulas in the appendix to this chapter.

The second question—Is the result significant?—can be answered in terms of the "tightness" of the observed points about the fitted line. If they are all very close to the line, and the fit is good (i.e., the sum of the squares of the errors is small), then the calculated relationship between $S$ and $E$ would be deemed statistically significant; if the points were very widely scattered around the line, it would be considered statistically insignificant.

This rather vague notion of a tightly or widely scattered set of points can be made much more precise by using the statistician's formula for the correlation coefficient, $R$ (this formula is also given in the appendix). Because of its mathematical definition, $R$ is a number between $-1.0$ and $+1.0$. A positive correlation means that the two variables, such as $E$ and $S$, move by and large in the same direction; a negative correlation means they move in opposite directions. (In Figures 5-1 and 5-2, the correlation is obviously positive. If we were to plot speed against weight, or against muddiness of the track, we would probably get negative correlations.) A correlation near zero means a loose, not very useful fit. Correlations near $+1$ or $-1$ indicate a tight fit that is statistically significant.[4]

Having found the relation between experience and speed, you may be content to rest on your laurels. But that would be a dangerous thing to do. Somebody might suspect that the horses in our sample were not all carrying the same weight, and that weight may very well also exert an influence on speed. Or, to return to our example, some of the jockeys could have been males and others females; and the condition of the horses may have varied in observable ways.

Can we analyze more than just one factor in a regression equation? In other words, could we calculate an equation that simultaneously accounts for jockey's experience, jockey's sex, weight carried, and horse's condition in "predicting" the speed of a horse? Could we calculate the coefficients $a, b, c, d, e$ in an equation:

Speed $= a + b$ (experience) $+ c$ (sex) $+ d$ (weight) $+ e$ (condition)

The answer is of course we can![5] (Statisticians are terrific people!) If we have data—that is, actual observations of all these variables for our sample of horses—this can be done almost as easily as in the simpler case when we worried only about the effect of experience on speed. Again we shall spare you the formulas and mathematical details. We note only that a least squares regression equation can be calculated from the data, and a correlation to judge its statistical significance can be obtained (this is analogous to the formulas in the appendix to this chapter).[6]

## Simulation Experiments

Imagine that we have listed and measured all the relevant variables that affect the speed of a race horse: jockey's experience, jockey's sex, weight carried, condition, track surface, class of the opposition, quality of each horse's recent performance, and so forth. Moreover, we have calculated a regression equation based on all these factors — perhaps as many as 10 or 12. Finally, imagine that our correlation is very high, say 0.9999, so that we have a great deal of confidence in our statistical results. Are we ready to clean up at the track?

One certainly might think so. After all, our regression equation predicts the speed of horses very reliably, and the fastest horse is bound to win! Of course, even a tightly fitting regression equation will make some erroneous predictions, and applying it will not always pick a winner. The reason is that there are *in reality* too many factors that bear on speed (including some that we may term "random") to take them all into account. Among other things, the jockey's mental concentration and attitude at the time of the race almost certainly have an effect; but what affects concentration — for example, a fight with a girlfriend or boyfriend — is something we cannot conceivably measure!

There is a further problem, however. *Even if the regression equation does a good job picking winners, profits are not assured.* So many bettors may have bet on the winner that the payoff is very small. If so, then even a few erroneous predictions (i.e., predicting that Old Siwash will win, betting on him, and losing) may wipe out our meager earnings in the successful cases. What we really need to do is to check out the profitability of the betting strategy that says simply: "Bet on the horse in each race that our regression equation predicts will be the fastest."

A handy way of doing this is by means of a simulation experiment (this is roughly what the handicappers mean when they advise you to try out a system "on paper"). We would begin by taking a new sample of horses and jockeys (one that was *not* used in deriving our regression equation to predict speed). Next we apply the equation to each horse over a series of races, and use it to predict which horse will win each race. At this point we *pretend* to bet, say, $2 on that horse. Since we have a historical sample, we know which horse actually won and how much it paid.

If the horse we selected in each race actually did win, we credit ourselves with the payoff; whether or not it wins, we charge ourselves with the price of the ($2) ticket. Repeating this procedure over perhaps 100 races will give us very good statistical information on the profit-and-loss implications of our system. If the system fails overall— that is, if it does not yield a profit, and perhaps does not even hold our losses to the amount implied by the track take—there may be two possible explanations. First, maybe our calculated regression equation did not hold up for a new sample of races and horses. It may have fit the data from which it was calculated rather well, but what it measured was an idiosyncratic relationship that could not be extrapolated to other situations. For example, the determinants of racing speeds at Belmont in 1983 may just not be quite the same as the determinants in 1984, or the predictors of speed at Belmont may differ from those at Saratoga or Gulfstream. Second, even if our equation does hold up, the payoffs may just not be big enough to compensate for the occasional inevitable losses.

We believe that such simulation experiments are a must if you want to "prove out" any type of betting strategy in an objective manner. We shall describe next the results of simulations we have performed to test the profitability of various betting strategies.

## The Nature of a "Good" Betting System

An enormous number of regression equations can be devised and employed to predict the winners of horse races; the only limit is the number of *combinations* of variables that you can dream up and measure! For example, you might wish to "run" (that is, compute) the equation:

$$X = a + b(\text{earnings per race}) + c(\text{change in class of race})$$
$$+ \ d(\text{jockey's experience}) + e(\text{jockey's sex})$$
$$+ \ f(\text{horse's fastest time at the distance})$$
$$+ \ g(\text{weight carried})$$

The letter $X$ in such an equation may be thought of as an index of the horse's quality, such as speed. If the equation is a "good" one, your system will be simply to bet on that horse with the highest value of $X$ among all entrants in any given race.

It is certainly possible that some regression equations will yield a "high" proportion of winners. Notice immediately one drawback, however. Regression analysis, especially when one examines numerous variables,[7] is quite costly in terms of both time and effort. Few of us can bring a portable computer to the racetrack, and even if we could, there may not be enough time to run all the necessary equations before each race. One must, therefore: (1) invest in the appropriate capital— computer hardware and software and (2) spend a good bit of time analyzing data before arriving at the track. Of course, you will recall from our discussion in Chapter 3 that the use of "canned" computer programs or hand-held calculators is not likely to do you much good. You will just have to take a few programming courses and design your own software!

The question at this point, as we have noted before, is not simply whether one's system "works" in some vaguely defined sense, but whether it yields *an adequate return* to one's expenditure of time and money.

*A brief digression*: Your reaction at this point may be to say: "Computer, hell! I can do all the analysis I need with a pencil in the margins of the *Racing Form*!" Our response is twofold. First: Sure you can! That is precisely what almost all racetrack bettors do; and almost all racetrack bettors lose money. If you can turn a profit, more power to you; but we're skeptical. And second: It is *not* the computers or calculators that *make it difficult* to pick winners—the task is intrinsically a tough one. It may be possible to perform adequate analysis without a little electronic help, but to do so may require that you undertake handicapping as a full-time job!

It is important to realize, as we have stressed at several points, that the "goodness" of any system of picking winners—whether or not it is based in regression equations—does *not* rest solely on the number (or proportion) of winners predicted. Ultimately, its success must be judged in terms of the "profit and loss" or "rate of return" statement, which is why one must simulate the system *via* a large series of hypothetical bets.

To illustrate, consider two hypothetical regression equations that will, with a substantial number of misses or errors, predict winners. Equation 1 bases its index of each horse's quality on the following variables: earnings per race, number of wins in the last six starts, goodness or badness of the most recent start, the jockey's in-the-money percentage during the current meet, and change in class of race. This system picks a "high" proportion of winners—let's say 35 percent— which is really quite impressive.[8] However, when we simulate the system based on this equation—that is, when we try it out by making hypothetical bets on the horses it selects—we find an unhappy result.

The horses we pick are heavy favorites of the betting public and are returning an average win payoff of only $5 to a $2 bet. If we make 100 bets, then we have:

Amount bet ($2 per horse)     = $200
Winning payoffs ($5 × 35)     = $175
Net loss                      = $ 25

In other words, our good-looking system loses 12.5 percent of the money we bet, a better-than-average performance (recall that the crowd as a whole loses 18 or 19 percent of its money), but hardly a "reasonable" or "adequate" rate of return to investment!

In contrast, consider regression equation 2, which predicts solely on the basis of sex of jockey, change in class of race, and change in horse's odds during the last eight minutes of betting. This system, when we simulate it, predicts only 10 percent of the winners—worse than a random selection. But the horses we pick are not popular with the crowd and pay an average of $21 to win on a $2 bet. We thus find, after 100 hypothetical bets:

Amount bet                    = $200
Winning payoffs ($21 × 10)    = $210
Net profit                    = $ 10

In other words, our not-so-hot-looking system, which picks only a small proportion of winners, gives us a positive 5 percent return to our money, far better than good-looking equation 1.

The lesson to be drawn is by now familiar. The name of the game isn't simply to pick winners, or, as our resident statistician might put it, to "maximize correlation coefficients." It is rather to *earn profits*, which isn't quite the same thing.

Of course, we cannot push this lesson too far. Obviously, picking winners is closely related to making money! A system that never produces a payoff must be a disaster; whereas one that "almost always" pays off must do relatively well. But within the extremes, as we keep saying, picking winners isn't enough. One must pick winners *that others don't pick*. Only then is there some hope of overcoming the track's hefty edge and winding up on the positive side of the ledger.

## Appendix

We assume that we have pairs of numbers for $n$ horses measuring jockey experience and speed. We denote the first pair by $(E_1, S_1)$, the second pair by $(E_2, S_2)$, and so on. It is handy to define a few quantities based on the $E$'s and $S$'s:

$$E = (E_1 + E_2 + \ldots + E_n)/n$$ the arithmetic mean of experience levels in the sample

$$S = (S_1 + S_2 + \ldots + S_n)/n$$ the arithmetic mean of speeds in the sample

$$C = (E_1 S_1 + E_2 S_2 + \ldots + E_n S_n)/n$$ the arithmetic mean of the "cross products" of $E$'s and $S$'s

$$V_E = (E_2^2 + E_2^2 + \ldots + E_2^2)/n$$ the average of the squares of the experience figures

Then, if we want to figure out what $a$ and $b$ in the straight-line equation $S = a + bE$ will make that the best-fitting (least squares) line, we calculate $a$ and $b$ as follows:

$$b = \frac{C - \overline{E}\,\overline{S}}{V_E - \overline{E}^2}$$

$$a = \overline{S} - b\overline{E}$$

Finally, we show how the correlation coefficient can be computed. We need to define $V_S$ (analogously to $V_E$) *as*

$$V_S = (S_1^2 + S_2^2 + \ldots + S_n^2)/n$$

Then the correlation coefficient is given by

$$R = \frac{C - \overline{E}\,\overline{S}}{\sqrt{V_E - \overline{E}^2}\ \sqrt{V_S - \overline{S}^2}}$$

## Endnotes

1. How do we pick at random? For practice we might write the names of the horses on separate slips of paper (of equal size, shape, color, and weight) and shake them up thoroughly in a box; then, with eyes closed, we might pull one slip out. There are better ways, but as a rough and ready method, this one will do.
2. Why, we don't know. It may be that the owners and trainers of "Secretariats" do not have much faith in female riders.
3. Let $d_1, d_2, \ldots, d_{99}, d_{100}$ denote the difference between the female and male winning percentages. The arithmetic mean is $m = (d_1 + d_2 + \ldots + d_{99} + d_{100})/100$. The variance of these numbers measures their dispersion around the mean and is defined as $V = [(d_1 - m)^2 + (d_2 - m)^2 + \ldots + (d_{99} - m)^2 + (d_{100} - m)^2]/100$. The standard deviation is $s = \sqrt{V}$. The arithmetic mean is significantly bigger than zero if it is true that $m/(s/\sqrt{100}) = 10m/s$ is bigger than 1.96, and it

is significantly smaller than zero if it is less than $-1.96$. If it is between these two values, we cannot reject the hypothesis that there is no difference between men and women (as far as riding abilities are concerned!).

4. The actual judgment of whether an $R$ is or is not statistically significant depends on fairly complicated mathematics and takes into account both the size of $R$ and the sample size $n$. To give you some notion, we present cutoff values for $R$ below which the relationship is not significant, and above which it is:

| Sample Size | R Needed for Significance |
|:-:|:-:|
| 10 | 0.632 |
| 20 | 0.444 |
| 30 | 0.362 |
| 60 | 0.254 |
| 120 | 0.152 |

5. Since equations of this sort make sense only if we have included *quantifiable* variables, we shall pretend that "sex" is measured as "0" if it is "female" and as "1" if it is "male"; "track condition" is measured as "0" if it is "muddy," "1" if it is "good," and "2" if it is "fast."

6. Note that the cutoff values in note 4 must be replaced by slightly different ones if there are two variables that do the "explaining" rather than just one.

7. When several variables are used as predictors (or explainers), we usually refer to our efforts as *multiple* regression analysis.

8. If eight horses run in the average race, a purely random selection method will pick only about 12.5 percent (one-eighth) of the winners. In contrast, simply betting favorites will produce about 33 percent winners, with some variation across times and places (tracks).

*Chapter 6*

# The Evidence from Win, Place, and Show Betting

## Preamble

In this chapter we begin a detailed examination of the empirical evidence on the profitability of betting on horses. The first question we ask is how to measure the betting public's subjective assessment of each horse's winning chances. It is clear that this is appropriately measured by the proportion of the entire betting pool that is bet on the individual horses. If the public (in the aggregate) thinks that a given horse has four out of ten chances of winning a given race, it will bet 40 percent of all the moneys bet in that race on the given horse. We call this proportion the *subjective probability* of winning, and it is closely related to the *odds* on the horse in question.

The public may or may not be right in its assessment. Horses that have 40 percent of all moneys bet on them may win more than 40 percent of the time or less than 40 percent of the time. We can calculate this *objective winning probability* by taking the historical record of all horses that have had 40 percent of the betting pool bet on them and simply counting the percentage of races they have actually won.

If the public's assessment of horses' winning chances were perfect, the subjective and objective probabilities would be the same. In fact, they tend to be close, but with one persistent quirk: Favorites (horses with high winning chances) have higher objective probabilities than subjective probabilities, with the reverse being true for longshots. We describe this empirical regularity by saying that favorites are underbet and longshots are overbet. The reasons for this phenomenon are open to speculation (read the remainder of the chapter), but the profound consequence is that you will make out better *on the average* (over many, many visits to the racetrack) by betting on favorites.

Is this kind of situation compatible with the assumption that bettors as a group are thoroughly informed about each horse's ability and winning chances and are out to maximize their gain? Clearly not. Everybody is just as able as we are (and as many other researchers who have found the same results) to determine the greater profitability of betting on favorites; if people *acted in their own self-interest*, they would increase the amounts bet on favorites relative to longshots. This would lower the payoffs on favorites relative to longshots, until on balance *no differentials* would exist among horses in different odds categories. We describe the actual situation by saying that the betting market is *not efficient,* since it does not use all useful information that is potentially available.

In fact, one can do even better than just betting on favorites. One can employ statistical models of various sorts to improve one's edge a bit even further. The most successful betting strategies built on these statistical models characteristically involve place betting and show betting and can actually show a long-term (modest) profit. (Win betting on favorites is, in contrast, a money-losing activity in the long run, although the losses are much smaller than betting on longshots.) All this tends to suggest that there may well be a class of bettors referred to as "smart money"—bettors who have information not available to us run-of-the-mill mortals.

We describe two of the more successful betting models in detail. The Asch-Malkiel-Quandt approach (our approach) focuses on two facts about each horse in a race: its betting odds and the way in which those odds *change* during the last few minutes of betting before the race. Using our approach is a fairly involved process that requires some last-minute calculations if followed carefully. But here is a rough approximation. First, forget the true longshots; horses whose odds are 15 to 1 or above are, on average, awful bets. Look at the rest of the entrants, with particular attention to those whose odds are relatively *low* and also are *coming down* in the last five minutes of betting. These horses tend to be quite good bets to place or show (not to win).

The "Dr. Z" System, developed by Ziemba and Hausch, focuses on discrepancies between patterns of betting in the win pool on the one hand, and the place and show pools on the other. This system is also pretty involved if you follow it to the letter. The basic idea, however, is to identify horses that are underbet to place or show *relative* to their position in the win pool. Suppose, for example, that a particular horse has 33 percent of the win pool bet on it (its win odds will be somewhere around 2 to 1). For some reason, however, this horse has only 15 percent of the place pool bet on it. Such a horse is a very interesting place bet according to Dr. Z.

One cautionary remark is in order. Even if you act according to some of the modestly profitable strategies described in this chapter, your winning days may be numbered if enough bettors decide to act the same way you do. The basic lesson is this: No system can remain profitable if enough people employ it, for by the very act of using the system, they depress the odds and the payoffs on the horses selected by that system. Since on the average only the racetrack (and the tax collector) wins, the betting public must lose.

## Some Basic Concepts

In this chapter we shall review the various strands of the "academic" literature on racetrack betting. We shall keep in mind many of the questions raised in earlier chapters, such as "Is it possible consistently to make money at the track?" or "What are winning strategies, if any?" or "Is the betting market efficient?"

To make this chapter easier to understand, we must introduce a small amount of mathematical notation. If you get turned off by formulas, read on anyway; you will be able to follow the gist of the arguments. You will, however, be at a disadvantage when it comes to taking advantage of the right kind of opportunities, since those opportunities beckon only to those who don't mind a bit of algebra.

We begin with a few definitions. Imagine that we are dealing with a particular race in which $N$ horses have been entered. $N$ is rarely less than 5 and rarely more than 12. Each of the horses has a certain amount bet on it to win; the amounts will be denoted by $B_1$ for horse number 1, by $B_2$ for horse number 2, and so on until we get to $B_N$, the amount bet on the last horse at the starting gate. The total win pool will be denoted by the letter $B$; thus obviously

$$B = B_1 + B_2 + \ldots + B_N$$

We shall also define the letter $t$ to stand for the track's take, expressed as a percentage including breakage. Thus $t$ is normally in the range of $0.17 - 0.185$. If horse $i$ wins, the total amount bet on all horses, minus the track's take, is paid out to the winning tickets. Thus, the payoff per dollar bet on horse $i$ (denoted by $M_i$) is

$$M_i = \frac{B(1 - t)}{B_i} \qquad (6\text{-}1)$$

Finally, the odds on horse $i$, to be denoted by $D_i$, are one less than the payoff, namely

$$D_i = M_i - 1 \qquad (6\text{-}2)$$

So, for example, if $1,642 is bet on Lucky Peter while the total amount bet on all horses in a race is $8,964, and if the track take exclusive of breakage is 17 percent, the payoff to Lucky Peter according to the formula would be $4.5311, which would then be rounded down to $4.50 (for a $1 bet; double this for the standard $2 bet). The odds displayed would then be 7 to 2.

Following this basic terminology, we have to introduce the notion of the probability that a particular horse, say horse $i$, will win. We have considered this concept before when we discussed how we evaluate evidence, statistical or otherwise, and how we might conclude that this or that horse is likelier to win. Now we must go a little more deeply into this matter.

The main distinction we want to draw is between the *objective* probability of a horse winning and the *subjective* probability. By the former, we mean an objectively verifiable property of the horse. If this objective probability were 0.3, this would mean that if this horse ran a very large number of comparable races, it would win very close to 30 percent of them. How we figure out the value of this objective probability for different horses remains to be seen; what we care about now is the meaning of the concept of objective probability. However we measure or "estimate" horse $i$'s objective probability of winning, we shall denote it by $p_i$.

In contrast, by subjective probability we do not mean a property of the horse but rather what the public *thinks* about the horse's future performance. Of course, if people are smart, what they *think* about a horse's future performance will correspond pretty well to the objective probability of the horse's winning, but there is clearly no necessity for this to be so. Richard, for example, has a coin that, based on both metallurgical studies and statistical testing, has exactly a 0.5 probability of "heads" and 0.5 probability of "tails." Unfortunately, he has succeeded in persuading his friend Peter that this is a trick coin that will come up "heads" 60 percent of the time. Since Peter is a trusting soul and believes this story, his subjective probability is 0.6 for "heads" and 0.4 for "tails." Richard now proposes the following game: They will flip the coin, and if it comes up heads, Peter wins; otherwise, Richard does. Suppose, finally, that it is agreed that when Peter loses, he has to pay Richard $1.

How much of a payoff will Peter require if the coin comes up heads in order to induce him to play the game at all? At least enough to break even in the sense of expected values. How much is that? Let us say it is an amount $A$. The expected value of a game where you win $A$ with probability 0.6 and lose $1 with probability 0.4 is

$$\text{Expected value} = 0.6A - 0.4$$

If this expected value were zero, $A$ would have to be 0.6667, or about 67¢. If Richard offered to play the game with $A = 0.80$, Peter would leap at the chance, since his expected value calculation, *based on his subjective probabilities,* convinces him that he will clean up at this game (shouldn't he be a mite suspicious at Richard's generosity in offering a payoff of 80¢?). Alas, the objective probabilities are 0.5, and Peter will in fact lose in the long run.

Since the ultimate outcomes are governed by objective probabilities and people's betting behavior, by subjective probabilities, it is important to compare the two, which is what we shall do next. First, it is important to note that the best and most sensible aggregate measure of people's subjective probabilities that various horses will win is simply the proportion of the total pool bet on each of the various horses. A few examples will suffice. Imagine that the entire betting pool is bet on horse 1, and nothing is bet on all the other horses. Pretty clearly, the public believes that horse 1 is sure to win. Now imagine that 50 percent of the pool is on horse 1, 50 percent on horse 2, and nothing is bet on the remaining horses. This clearly means that the public believes that horses 1 and 2 are equally likely to win and horses 3, 4, . . . etc. have zero chance. For if, in fact, somebody believed that horse 3 had a tiny chance, say 1 in 100, of winning, it would surely be worthwhile to bet a little on horse 3: The person believes that the horse has a 0.01 chance of winning, but the odds and prospective payoff are astronomical. A $2 bet on a given horse out of a betting pool of, say, $20,000 implies a payoff of over 8,000 to 1 (remember the track take; this is why the payoff is not 10,000 to 1). Since this bet is so profitable in the expected value sense, the bet will be made. If nobody has bet even a penny on horse 3, it must mean that horse 3 is thought to have exactly zero chance of winning. This reasoning can be equally well applied to less "round" numbers, and so we shall compute the subjective probability of horse $i$ winning as

$$s_i = \frac{B_i}{B} \qquad (6\text{-}3)$$

We have mentioned several times before that it is plausible that people are expected utility maximizers and that under many circumstances this implies that they make decisions by looking at both the expected value of a bet and the variance of the possible returns from the bet, which is a measure of how widely dispersed the outcomes are about the mean. We now have all the tools to calculate these quantities for a particular horse, say horse $i$.

Recall that you calculate an expected value by taking each possible outcome of a bet, multiplying it by the probability that that outcome will occur, and adding up all these products. In racetrack betting there are only two outcomes: If horse $i$ wins, the bettor obtains a payoff of $D_i + 1$ dollars per dollar bet; since the bettor had to lay out one dollar to make the bet, the net payoff is $D_i$ dollars. If horse $i$ loses, you are out your investment; that is to say, your payoff is $-1$ (minus one) dollar per dollar bet. It follows that the expected value of this bet is

$$E_i = p_i D_i - (1.0)\,(1 - p_i)$$

Another way of writing this formula is to note that $D_i = M_i - 1$, and since $M_i = B(1 - t)/B_i$ and $B/B_i = 1/s_i$, we have:

$$E_i = p_i \frac{1 - t}{s_i} - 1 - (1 - p_i)$$

$$= \frac{p_i}{s_i}(1 - t) - 1 \qquad (6\text{-}4)$$

This formula says that the expected value (or payoff) of a bet on horse $i$ depends on the ratio of the objective to subjective probabilities that the horse will win, and upon $(1 - t)$, the amount of money left for distribution to bettors after the track take is subtracted. Notice why this makes sense. A "good" bet—one with high expected value—exists if a horse's true (objective) chance of winning is substantially *higher* than the crowd (subjectively) believes—that is, the ratio $p_i/s_i$ is "large."

It follows immediately that if the subjective and objective probabilities are the same $(p_i = s_i)$, the expected value is $-t$; that is to say, on the average you will lose an amount equal to the track take (we return to this case later). Through similar reasoning, but with a little more algebra, we can obtain the variance $V_i$ as

$$V_i = \frac{p_i(1 - p_i)(1 - t)^2}{s_i^2} \qquad (6\text{-}5)$$

Hence, both the mean and the variance depend only on the objective probability, the subjective probability, and the track take.

## The Subjective and Objective Probabilities of Winning

The measurement of subjective probabilities is easy. All we have to do is to divide the amount bet on a horse by the total win pool. It is obviously very difficult to measure a horse's objective probability of winning. The best we can probably do without an enormous amount of effort is to consider groups of comparable horses and see what fraction of them actually won.

The next obvious question is how we should find groups of comparable horses. One device that has been used several times by various investigators (Ali [1977], Asch, Malkiel, Quandt [1982], and Snyder [1978]) is to assume that horses with the same or very similar odds tend to be comparable. What we therefore do is to group horses by their odds. We take a set of many races and put the horse with the lowest odds in each race into Group 1, the horse with the second-lowest odds in each race in Group 2, and so on. Each horse in Group 1 has its own particular odds, and they are all slightly different, ranging perhaps from 1 to 2 to, say, 3 to 2. In Group 2, the odds might range from 1 to 5 to 2, and so on. We can convert these odds to subjective probabilities by using the formula

$$s_i = \frac{1 - t}{D_i + 1} \qquad (6\text{-}6)$$

which follows from the definitions given earlier.[1] Then, within each group, we can average these subjective probabilities together. This is the procedure for estimating the subjective winning probability of the horses in each group.

Now, how do we get an estimate of the objective probability of winning in each group? The simplest way is to let the record speak for itself! We shall just count how many horses in each group actually won, as a percentage of the total number of horses in that group. Table

Table 6-1    Objective and Subjective Probabilities

| Groups | Number of Horses in Group | Objective Probability | Subjective Probability |
|---|---|---|---|
| Favorites | 729 | .361 | .325 |
| Second-lowest odds | 729 | .218 | .205 |
| Third-lowest odds | 729 | .170 | .145 |
| Fourth-lowest odds | 724 | .115 | .104 |
| Fifth-lowest odds | 692 | .071 | .072 |
| Sixth-lowest odds | 598 | .050 | .048 |
| Seventh-lowest odds | 431 | .030 | .034 |
| Eighth-lowest odds | 289 | .017 | .025 |
| Ninth-lowest odds | 165 | .006 | .018 |

6-1 illustrates this comparison for 729 races in Atlantic City, N.J. in 1978, including a total of 5,805 horses (Asch, Malkiel, Quandt [1982]).

First, note that the groups in Table 6-1 are based on different numbers of horses; this is obvious when you consider that some races have only six or seven horses running, and in such races there cannot be a horse with "eighth-lowest odds" or "ninth-lowest odds." Second, it is interesting to observe that the subjective and objective probabilities are apparently quite close. The third and most interesting thing to note is that for horses with low odds (favorites and near-favorites), the objective probability of winning is quite a bit higher than the subjective probability, whereas for longshots (in our table, horses with seventh-, eighth-, and ninth-lowest odds), the exact reverse is true. What this says is that the betting public consistently overestimates the winning chances of longshots (horses with low objective probabilities of winning) and consistently underestimates the winning chances of favorites.[2]

This is perhaps the most fundamental and well-confirmed empirical regularity in racetrack betting. For example, Fabricand (1965, 1979) has obtained the detailed data in Table 6-2 (based on 10,000 races) in which the groups are explicitly identified as ranges of odds. Exactly the same phenomenon is observable in Table 6-2 as in Table 6-1: Favorites or near-favorites are "underbet" and longshots are "overbet." (Table 6-2 also contains an extra column on the right-hand side; more on that later.) We say that favorites are "underbet" because if more had been bet on them, the subjective probability computed for these horses would have risen to be more nearly equal to the objective probability (which, of course, remains unaffected by how much people bet).[3]

**Table 6-2    Fabricand's Data**

| Odds | Number of Horses Entered | Objective Probability | Subjective Probability | Expected Profit per Dollar Bet |
|---|---|---|---|---|
| 0.40–0.55 | 129 | 0.713 | 0.569 | 0.034 |
| 0.60–0.75 | 295 | 0.553 | 0.502 | −0.071 |
| 0.80–0.95 | 470 | 0.513 | 0.449 | −0.038 |
| 1.00–1.15 | 615 | 0.470 | 0.406 | −0.024 |
| 1.20–1.35 | 789 | 0.403 | 0.371 | −0.081 |
| 1.40–1.55 | 874 | 0.379 | 0.341 | −0.061 |
| 1.60–1.75 | 954 | 0.355 | 0.315 | −0.048 |
| 1.80–1.95 | 1,051 | 0.309 | 0.293 | −0.105 |
| 2.00–2.45 | 3,223 | 0.289 | 0.263 | −0.065 |
| 2.50–2.95 | 3,623 | 0.230 | 0.228 | −0.135 |
| 3.00–3.45 | 3,807 | 0.209 | 0.201 | −0.110 |
| 3.50–3.95 | 3,652 | 0.186 | 0.180 | −0.116 |
| 4.00–4.45 | 3,296 | 0.161 | 0.162 | −0.153 |
| 4.50–4.95 | 3,129 | 0.155 | 0.148 | −0.106 |
| 5.00–5.95 | 5,586 | 0.123 | 0.132 | −0.201 |
| 6.00–6.95 | 5,154 | 0.110 | 0.114 | −0.180 |
| 7.00–7.95 | 4,665 | 0.099 | 0.100 | −0.164 |
| 8.00–8.95 | 3,990 | 0.082 | 0.090 | −0.218 |
| 9.00–9.95 | 3,617 | 0.082 | 0.081 | −0.147 |
| 10.00–14.95 | 12,007 | 0.060 | 0.065 | −0.207 |
| 15.00–19.95 | 7,041 | 0.040 | 0.047 | −0.264 |
| 20.00–99.95 | 25,044 | 0.014 | 0.025 | −0.540 |

A major unresolved question is why this type of discrepancy is observed over and over again. It is practically an empirical "law" in racetrack betting, and many academic studies have speculated on the possible reasons for it. We shall briefly examine the principal theories.

The first and perhaps oldest theory is that the betting public has a special taste, a "yen," for betting on longshots, at the same time that it has a special distaste for betting on favorites. Betting on favorites may be perceived as a stodgy thing to do, while betting on longshots has a certain zip to it; moreover, if you win, you can tell all your friends about it and gain admiration! If this is true, we would expect to see pretty much what we do observe. Consider a suggestive, although slightly incorrect, analogy involving shares of common stock. Say that two companies are very much (exactly?) the same with respect to product, earnings expectations, and what have you. One of them is called Peter Piper, Inc., and the other is called Picked a Peck of Pickled Peppers, Inc. The shares of these two companies would sell for the same price (since they are in effect identical companies). But members of the investing public derive a real disutility from owning shares in a company with a cumbersome name such as Picked a Peck of Pickled Peppers; in fact, most people can't even pronounce the name to their brokers, and it causes them real pain to have to stumble over the awkward words. We would expect that this—perhaps rational, perhaps irrational—preference will indeed affect the relative prices of the shares. In just the same way, if there is a real preference for longshots, their "price" should rise relative to favorites, and, of course, it does. In horseracing the "price" is measured by the subjective probability (in effect, the reciprocal of the odds), which is too high for longshots relative to their objective probabilities.

A second possibility that has been suggested is that people are just not very good at estimating objective probabilities and that there tends to be a systematic bias in the direction of overestimating the chance of winning a low-probability bet and underestimating it for a high-probability bet. Tversky and Kahneman (1974) have suggested that when people make errors about probabilities, they employ rules of thumb that can seriously lead one astray. For example, people might judge the probability of a general class of events ("do horses with 50 to 1 odds win?") on the basis of what happened in the last race (in which a 50 to 1 horse perhaps did win). Starr and Kleinman (1984) have performed experiments with experimental subjects that seem to confirm the existence of those errors generally, not only in racetrack betting.

A third theory, proposed by Mitzak, Kusyszyn, and Starr (1981), questions whether the under/overbetting phenomenon exists at all, except to the extent that it is associated with "informed betting." Their statistical results appear to show that if we restrict our attention to relatively predictable horses—horses whose odds can be fairly accurately predicted by track conditions, previous running experience, and so on—the under/overbetting bias disappears. If we consider horses for which a lot of uncertainty remains even after we have accounted for the objective factors that influence a horse's winning chances, the under/ overbetting bias does exist and is presumably due to the existence of a small set of bettors with better information than the general public; this "smart money" takes advantage of its special information and tilts the odds in the direction of underbetting favorites and overbetting longshots.

It is not possible to decide this issue definitively. Each of the theories has something going for it, and the end result we observe may well contain germs of truth from each. The most important thing is that this empirical regularity exists, and we can now ask whether it is possible to take advantage of it.

## Rates of Return

If we are to compare the profitability of racetrack betting with any other kind of investment activity, we must define the rate of return from each of these activities. This may not be so easy for an investment that has a "lifetime" of many years and provides the owner an income stream over such a long period. Since a rate of return calculation for such an investment involves the comparison of present-day dollars with future dollars, it must make use of the interest rate which is the rate at which future and present dollars can be transformed into each other.

Fortunately, our racetrack case is simpler because we usually want to compare the rate of return from investing in one horse to that of another horse in the same race. Betting on a horse is an "investment," with at most 20 minutes duration; thus, all we need to calculate is how much return we get per dollar bet. Our net return is simply

$$(payoff) - (amount\ bet)$$

and the rate of return is this quantity, divided by the amount bet:

$$Rate\ of\ return = \frac{payoff - amount\ bet}{amount\ bet}$$

We calculated the rates of return for the sample of horses discussed in Table 6–1, but now we have aggregated the horses into groups a little differently, by odds-levels, and a little more coarsely than in Table 6–2. We did this twice: once for all the races and once only for the late races (i.e., the eighth and ninth races of each racing day). Our purpose was to see if rates of return in late races differ from their average in all races. The results are continued in Table 6–3.

Note that *all rates of return are negative*; hence, on the average, bettors lose no matter what odds horse they bet on. Interestingly, the loss is only −13.7 percent if you bet on horses with odds less than 2, which is quite a bit less than the 17 to 18 percent loss that bettors in the aggregate *must* lose because of the track's take. Looking down the middle column of the table, we see that the returns fluctuate in no particularly orderly manner, but it is noteworthy that longshots — that is, horses with odds higher than 25 — make a whopping 64 percent

Table 6-3    Rates of Return from Asch-Malkiel-Quandt Study

| Odds Level D | Average Rate of Return in All Races | Average Rate of Return in Late Races |
|---|---|---|
| $D \leq 2$ | $-.137$ | $-.043$ |
| $2 < D \leq 3.5$ | $-.318$ | $-.321$ |
| $3.5 < D \leq 5$ | $-.176$ | $-.029$ |
| $5 < D \leq 8$ | $-.224$ | $-.524$ |
| $8 < D \leq 14$ | $-.160$ | $-.170$ |
| $14 < D \leq 25$ | $-.326$ | $-.378$ |
| $25 < D$ | $-.637$ | $-.686$ |

loss on every dollar bet! This certainly confirms what we discussed in the previous section: Longshots are overbet—that is, their odds and payoffs are lower than is justified by their objective chances of winning (and the converse is true for favorites). This tendency, if anything, is all the more apparent for the late races. Here, betting on the short-odds horses is almost a fair (break-even) game, and the loss on the longshots is greater still.

Why should the late races be any different from the earlier ones? One speculation advanced a long time ago by McGlothlin (1956) is based on the following. When Peter goes to the track, the normal expectation is that he will lose money. By the time the seventh race is over, Peter has lost $50, and he is worried that when he gets home his wife Rita will apply a rolling pin to his backside. He must, at all costs, recoup. Betting on favorites will hardly make him recoup because their payoffs are so low; even though he would be relatively likely to win, he would diminish his losses from $50 to, say, only $40 or $30, and that is not enough to avert the dreaded specter of the rolling pin! He must bet on longshots to have any chance of winning or even breaking even. So longshots are overbet in late races even more than in the early ones.

Look now at the far right column of Table 6-2, based on Fabricand's data. These are the average rates of return for that particular sample, and they tell a very similar story to that of Table 6-3; the only exception is that the rate of return to horses with odds less than 0.55 is actually positive! This seems to suggest that betting on such horses— very heavy favorites—will actually make money in the long run. Note, however, that one would have to do a lot of waiting to take advantage of this, since most races do not have horses with odds that low. In fact, only 129 out of the 93,011 horses analyzed in Fabricand's study had odds less than 0.55 (roughly 1 to 2).

## The Question of Efficiency in Betting

We have described earlier what we mean by market efficiency in the stock market as well as the racetrack "betting market." Remember that in an efficient market, all information that has any bearing on the profitability of an investment is already accounted for in the price of that investment opportunity, so that no above-average profits can be derived from it. You may also remember that this apparently simple notion of efficiency was slightly muddled by two ways of looking at it. According to the first view, a market is inefficient if investment opportunities yielding above-average profits exist. According to the second view, inefficiency would exist only if above-average profits were possible *after* we have adjusted for the fact that some investment opportunities are riskier than others.

Scholars writing about racetrack betting have characteristically interpreted racetrack betting efficiency in the first sense. Thus, Mitzak, Kusyszyn, and Starr (1981) say that ". . . a system is . . . efficient if all prior information can be used to accurately estimate the objective probability distribution for some future event. At this level of efficiency no individual can aspire to produce substantial long-term profit beyond the expected norms." Ziemba and Hausch (1984, p.73) consider efficiency to exist if the (objective) probability that a horse will win is equal to the fraction of money bet on that horse (i.e., the subjective probability). This way of looking at efficiency is less stringent than the alternative, which requires that the variability (riskiness) of profits or returns be taken into account. Even by this less stringent criterion, the betting market seems to have some inefficiency in it. Objective and subjective probabilities, although close to each other, are not the same, and for both favorites and longshots these probabilities are sufficiently far apart so that the differences between them are statistically significant.

The rates of return, or profitability, of betting on favorites and longshots are very different. These rates of return are, in turn, massively different from the average return to the public as a whole, which equals the take and is minus 17 to 18 percent. Although we shall explore later just how big the rate of return can be with judicious betting strategies, we can already conclude, at least tentatively, that the betting market is in a sense inefficient. What we have not shown yet is whether this inefficiency is worth bothering about from the point of view of personal gain and profit, or whether it is merely an academic curiosum.

Since the betting market appears to contain some inefficiency on our simple criterion, it is not surprising that it appears to be inefficient on the more stringent criterion as well. It is worth looking at this in a little more detail because the argument is quite persuasive and important.

Imagine that only two investment opportunities exist. For the moment we don't care whether they are stocks in two companies or bets on two horses. Imagine further that we can calculate the expected return to each investment (i.e., the average profit we would make per dollar invested if we invested in similar opportunities many times) and the variance of the returns (which, as you may remember, is a measure of how dispersed the returns are around the average value). Finally, imagine the following *fact*: both investments are willingly purchased by some investors.

What must be true of the expected returns and variances of these two investments? Let us denote by $e_1$ and $e_2$ the expected values and by $v_1$ and $v_2$ their variances, and suppose that $e_1$ is bigger than $e_2$ — that is, Investment 1 has a bigger expected return. If people are risk averse, if they dislike variability, then $v_2$ must be smaller than $v_1$. Why is this so? Because, if people dislike variability in returns, for some people the lower value of $v_2$ provides enough psychic compensation to make them endure the lower expected return $e_2$. If $e_2$ were smaller than $e_1$ as we supposed, and at the same time $v_2$ were bigger than $v_1$, Investment 2 would be a worse investment than Investment 1 on both counts; we can express this by saying that Investment 1 would *dominate* Investment 2. In fact, nobody would buy Investment 2 at all, because everybody could do better by buying Investment 1. But this contradicts our supposed *fact* that both investments are willingly purchased by *some* people! So, if both investments are willingly purchased by people, $e_1 > e_2$ implies that $v_1 > v_2$.

The argument is very similar if people are risk lovers. In this case they *like* variability (and, of course, they still like high expected returns). If, then, both investments are willingly purchased by some people and $e_1$ is bigger than $e_2$, then $v_1$ must be smaller than $v_2$. If this condition fails, there would exist a pair of investments, that is, horses, in which one of the two had both higher expected return and higher variance. That, in turn, implies inefficiency because efficiency requires risk-adjusted returns to be equal: If one horse has a low variance (riskiness) of returns (which is *bad* from the risk lovers' point of view), investors must be compensated for this "bad" by a higher expected return on that horse.

**Table 6-4    Expected Values and Variances**

| Odds | Expected Values | Variances |
|---|---|---|
| 0.40- 0.55 | 0.028 | 0.425 |
| 0.60- 0.75 | -0.097 | 0.660 |
| 0.80- 0.95 | -0.063 | 0.833 |
| 1.00- 1.15 | -0.051 | 1.016 |
| 1.20- 1.35 | -0.109 | 1.175 |
| 1.40- 1.55 | -0.089 | 1.361 |
| 1.60- 1.75 | -0.076 | 1.552 |
| 1.80- 1.95 | -0.135 | 1.672 |
| 2.00- 2.45 | -0.099 | 1.997 |
| 2.50- 2.95 | -0.173 | 2.291 |
| 3.00- 3.45 | -0.147 | 2.751 |
| 3.50- 3.95 | -0.153 | 3.142 |
| 4.00- 4.45 | -0.185 | 3.461 |
| 4.50- 4.95 | -0.141 | 4.021 |
| 5.00- 5.95 | -0.236 | 4.163 |
| 6.00- 6.95 | -0.209 | 5.065 |
| 7.00- 7.95 | -0.188 | 5.998 |
| 8.00- 8.95 | -0.253 | 6.249 |
| 9.00- 9.95 | -0.170 | 7.715 |
| 10.00-14.95 | -0.243 | 8.976 |
| 15.00-19.95 | -0.302 | 11.689 |
| 20.00-99.95 | -0.541 | 14.851 |

The obvious thing to do is to compute the expected values and the variances of horses in different odds categories. If these are arranged in increasing order of variance, their corresponding expected values must be decreasing if the "betting market" from which we have gathered the data was efficient. We have performed this computation with the objective and subjective probabilities in Table 6-2, and the results are shown in Table 6-4. In computing the expected values and variances, we have used Formulas (6-1) and (6-2) from earlier in this chapter; we also employed a track take $t$ of 0.18 (although alternative values such as 0.17 give qualitatively similar answers). Note that our expected values are slightly different from those in Table 6-2 in the column labeled "Expected Profit per Dollar Bet"; the reason is that the Table 6-2 figures are based on actual profit experience, while our figures were computed from the theoretical formulas (which, of course, do employ objective winning probabilities). The variances in Table 6-4 are in fact in increasing order (the greater the odds, the greater the variability of returns), but the expected values are nowhere near in decreasing order, as would be required for efficiency. For example, horses with odds in the 1.40 to 1.55 range dominated horses in the

1.20 to 1.35 range, since the latter have both lower expected value and lower variance. It may be objected that tables of this kind involve "aggregation" or averaging over groups of horses with nonidentical odds since we classify horses by odds-ranges; moreover, the expected values and variances in the table are never simultaneously available in a single race in which choices among them can be made. We agree that there is room for doubt, but note that similar results are obtained for other samples and similar results are seen even if we "disaggregate" as much as possible—for example, if we restrict our attention exclusively to races in which, say, six horses were running and repeat these same calculations.

The conclusion that we have reached so far—tentatively and with qualifications—is that the betting market is not efficient, at least not completely. This means that all the information that exists about a race is not fully reflected in the odds; one might therefore be able to take profitable advantage of this. Before we discuss how this could be done, however, we return briefly to the under/overbetting bias discussed earlier. Consider this question: Is it possible, hypothetically speaking, that in some situations the objective and subjective probabilities of winning are exactly equal to one another, horse by horse? Using our notation of $p_i$ and $s_i$ for the objective and subjective probabilities of winning for horse $i$, this would mean that $p_1 = s_1, p_2 = s_2, \ldots, p_N = s_N$. What happens then to the expected return and the variance of return? If $p_i = s_i$, Formulas (6–1) and (6–2) become

$$E_i = -t$$

$$v_i = \frac{(1 - p_i)(1 - t)^2}{p_i}$$

We get the unsurprising result that in that case the expected return no longer depends on the probability (objective or subjective) of winning; it is exactly equal to the track take and is *the same for every horse*! The variance does depend on the probability of winning, and it is easy to see that the smaller the probability, the greater the variance. *That means that such a situation is totally incompatible with market efficiency*, which, we have seen, requires that if a horse has higher variance, it *must* have lower expected return. In fact, it has been shown (Quandt [1986]) that without some under/overbetting bias, efficiency in the stringent sense cannot be obtained at all; although the under/overbetting bias does not ensure that efficiency will exist (as we have seen from Table 6–4), without it efficiency surely cannot exist. This also suggests that the betting market operates as if it were "trying" to be efficient by making prices (odds) reflect all information; it just does not quite make it.

## How Well Do Odds Predict Winners?

We already know that horses with low odds have a relatively high probability of winning, and in this sense, the odds obviously are of some help in picking winners. (Similar results were found by Hoerl and Fallin as early as 1974.) The question we want to ask now is whether any refinements are possible that would allow us to do better. That is, can we coax more evidence out of the odds?

Notice first that there are various kinds of odds that one could look at. Thus far, when we use the term "odds," we have meant *the final odds*—that is, the odds at the end of the betting, when the race begins. We could also examine the *morning line* odds, $D_i^{ML}$, which represent professional handicappers' estimates concerning the various horses. Finally, if we were interested in how betting patterns might change during the late betting, we might wish to calculate odds that are implied by the betting in, say, the last 5 minutes before the race starts. These odds, which we shall refer to as *marginal odds*, cannot be obtained in a simple fashion and are not displayed by the racetrack. To calculate them we have to know how much was bet on each horse in the last 5 minutes (rather than in the entire betting period). We can then calculate odds for the horses *attributable to the last 5 minutes of betting* by exactly the same formulas as were used before. These marginal odds (for horse $i$) will be denoted by $D_i^{M5}$.

To the extent that people act on information, the various odds will reflect that information to a greater or smaller extent. It would be interesting to know which set of odds displays the most information or which is most "efficient." To examine this, we show in Table 6–5 the ratios of the final odds $D$ to the morning line odds $D^{ML}$ and also the ratio of the marginal odds $D^{M5}$ to the morning line odds.

Table 6–5   Ratios of Odds at Atlantic City, N.J. Racecourse, 1978

| Horses Finishing | $D/D^{ML}$ | $D^{M5}/D^{ML}$ |
|---|---|---|
| First | 0.96 | 0.82 |
| Second | 1.16 | 1.06 |
| Third | 1.22 | 1.17 |
| Fourth and below | 1.59 | 1.63 |

The numbers in Table 6–5 are extremely interesting. In the first column, note that on the average the final odds for winners are slightly below the corresponding morning line odds; the worse the horse does, the bigger this ratio gets. Since odds and the subjective probability of winning are in an inverse relationship, this means that the public considers (future) winners subjectively more probable to win than the professionals responsible for the morning line odds, and that the public considers losers substantially less probable to win than do the experts. The upshot is that the final odds appear to be much more efficient than the morning line odds.

Turning to the second column, we see that all these effects are even stronger when we compare the marginal odds (implied by the last 5 minutes of betting) to the morning line odds. This suggests that the marginal odds contain even better information than the final odds; in other words, the people who bet in the last 5 minutes are somehow better informed than the public at large. This responds directly to the conjecture that there exists "smart money" and that the "smart money" is "late betting money." Why would people who have better information bet late? Betting on a horse changes the odds; if you expect that potential bettors watch the odds and tend to bet on horses that have falling odds, you will want to postpone betting as long as possible. This will reduce the time left for others to follow your bet and thus depress the odds on your horse even further. The figures in Table 6–5 are compatible with this scenario and suggest not only that both the final and marginal odds contain more information than the morning line odds but also that there may, indeed, exist some smart money. The existence of smart money means that there is some information *not known* to everybody, which may also be responsible for some of the inefficiency identified earlier.

We now attack the problem of identifying future winners more directly. There are two procedures that we should consider: (1) Find a statistical relationship between winning and a host of objective factors such as the distance of the race, the quality of the horse's previous race, change in class if any, layoff, track condition, percentage of wins in the last umpteen races, and so on. (2) Make the assumption that all these objective factors are somehow "congealed" in the various types of odds we have noted above, and find the relationship between winning and the behavior of those various odds. The former method is cumbersome and requires incredible amounts of data, and for that reason is an unlikely candidate for easy computation. Since we already have some evidence that the odds do contain a lot of information, the latter seems an easier and more promising approach.

In Chapter 5 we discussed regression analysis, an appropriate statistical procedure to find the relationship between a dependent variable and several independent variables. Here our independent variables will be based on the morning line odds and the final odds.[4] We could use the odds themselves, but it is more convenient to translate the odds into probabilities according to the formula discussed earlier in the chapter. There we said that the (subjective) probability $s_i$ was given by

$$s_i = \frac{1-t}{D_i + 1}$$

We shall thus use $s_i$ instead of $D_i$ and $s^{ML} = (1-t)/(D^{ML}+1)$ instead of the morning line odds. Our dependent variable is whether a horse in question has won or not; if it has won, the value of the dependent variable will be 1.0; otherwise it will be 0.0. For purposes of analyzing the problem, we take our sample of 5,714 horses from the 1978 racing season in Atlantic City, N.J. (a small number of races included in Table 6–1 were eliminated because they involved dead heats and other anomalies). For each horse $i$ we have the following measurements: the dependent variable $w_i$, which is either 0 or 1; the subjective probability $s_i$, based on the final odds $D_i$; and the subjective probability $s_i^{ML}$ based on the morning line odds. Our aim is to find coefficients $a$, $b$, $c$ in an equation

$$w_i = a + bs_i + cs_i^{ML}$$

If we obtain a statistically significant relationship, we can use the equation to "predict" $w_i$ for a horse that has not run yet but for which we already have the final odds and the morning line odds; we would then bet on that horse or not, depending on whether the predicted $w_i$ was close to 1 or close to 0.

Two important qualifications must be made immediately. The first one has to do with what you have probably noticed at the track: The final odds are on the toteboard just after the race begins (and if we need the marginal odds as well, they too could be calculated only at that instant); but at this moment, one can no longer make any bets! So we must "cheat" a little. We shall take the odds 1 minute before race time (they usually do not change much in the last minute) and using a handy hand-held calculator in which the values of $a$, $b$, and $c$ have been prestored, compute the $w$-predictions for the horses. Even this would require very nimble fingers but becomes a definite possibility with a programmable calculator: We shall have stored in it $a$, $b$, $c$, and the morning line odds; the almost "final" odds (say, 1 minute before race time) can be entered in 20 seconds, the program run, and the results obtained in 10 seconds; that still leaves us half a minute to make a bet.

The more important qualification is that when the dependent variable has only two values, namely 0 and 1, it is not strictly correct (for rather esoteric mathematical reasons) to apply standard regression analysis. Instead, we have to apply a variant called logit analysis, which allows us to predict the probability that any given horse, say the $i$th, in a race will win. Logit analysis still computes the $b$ and $c$ coefficients ($a$ plays no role) from the relationship between the odds of the horses and the fact that they have or have not won; but it then computes the probability that the $i$th horse in a race of $N$ horses will win from the following formula:

$$\text{Probability that horse } i \text{ wins} = \frac{e^{bs_i + cs_i^{ML}}}{e^{bs_1 + cs_1^{ML}} + e^{bs_2 + cs_2^{ML}} + \ldots + e^{bs_n + cs_n^{ML}}}$$

$$(6\text{--}7)$$

where $e$ is the base of the natural logarithms and is approximately 2.71828. The formula thus says the following: Compute $bs + cs^{ML}$ for each and every horse, raise the mysterious number $e$ to the $(bs_1 + cs_1^{ML})$-power, raise it to the $(bs_2 + cs_2^{ML})$-power, and so on, and finally form the ratios of each of these powers to the sum of all these powers. In our calculations for Atlantic City, $b$ turned out to be 4.26 and $c$ was 4.15; both were statistically highly significant, which shows that each contains some information not contained in the other. It is interesting that the corresponding calculations for data from the Meadowlands Racetrack in 1984 turn out to be rather similar: $b$ is 3.56 and $c$ is 5.67. The two samples are from different places and times and cover different types of racing (the Meadowlands data were for harness racing); yet the relationship that the various kinds of odds have to the probability of winning is much the same! The "output" of such an exercise is shown in Table 6–6, which lists the horses in a hypothetical race. Columns 2 and 3 show the probabilities implied by the final and morning line odds; the final odds themselves are in column 4, and the predicted probability is in the last column.

An interesting consequence of the logit prediction in this case is that the predicted winning probability for horse 1 is much higher than one would think from the morning line or the final odds-based probabilities alone, whereas for horse 3, which is by no means a longshot, the reverse is true!

Table 6-6   Logit Predictions of Winning Probabilities for a Hypothetical Race

| Horse | Subjective Probability | Morning-Line-Odds-Based Probability | Final Odds | Winning Probability |
|-------|-----------------------|-------------------------------------|------------|---------------------|
| 1 | .30 | .40 | 1.73 | .479 |
| 2 | .25 | .30 | 2.28 | .256 |
| 3 | .20 | .20 | 3.10 | .136 |
| 4 | .15 | .05 | 4.47 | .059 |
| 5 | .07 | .03 | 10.71 | .039 |
| 6 | .03 | .02 | 26.33 | .031 |

To summarize: We have taken a large number of races and recorded the morning line odds, the final odds (and the marginal odds as well) for every horse. We also recorded which horse won in each race. We then found the statistical relationship between the odds and the likelihood of winning. This relationship is crystallized in statistical estimates of the coefficients $b$ and $c$. We can now plug these values of $b$ and $c$ into the probability Formula (6-7) and compute the estimated winning probability of each horse. How good are these predictions and how useful? Read on.

## Simulations: How Good Are the Predictions?

Since we have a large sample of races, we could easily perform the following test. Take each race and, using the probability formula, predict which horse in that race has the highest probability of winning. Then bet $2 on that horse. If we did this for all races in our sample, we would win some, lose some, and in the end we could calculate our rate of return—that is, our average gain as a percentage of the money we placed at risk. We would thus simulate what would have happened over a racing season if we had actually used such a strategy at Atlantic City or at Meadowlands, or what have you.

However, there is a possibility of a subtle bias in what we have just proposed. We derived the statistical estimates for $b$ and $c$ from the very same races for which we are proposing to make probability predictions! But we have no knowledge that these races are not "flukey" in some way so that we could be making excellent predictions, yet they would be useless for any other races. To guard against this danger, we have to proceed more cautiously, if more cumbersomely, in devising our simulation test. We shall, first of all, divide our 712 races in our Atlantic City sample into two groups of 356 each and label these Group A and B, respectively. We shall do the statistical analysis that provides us with coefficients $b$ and $c$ on the horses in Group A. We shall then use these to make predictions for and run our simulations on the horses in Group B. This is called "out-of-sample-forecasting" in that the data from which we derive the statistical relationship are completely separate from the data to which we apply it subsequently. As an analogy, imagine that we take astronomical measurements of the earth's position, from which we conclude that the earth's orbit around the sun is elliptical. It is nice to know that this allows us to predict the position of the earth in the future, but it really enhances our confidence in our theory if this allows us to predict the future position of Mars! Coming back to horseracing, we can of course also do the reverse: get the statistical relationship from Group B and use this to do simulations on Group A. So we shall have two sets of simulations by which we can judge the goodness of our procedures.

Before we present the results of simulations, we must pause and think about two things: (1) Just how good are the predictions made by our statistical analysis? and (2) What alternative strategies are there, other than just betting \$2 to win on the horse in each race that has the highest predicted winning probability?

## How Good Are the Predictions?

We can provide a simple answer to this question: We merely count up how many horses with the highest predicted probability in each race actually did win. It turns out that in Group A 114 out of the 356 predicted winners (remember, there are 356 races and one predicted winner in each race)—that is, 32 percent, actually won. In Group B, 118, or 33 percent, actually won. We think that on the face of it that is not stupendously impressive. If you bet on every favorite to win, you would do comparably well in just picking winners. But as you remember, it is not enough to pick winners; you must also make money, and these two aims are not synonymous. This leads us to think about betting strategies.

## Betting Strategies

The simplest strategy is to bet to win on the horse with the highest predicted winning probability. We shall call this Strategy $1/W$. A little thought should convince you that this is not necessarily a very good strategy. Imagine that we have a race with six horses and that their predicted winning probabilities are 0.25, 0.15, 0.15, 0.15, 0.15, and 0.15. True, horse number 1 has the highest winning probability, but even this highest probability gives you only one chance in four. So perhaps we should not bet in a race like this at all! We therefore concoct an alternative strategy called Strategy 2/W: Bet to win on the horse with the highest winning probability, but only if this probability is at least as high as 0.5; otherwise, make no bet on the race. (There is nothing magical about 0.5; we could just as well have picked 0.4 or some other number. The results would have changed somewhat, but the principle remains the same.)

Next consider another race with six horses, with predicted winning probabilities of 0.45, 0.43, 0.03, 0.03, 0.03, and 0.03. To be sure, horse number 1 has a healthy predicted winning probability, but the winning probability of horse number 2 is so close to that of horse 1 that we may not feel too sanguine about horse 1. So we concoct Strategy 3/W: Bet to win on the horse with the highest predicted probability, but only if this probability is at least 3.5 times greater than the predicted probability of the second most likely horse to win (again, nothing magical about 3.5; we could have used some other number such as 2, 3, or 4).

Once we have defined our Strategies 1/W, 2/W, 3/W, it is easy to realize that we do not necessarily have to bet to win. We could just as easily use the selection procedures in these strategies but then proceed to bet the chosen horse to place or to show. This gives rise to Strategies 1/P, 2/P, 3/P, 1/S, 2/S, 3/S, where the notation should be self-explanatory. The fact that encourages us to consider these strategies is this: The horse with the highest predicted probability placed 182 times (51 percent) and showed 219 times (62 percent) in Group A and 199 times (56 percent) and 250 times (70 percent), respectively, in Group B.

Table 6–7 displays the average rates of return per dollar invested; for reasons we shall explain shortly, we also show the variance of the returns. We see right away that placing win bets is not profitable. Although the average rates of return are all better than the track take, they are all negative. Among them, Strategy 2/W does best: It is not far from breaking even. Notice that if we "play" Strategies 2/? or 3/?, we bet much more infrequently, once in every five or six races, since the conditions for using these strategies do not occur all the time.

The picture is somewhat more favorable for place and show betting. For some of the strategies the returns are positive, which means that on balance we make money but only moderately; the positive returns

Table 6-7    Results of Simulations: Average Rates of Return and Variances
             for Atlantic City Sample

| | Statistical Analysis from Group A Simulations Based on Group B | | | Statistical Analysis from Group B Simulations Based on Group A | | |
|---|---|---|---|---|---|---|
| Strategy | Number of Races Bet On | Average Rate of Return | Variance of Return | Number of Races Bet On | Average Rate of Return | Variance of Return |
| 1/W | 356 | −0.160 | 3.170 | 356 | −0.168 | 3.345 |
| 2/W | 62 | −0.077 | 1.650 | 57 | −0.002 | 1.614 |
| 3/W | 52 | −0.150 | 1.655 | 51 | −0.047 | 1.685 |
| 1/P | 356 | −0.043 | 1.634 | 356 | −0.047 | 1.742 |
| 2/P | 62 | 0.023 | 0.780 | 57 | 0.028 | 0.805 |
| 3/P | 52 | −0.049 | 0.970 | 51 | 0.027 | 0.653 |
| 1/S | 356 | −0.037 | 1.180 | 356 | −0.102 | 1.439 |
| 2/S | 62 | 0.073 | 0.734 | 57 | −0.057 | 0.935 |
| 3/S | 52 | −0.021 | 0.871 | 51 | 0.062 | 0.963 |

range from 2 to 7 percent. The principal conclusion is that all the strategies (except for 1/W) do quite a bit better than the average 17 to 18 percent loss you could expect due to the track take; however, the results are nothing to write home about if you are after serious money. Nevertheless, it appears that the place and show pools contain some "inefficiency"—not enough to get rich on but enough to come close to breaking even. This is confirmed by performing similar calculations for our Meadowlands sample of 706 races. There the strategies involved in win bets have rates of return ranging from 0.037 to −0.209; for place and show betting they range from −0.142 to +0.030—slightly lower than at Atlantic City but nevertheless comparable.

Finally, it is interesting to compare our strategies with the naive strategy of simply betting on the favorite in each race. If we bet to win, the return is −0.173; the returns to place and show bets return −0.109 and −0.087, respectively. Our strategies in fact do modestly better than this naive strategy, but even the naive strategy (in place and show betting) does better than the overall expected loss. Of course, this is a very stodgy way of betting—it may be "safe," but you are unlikely to have much fun!

This brings us back to the question of "market efficiency"—the reason that we displayed the variances of the returns in Table 6-7. Let us consider Strategy 2/P again. Depending on whether we look at the Group B or Group A simulations, it has a return variance of about 0.8. This strategy has a relatively high average return, which is something that people *like*. If it had an exceptionally low variance, which racetrack bettors *do not like* (the "stodginess factor"), then the presence of the high average return could not be used to infer that the market is inefficient, because the *risk-adjusted* return would *not be out of line*. So let us compare the variance(s) of Strategy 2/P with the list of variances of single horse bets to win, by odds class, in Table 6-4. From that table we see that horses with a variance of around 0.8 have an average return between $-0.06$ and $-0.10$ (falling between variances of 0.66 and 0.83). Our Strategy 2/P therefore *dominates* straight win betting.

This suggests that the betting market is inefficient—that is, the public fails to take advantage of all the information available (specifically, that it is relatively profitable to make place bets on horses with high winning probabilities predicted by a logit analysis). Basically, the same argument can be made for any of the place and show strategies but not for the win strategies: For example, Strategy 1/W has in Group B a variance of 3.171 and an average return of $-0.160$, *which is almost exactly the same* as placing a win bet on a horse with odds in the 3.50 to 3.95 range! (See Table 6-4.) Strategies 2/W and 3/W are very nearly equivalent to straight win bets on horses in the odds ranges of 1.60 to 1.75 and 1.80 to 1.95, respectively. It thus seems that (in spite of some inefficiency discussed earlier in this chapter) the odds and, therefore, the payoffs to win bets reflect sufficiently the information available about winning chances that special strategies cannot improve on them. This appears to be less true for place and show bets and may well be due to the great difficulty of calculating the payoffs to place and show bets.

## Some Cautionary Remarks

There are two warnings that you ought to heed. First of all, the coefficient values for $b$ and $c$ that we derived by logit analysis are not "universal constants" of nature, unchanging and eternal, and applicable to any racetrack at any time. Underlying conditions differ from track to track and may even differ from year to year (although we think that the latter is less likely). The safe thing to do if you want to use such strategies at Aqueduct or Belmont or Saratoga is to gather a data set from the racetrack in question and *redo* the logit analysis. It would not surprise us if at some tracks the statistically correct values of $b$ and $c$ were 2.0 or 6.0, or anywhere in between. Whatever they are, they will affect the outcome of the strategies.

Second, this seems to be a good place to say a little more about how betting can "spoil" your chances of winning. (Of course, we do not mean that betting can affect the chances that a particular horse will win the race; rather, we mean that it can spoil your chance of winning *money*.) Consider a hypothetical race at which the total handle is fairly small. We assume that the win, place, and show bets (5 seconds before the race starts) are as follows:

| Horse | Win Bets | Place Bets | Show Bets |
|-------|----------|------------|-----------|
| 1 | 5,000 | 2,083 | 1,250 |
| 2 | 3,000 | 1,250 | 750 |
| 3 | 2,000 | 833 | 500 |
| 4 | 1,000 | 417 | 250 |
| 5 | 500 | 208 | 125 |
| 6 | 300 | 125 | 75 |
| 7 | 200 | 83 | 50 |

You will note that at this hypothetical track odd-numbered bets (e.g., one dollar) are allowed (otherwise the amounts bet on a horse would always be even numbers). Also, we have fixed the numbers so that the proportions bet on the various horses are nearly the same for the win, place, and show pools.

Let us finally assume that payoffs are rounded down to the nearest 10 cents. The payoffs to each of the seven horses, should they win, are $1.90, $3.20, $4.90, $9.80, $19.60, $32.80, and $49.20. Now consider the effect of making a $20 bet. If you bet on horse 1 or 2, none of the payoffs changes. If you bet on horse 3, its payoff declines to $4.80, not a major change. But if you bet on horse 7, its payoff drops from $49.20 to $44.80, which is no longer negligible. What if you had bet $200? If you bet on horse 1, there is still no change in its payoff. If you bet on number 3, its payoff drops to $4.50. If you bet on number 7, its payoff is down to $25.00! Before you bet on it, the promised payoff, together with your estimate of its objective winning probability, made it seem like a good bet, but after you have bet $200 on it, it is a very different story. If you should be a really high roller and want to bet $2,000, you will appreciably affect the odds and payoffs of whatever horse you bet on: If you bet on number 2, its payoff drops to $1.60 and with number 7, it drops to $5.20: Your bet has made the longshot practically the favorite.

A very similar story can be told about place and show betting. Although we have not explained yet how the payoffs to place and

Table 6-8    Effect of Place Bets of Various Sizes on Payoffs

| Assumed Winner and Runner-up | Bet on Winner | | Bet on Runner-up | |
|---|---|---|---|---|
| | Payoff to Winner | Payoff to Runner-up | Payoff to Winner | Payoff to Runner-up |
| Nos. 1 & 3, bet $2 | 1.20 | 1.70 | 1.20 | 1.70 |
| Nos. 1 & 3, bet $20 | 1.20 | 1.70 | 1.20 | 1.70 |
| Nos. 1 & 3, bet $200 | 1.20 | 1.60 | 1.20 | 1.50 |
| Nos. 3 & 4, bet $2 | 2.70 | 4.40 | 2.70 | 4.40 |
| Nos. 3 & 4, bet $20 | 2.60 | 4.40 | 2.70 | 4.20 |
| Nos. 3 & 4, bet $200 | 2.30 | 4.30 | 2.60 | 3.20 |
| Nos. 5 & 6, bet $2 | 9.90 | 16.00 | 10.00 | 15.80 |
| Nos. 5 & 6, bet $20 | 9.20 | 16.00 | 10.00 | 13.90 |
| Nos. 5 & 6, bet $200 | 5.50 | 15.90 | 9.90 | 6.70 |
| Nos. 7 & 5, bet $2 | 23.30 | 10.10 | 23.80 | 10.00 |
| Nos. 7 & 5, bet $20 | 19.40 | 10.10 | 23.80 | 9.30 |
| Nos. 7 & 5, bet $200 | 7.60 | 10.00 | 23.60 | 5.60 |

show bets are calculated (this will be covered in detail in the next section), we can illustrate the effect on payoffs of bets of particular sizes (see Table 6-8). Keep in mind that the payoffs to place bets depend on which two horses come in first and second (and the sizes of show payoffs depend on which three horses come in first, second, and third). As before, if you bet on relative favorites, the effect is fairly small, but if you bet on longshots, even a $20 bet may have a nonnegligible effect on the payoff. The same general conclusion holds for show betting, but we shall not belabor the issue further. We just note that you should always be aware of this problem. If you are contemplating a fairly sizable bet, consider the effect of your bet on the payoffs. This can be done exactly for win bets, and the range of effects can be approximated for place and show bets from the betting pool figures displayed at the track.

The moral is obvious, and we have harped on this before: If enough people attempt to take advantage of any potentially winning strategy, the differential profit from that strategy *must disappear*. The key to making money is *restraint*, individually, and by the public at large. If this seems to you another sign of stodginess, we are sorry, indeed, and we feel that you should amuse yourself, if you so wish, with wild things. But you must then be aware of the fact that you are seeking fun, not money.

## More Inefficiency in the Place and Show Pools:
## The Ziemba-Hausch ("Dr. Z") System

### How Place and Show Payoffs Are Calculated

We have already seen that there is reason to believe that inefficiencies in place and show betting might be exploited for modest profit (whereas there is some inefficiency in win betting, it is not enough to make money). A new and promising approach to exploiting this inefficiency was devised by Hausch, Ziemba, and Rubinstein (1981), and by Ziemba and Hausch (1984) and Hausch and Ziemba (1985). The key to understanding how this system works is the formula for determining the payoffs to place and show bets.

Once again, we need a little bit of algebraic notation. Recall that we used $B$ to denote the total amount bet on all horses in the race. Analogously, we shall define $P_i$ to be the amount bet to place on horse $i$, and $P$ the total place pool on all horses; also, we shall use $S_i$ to denote the amount bet to show on horse $i$, and $S$ the total show pool.

Everybody knows that the payoff on a win bet can be determined at a glance. If Peter's favorite horse, Aunt Louise, has $8,462 bet on it out of a total win pool of $25,698 and the track take is 18 percent (not including breakage), the payoff is $4.80 to a $2 bet. But what about place betting?

The problem here is that a place bet pays off whether the horse comes in first or second. Since any horse that has come in first or second has won its place bet, it is generally (but not always) true that there are two horses in every race on which place bets must be paid off (if there is a tie for second place, place bets on three horses have to be paid). This means that the total place pool must be divided between two horses. The first rule in dividing the pool is that everybody who has bet on either of the placing horses gets his or her investment refunded. The second rule is that the remainder of the money is divided equally between the two groups of people who have bet on one or the other horse, respectively. This means that the payoff to horse $i$ depends on which other horse also placed.

Let us look at an example. Imagine that the total place pool is $20,000 ($P = 20{,}000$) and that the amounts bet on horses 1, 2, and 3 are $P_1 = \$1{,}000$, $P_2 = \$4{,}000$, $P_3 = \$8{,}000$ (we do not care at this point how much is bet on each of the remaining horses). Finally, we assume that the track take is 18 percent.

Suppose that horse 1 places. The amount available for distribution is $(0.82)(20,000) = 16,400$. Suppose horse 2 also places. First, the track refunds the amounts originally bet on horses 1 and 2, which is $1,000 + \$4,000 = \$5,000$. That leaves $\$16,400 - \$5,000 = \$11,400$ to be distributed equally between bettors on horse 1 (as a group) and bettors on horse 2 (as a group). Hence each group gets $\$11,400/2 = \$5,700$. Since a total of $1,000 was bet on horse 1 (which is refunded), the total payment to holders of place bets on number 1 is $6,700; that is, the payoff is $6.70 per dollar bet. For the same reason, the total paid to the group holding place bets on number 2 is $9,700, and the payoff *per dollar bet* is $\$9,700/\$4,000 = \$2.425$ (which does not yet take breakage into account; this payoff would in fact be rounded down to $2.40). The general formula for the payoff to the group holding tickets on horse $i$ can be written down from the above reasoning. First the total available for distribution is $P(1 - t)$. If horse $j$ was the other horse that placed, we first refund the tickets that were bought on horses $i$ and $j$; after this refunding we have $P(1 - t) - P_i - P_j$ left over. Half of that is $[P(1 - t) - P_i - P_j]/2$. The holders of tickets on horse $i$ collectively get $P_i + (P(1 - t) - P_i - P_j)/2$. *Per dollar*, the payoff is

$$1 + \frac{P(1 - t) - P_i - P_j}{2P_i}$$

if $i$ and $j$ place, and zero if $i$ does not place.

Exactly the same principles govern the payoffs to show betting except that we now have to account for three "showers." Everybody who holds a show bet on a horse that comes in first, second, or third gets his or her money refunded; the remainder is divided equally among the three groups. Thus, the payoff *per dollar bet* to holders of show tickets on horse $i$ is

$$1 + \frac{S(1 - t) - S_i - S_j - S_k}{3S_i}$$

if horses $i, j$, and $k$ all show, and zero if horse $i$ does not come in among the first three.

We note parenthetically that these rules are not sacred and eternal laws; in other countries different ones may be followed. For example, in New Zealand there is no place betting at all, and in show betting, which does exist, the payoff is determined as follows: The total show pool (after the take) is apportioned equally among the three groups of people holding show tickets on the first three finishers. Thus the per dollar payoff to show bettors on horse $i$ is

$$\frac{(1 - t)S}{3S_i}$$

Under these circumstances, it is in theory possible to have a winning show bet and still lose money (McCulloch and van Zijl [1984]). If the total show pool is \$12,000, the take is 18 percent, and the amount bet on horse 1 is greater than \$3,280, holders of tickets on number 1 will get back less than a dollar for each dollar bet because

$$\frac{(0.82)\,12,000}{3S_1} = \frac{3,280}{S_1}$$

which is less than 1 if $S_1$ is greater than 3,280.

The British system is different still. There are only two types of bets: win and place. Here, however, "place" means simply "in the money," and the number of horses in the money depends on the number of entrants in the race. If, for example, there are four or fewer starters, only the winner pays off; but if there is a very large field — 16 or more — bettors on the first *four* finishers collect money.

In any event, we can now calculate the place payoffs. To calculate the expected payoff, we need two things: the payoff itself and the probability that a particular pair of horses will place. We now turn to this latter problem.

## The Probability That Two Particular Horses Will Place

Once again we are considering horses $i$ and $j$. We first need to know the objective probability that, say, horse $i$ will win. In general, we already know that the public perception of the horses' quality, as expressed in the odds, is a pretty good guide to the objective winning probability. So we might simply convert the odds to a (subjective) probability figure as we had done earlier in this chapter and pretend that these are the objective probabilities. The astute reader will immediately notice that this completely omits the problem of the over/underbetting bias that we discussed in such detail! So, perhaps we can actually do better by explicitly recognizing the existence of this bias!

How do we do this? Consider Table 6–2 in which we show the objective and subjective probabilities for a wide variety of horses. If we drew a diagram in which we measure subjective probability along the horizontal axis and objective probability along the vertical axis,

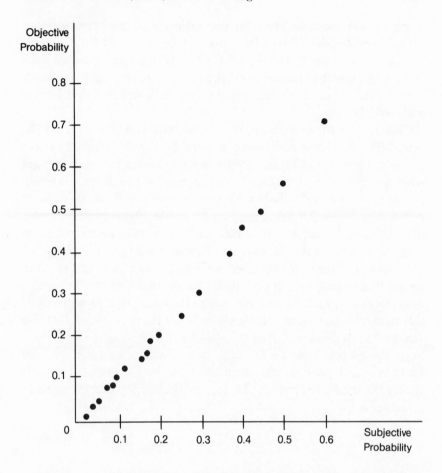

Figure 6-1 A Scatter Diagram of Objective and Subjective Probabilities.

and plotted a dot to represent each pair of probabilities from Table 6–2, we would get a "scatter diagram" such as Figure 6–1. The dots lie almost perfectly along a straight line, and we have calculated the regression equation from which we could predict the objective probabilities $p$ from the subjective probabilities $s$. The "best" straight line is given by

$$p = -0.0279 + 1.2097s$$

and the measure of the goodness of the "fit," the coefficient $R^2$, is 0.9931, which indicates an excellent fit (a perfect fit would be indicated by $R^2 = 1.0000$). Having such an equation allows us to estimate the objective probability for each horse from the odds.

Take as an example a horse that has $4,000 bet on it out of a total pool of $20,000. The subjective probability is $4,000/20,000 = 0.2$.

Applying the equation gives for our estimate of the corresponding objective probability: $-0.0279 + 0.2 \times 1.2097 = 0.2140$.

Now suppose we do this for all the horses in a race; thus we have estimated objective probabilities $p_1$, $p_2$, ..., $p_N$ for each of the $N$ horses. What is the probability that horse $i$ will win *and* that horse $j$ will come in second?

Clearly, $p_i$ is the probability that horse $i$ will win. But $p_j$ is *not* the probability that horse $j$ will come in second, but the probability that $j$ will win! Harville (1973) has proposed the following calculation to get what we are really after. Horse $j$ coming in second in the race is really the same as winning in that race if horse $i$ were somehow not there. If $p_i = 0.3$ and $p_j = 0.2$, we are saying that $i$ has 30 out of 100 chances of winning and $j$ has 20 out of 100 chances. If horse $i$ were not to be counted, horse $j$ would still have 20 chances of winning, but not out of 100 but out of only 70 (since we are disregarding $i$'s chances). That means that to get a proper probability for the fictitious race in which $i$ does not count, we have to scale up $j$'s chances so that its winning of this fictitious race again represents so many chances out of 100. We can do this by dividing 0.2 by 0.7 — that is, by dividing $p_j$ by $(1 - p_i)$. Since the events "horse $i$ wins" and "horse $j$ wins among the rest" are likely to be independent, the probability that both events will occur is simply the product of the two. Hence, the probability that $i$ wins and $j$ is second is

$$\frac{p_i p_j}{1 - p_i} \qquad (6\text{--}8)$$

and the probability that $j$ wins and $i$ comes in second is

$$\frac{p_i p_j}{1 - p_j} \qquad (6\text{--}9)$$

Statistical evidence has shown that these formulas are pretty good approximations to the actual probabilities of the events in question. Furthermore, since these two events are mutually exclusive, the probability that $i$ and $j$ both place (i.e., come in first and second in either order) is the sum of these two, $p_i p_j/(1 - p_i) + p_i p_j/(1 - p_j)$.

## Why May Profit Opportunities Exist?

We now know, at least in principle, how to calculate the payoffs for every possible placing combination, and we also know how to estimate the objective probabilities that these particular combinations will actually come in. These are the only two ingredients we need to evaluate the expected value or expected payoff of a bet. Just as in all the previous examples, the expected value is calculated by first multiplying together the magnitude of each possible outcome (payoff) with the corresponding probability and then adding up the products. The practical problem here is that there are now many possible outcomes — more than the two of our previous examples. If you were to bet on horse 1 to place, you would have to consider *all* of the following outcomes:

> Horse 1 wins and horse 2 is second
> Horse 1 wins and horse 3 is second
>
> .
>
> .
>
> .
>
> Horse 1 wins and horse $N$ is second
> Horse 2 wins and horse 1 is second
> Horse 3 wins and horse 1 is second
>
> .
>
> .
>
> .
>
> Horse $N$ wins and horse 1 is second

If there are 10 horses in the race, there are 18 possible favorable outcomes, each with its payoff and probability of realization. If we decide to neglect the breakage in our expected value formula, things become a little simpler, but it is still fairly laborious. Let us see what the expected value formula really is.

Suppose we want to find the expected value of a place bet on horse 1. We have previously developed formulas both for the payoffs and for the probabilities of the various occurrences. We have:

| If the Two Placers Are | The Payoff Per Dollar Invested Is | The Probability Is |
|---|---|---|
| Horses 1 and 2 | $1 + \dfrac{P(1-t) - P_1 - P_2}{2P_1}$ | $\dfrac{p_1 p_2}{1 - p_1} + \dfrac{p_1 p_2}{1 - p_2}$ |
| Horses 1 and 3 | $1 + \dfrac{P(1-t) - P_1 - P_3}{2P_1}$ | $\dfrac{p_1 p_3}{1 - p_1} + \dfrac{p_1 p_3}{1 - p_3}$ |
| Horses 1 and 4 | $1 + \dfrac{P(1-t) - P_1 - P_4}{2P_1}$ | $\dfrac{p_1 p_4}{1 - p_1} + \dfrac{p_1 p_4}{1 - p_4}$ |
| . | | |
| . | | |
| . | | |
| Horses 1 and $N$ | $1 + \dfrac{P(1-t) - P_1 - P_N}{2P_1}$ | $\dfrac{p_1 p_N}{1 - p_1} + \dfrac{p_1 p_N}{1 - p_N}$ |

By multiplying payoffs by probabilities and adding, we get for the expected value of a place bet on horse 1:

$$\text{Expected value} = \left(\frac{p_1 p_2}{1-p_1} + \frac{p_1 p_2}{1-p_2}\right)\left(1 + \frac{P(1-t) - P_1 - P_2}{2P_1}\right)$$

$$+ \left(\frac{p_1 p_3}{1-p_1} + \frac{p_1 p_2}{1-p_3}\right)\left(1 + \frac{P(1-t) - P_1 - P_3}{2P_1}\right)$$

$$\cdots$$

$$+ \left(\frac{p_1 p_N}{1-p_1} + \frac{p_1 p_N}{1-p_N}\right)\left(1 + \frac{P(1-t) - P_1 - P_N}{2P_1}\right)$$

If we computed the expected values of place bets on each horse in a race, there might well be one with a very high expected value. Betting on such horses consistently would tend to earn one a lot of profit.

All this sounds like a lot of laborious and complicated calculating. To give you an idea of what to look for, we present a few hypothetical examples. Our hypothetical races will have five horses in them, a take of 0.18, and we shall neglect breakage. We shall also assume for simplicity that the objective probability that a horse wins is identical to the subjective probability—that is, the ratio of the amount bet on it to win to the total win pool. (See Tables 6-9, 6-10, and 6-11.)

First, notice in Table 6-9 that the favorite (number 5), on which 51.6 percent of the entire win pool was bet, has a much smaller

Table 6-9   Pools, Win Probabilities, and Expected Value of Place Bets

| Horse | Win Pool | Place Pool | Win Probability | Expected Value of Place Bet |
|-------|----------|------------|-----------------|------------------------------|
| 1 | 1000. | 1000. | 0.032 | 0.38 |
| 2 | 2000. | 2000. | 0.065 | 0.41 |
| 3 | 4000. | 3000. | 0.129 | 0.59 |
| 4 | 8000. | 4000. | 0.258 | 0.89 |
| 5 | 16000. | 5000. | 0.516 | 1.15 |
| Total | 31000. | 15000. | | |

Table 6-10   Probabilities That a Given Combination of Horses Places

| Horse | 1 | 2 | 3 | 4 | 5 |
|-------|-----|-----|-----|-----|-----|
| 1 | 0.0 | 0.004 | 0.009 | 0.020 | 0.052 |
| 2 | 0.004 | 0.0 | 0.018 | 0.040 | 0.104 |
| 3 | 0.009 | 0.018 | 0.0 | 0.083 | 0.214 |
| 4 | 0.020 | 0.040 | 0.083 | 0.0 | 0.455 |
| 5 | 0.052 | 0.104 | 0.214 | 0.455 | 0.0 |

Table 6-11    Payoffs to Winning Place Bets

|            |      | Other Placing Horse Is |      |      |      |
| :--------: | :--: | :--: | :--: | :--: | :--: |
| Bet on Horse | 1    | 2    | 3    | 4    | 5    |
| 1          | 0.0  | 5.65 | 5.15 | 4.65 | 4.15 |
| 2          | 3.32 | 0.0  | 2.82 | 2.57 | 2.32 |
| 3          | 2.38 | 2.22 | 0.0  | 1.88 | 1.72 |
| 4          | 1.91 | 1.79 | 1.66 | 0.0  | 1.41 |
| 5          | 1.63 | 1.53 | 1.43 | 1.33 | 0.0  |

proportion (33.3 percent) of the place pool bet on it. The payoffs to place bets on number 5 are quite low because a substantial amount has been bet on this horse, but the probabilities of its placing are sufficiently high so that its expected value per dollar of investment in place betting is slightly bigger than 1.0. By contrast, numbers 1 and 2 are both unlikely to place and account for a relatively larger portion of the place pool than of the win pool; their expected values are quite a bit smaller than 1.0.

We have rigged the numbers in Tables 6-12, 6-13, and 6-14 so that the win bets and probabilities are the same as in Table 6-8. But here the amounts bet to place on numbers 1 and 2 are much smaller percentages of the win bets on these horses than is the case for numbers 3, 4, and particularly 5. The result is that betting on number 1

Table 6-12    Pools, Win Probabilities, and Expected Value of Place Bets

| Horse | Win Pool | Place Pool | Win Probability | Expected Value of Place Bet |
| :---: | :------: | :--------: | :-------------: | :-------------------------: |
| 1     | 1000.    | 100.       | 0.032           | 2.09                        |
| 2     | 2000.    | 400.       | 0.065           | 1.06                        |
| 3     | 4000.    | 1200.      | 0.129           | 0.77                        |
| 4     | 8000.    | 3200.      | 0.258           | 0.70                        |
| 5     | 16000.   | 8000.      | 0.516           | 0.85                        |
| Total | 31000.   | 12900.     |                 |                             |

Table 6-13    Probabilities That a Combination of Horses Places

| Horse | 1     | 2     | 3     | 4     | 5     |
| :---: | :---: | :---: | :---: | :---: | :---: |
| 1     | 0.0   | 0.004 | 0.009 | 0.020 | 0.052 |
| 2     | 0.004 | 0.0   | 0.018 | 0.040 | 0.104 |
| 3     | 0.009 | 0.018 | 0.0   | 0.083 | 0.214 |
| 4     | 0.020 | 0.040 | 0.083 | 0.0   | 0.455 |
| 5     | 0.052 | 0.104 | 0.214 | 0.455 | 0.0   |

Table 6-14    Payoffs to Winning Place Bets

|              | Other Placing Horse Is | | | | |
| Bet on Horse | 1     | 2     | 3     | 4     | 5     |
| --- | --- | --- | --- | --- | --- |
| 1 | 0.0   | 51.39 | 47.39 | 37.39 | 13.39 |
| 2 | 13.60 | 0.0   | 12.22 | 9.72  | 3.72  |
| 3 | 4.87  | 4.74  | 0.0   | 3.57  | 1.57  |
| 4 | 2.14  | 2.09  | 1.97  | 0.0   | 0.90  |
| 5 | 1.15  | 1.14  | 1.09  | 0.96  | 0.0   |

produces a very large payoff and a very sizable expected value (betting on number 2 produces an expected value just in excess of 1.0). As a last example, we assume that exactly the same amount is bet on each horse to place as is bet on it to win (see Tables 6-15, 6-16, and 6-17). You can check that all the expected values are quite a bit below 1: There is no money to be made if place bets on horses are the same proportion of the place pool as win bets are of the win pool.

Table 6-15    Pools, Win Probabilities, and Expected Value of Place Bets

| Horse | Win Pool | Place Pool | Win Probability | Expected Value of Place Bet |
| --- | --- | --- | --- | --- |
| 1 | 1000.  | 1000.  | 0.032 | 0.61 |
| 2 | 2000.  | 2000.  | 0.065 | 0.63 |
| 3 | 4000.  | 4000.  | 0.129 | 0.68 |
| 4 | 8000.  | 8000.  | 0.258 | 0.77 |
| 5 | 16000. | 16000. | 0.516 | 0.92 |
| Total | 31000. | 31000. | | |

Table 6-16    Probabilities That a Combination of Horses Places

| Horse | 1 | 2 | 3 | 4 | 5 |
| --- | --- | --- | --- | --- | --- |
| 1 | 0.0   | 0.004 | 0.009 | 0.020 | 0.052 |
| 2 | 0.004 | 0.0   | 0.018 | 0.040 | 0.104 |
| 3 | 0.009 | 0.018 | 0.0   | 0.083 | 0.214 |
| 4 | 0.020 | 0.040 | 0.083 | 0.0   | 0.455 |
| 5 | 0.052 | 0.104 | 0.214 | 0.455 | 0.0   |

Table 6-17    Payoffs to Winning Place Bets

|              | Other Placing Horse Is | | | | |
| Bet on Horse | 1     | 2     | 3     | 4     | 5     |
| --- | --- | --- | --- | --- | --- |
| 1 | 0.0   | 12.21 | 11.21 | 9.21  | 5.21  |
| 2 | 6.60  | 0.0   | 5.85  | 4.85  | 2.85  |
| 3 | 3.55  | 3.43  | 0.0   | 2.68  | 1.68  |
| 4 | 2.03  | 1.96  | 1.84  | 0.0   | 1.09  |
| 5 | 1.26  | 1.23  | 1.17  | 1.04  | 0.0   |

This, then, gives us the clue as to what we should look for: Generally, make place bets on horses whose share of the place pool is substantially smaller than their share in the win pool. In many races no such horse may exist, and in such races it might be smarter (though less fun) not to bet at all. In principle, we should determine the expected value of betting on each horse and bet only on the "bargains." What is a satisfactory bargain may differ from person to person, but we would be not inclined to bet if the expected value were less than about 1.20. Now, the evaluation of the expected value formula is quite cumbersome. Ziemba and Hausch (1984) have provided a reasonable approximate formula (based on statistical analysis) that will serve well enough (if not exactly). The formula is:

Approximate expected value of place bet on horse $i =$

$$0.319 + 0.559 \frac{B_i/B}{P_i/P} + \left[ 2.22 - 1.29 \frac{B_i}{B} \right] (0.171 - t)$$

Our discussion so far has been devoted solely to place betting. The situation is similar (even though the formulas become more complicated) if we consider show betting. The Harville formulas that give the probability that horse $i$ wins and $j$ comes in second can be adapted to give the probability that $i$ wins, $j$ comes in second, and $k$ comes in third. This probability is

$$\frac{p_i p_j p_k}{(1 - p_i)(1 - p_i - p_j)}$$

From the payoffs to show betting and these probabilities we can again calculate the expected value of a show bet on horse $i$. The precise formula is a monster, but once again, Ziemba and Hausch (1984) have provided an approximate formula that will work fairly well:

Approximate expected value of show bet on horse $i =$

$$0.543 + 0.369 \frac{B_i/B}{S_i/S} + \left[ 3.60 - 2.13 \frac{B_i}{B} \right] (0.171 - t)$$

The combination of the two formulas may maximize your chances of making a reasonable bet in a race; even if you do not find a suitable place bet (because all the place expected values are less than 1.20), you may still find an acceptable show bet.

## How Much Should You Bet?

Any number of rules of thumb can be employed. Some people might want to bet a fixed amount in each race. Others double the bet every time they lose. Ziemba and Hausch (1984) strongly endorse the so-called "Kelly criterion," which will maximize the long-run expected growth rate of your wealth.

Ziemba and Hausch (1984) present complicated formulas for the optimal amount to bet, both for show bets and place bets. These formulas take into account (1) the estimate of the objective probability that the horse will win $(B_i/B)$; (2) the track take; (3) the size of the place pool, $P$, for place betting and the size of the show pool, $S$, for show betting; (4) the fraction of the place pool on the horse to be bet on $(P_i/P)$ or, for show betting, the fraction of the show pool bet on the horse in question $(S_i/S)$; and (5) the current "wealth" of the individual (i.e., the money the individual came to the track with). Since the formulas are complicated and there are, in fact, many of them, each for a different set of circumstances, we present tables to show the optimal bet size under some simplifying assumptions. Radical departures from the assumptions are a clear indication that you should consult Ziemba and Hausch (1984).

Our assumptions are as follows: (1) the track take is 0.171; (2) the individual's wealth is $500; (3) the total place pool is between $10,000 and $150,000; and (4) the total show pool is between $6,000 and $94,000. The bettor would proceed as follows: First, he or she would compute the expected return on each horse in the race. If none of the expected returns exceeded our conservative figure of 1.20, no bet would be made. If one or more expected returns exceeded 1.20, the bettor would choose the largest. The bettor would ascertain the values of $B_i/B$, of $P$ and $P_i/P$ (or of $S$ and $S_i/S$ for show betting), and look up the appropriate part of Table 6–18 or Table 6–19. So, for example, if $B_i/B$ were 0.3 and $P_i/P$ were 0.1 and the entire place pool were $30,000, the optimal bet would be $128.

Looking at the figures in either Table 6–18 or 6–19, the user must be struck by how they change, as $B_i/B$, $P$, $P_i/P$ (or $S$ and $S_i/S$) vary. We note right away that the larger the pool, the greater the optimal bet. Obviously, also as the winning probability rises, so does the bet. Finally, if the proportionate amount of place (show) betting on the horse becomes very small, the bet is again very large. All these features make good sense; the last in particular says that if there is a big inefficiency in place or show betting, you should bet a lot. What may surprise you is how large the optimal bets can become: If the place pool is $150,000, the probability of the horse winning is 0.5, and the place bets on your horse are a tiny fraction of the place pool, namely 0.025, you should wager $374, namely 75 percent of your

**Table 6-18  Optimal Place Bets**

*Winning probability is = 0.050*

| $P_i/P$ | | | | | | Place pool in tens of thousands | | | | | | | | | |
|---|---|---|---|---|---|---|---|---|---|---|---|---|---|---|---|
| | 1 | 2 | 3 | 4 | 5 | 6 | 7 | 8 | 9 | 10 | 11 | 12 | 13 | 14 | 15 |
| .025 | 10. | 10. | 10. | 10. | 11. | 11. | 11. | 11. | 11. | 12. | 12. | 12. | 12. | 13. | 13. |

*Winning probability is = 0.100*

| $P_i/P$ | | | | | | Place pool in tens of thousands | | | | | | | | | |
|---|---|---|---|---|---|---|---|---|---|---|---|---|---|---|---|
| | 1 | 2 | 3 | 4 | 5 | 6 | 7 | 8 | 9 | 10 | 11 | 12 | 13 | 14 | 15 |
| .025 | 35. | 35. | 36. | 37. | 37. | 38. | 39. | 39. | 40. | 41. | 42. | 42. | 43. | 44. | 44. |
| .050 | 22. | 22. | 23. | 23. | 24. | 24. | 25. | 25. | 26. | 26. | 26. | 27. | 27. | 28. | 28. |

*Winning probability is = 0.150*

| $P_i/P$ | | | | | | Place pool in tens of thousands | | | | | | | | | |
|---|---|---|---|---|---|---|---|---|---|---|---|---|---|---|---|
| | 1 | 2 | 3 | 4 | 5 | 6 | 7 | 8 | 9 | 10 | 11 | 12 | 13 | 14 | 15 |
| .025 | 60. | 62. | 63. | 64. | 65. | 66. | 67. | 69. | 70. | 71. | 72. | 73. | 75. | 76. | 77. |
| .050 | 50. | 51. | 52. | 53. | 54. | 55. | 56. | 57. | 58. | 59. | 60. | 61. | 62. | 63. | 63. |
| .075 | 37. | 37. | 38. | 39. | 39. | 40. | 41. | 42. | 42. | 43. | 44. | 44. | 45. | 46. | 46. |

*Winning probability is = 0.200*

| $P_i/P$ | | | | | | Place pool in tens of thousands | | | | | | | | | |
|---|---|---|---|---|---|---|---|---|---|---|---|---|---|---|---|
| | 1 | 2 | 3 | 4 | 5 | 6 | 7 | 8 | 9 | 10 | 11 | 12 | 13 | 14 | 15 |
| .025 | 89. | 90. | 92. | 94. | 95. | 97. | 98. | 100. | 102. | 103. | 105. | 107. | 108. | 110. | 112. |
| .050 | 80. | 81. | 82. | 84. | 85. | 87. | 88. | 89. | 91. | 92. | 94. | 95. | 97. | 98. | 99. |
| .075 | 68. | 70. | 71. | 72. | 73. | 74. | 75. | 77. | 78. | 79. | 80. | 81. | 82. | 84. | 85. |
| .100 | 54. | 55. | 56. | 57. | 58. | 59. | 60. | 61. | 62. | 62. | 63. | 64. | 65. | 66. | 67. |
| .125 | 36. | 36. | 37. | 38. | 38. | 39. | 40. | 40. | 41. | 42. | 42. | 43. | 44. | 44. | 45. |

*Winning probability is = 0.250*

| | | | | | | Place pool in tens of thousands | | | | | | | | | |
|---|---|---|---|---|---|---|---|---|---|---|---|---|---|---|---|
| $P_i/P$ | 1 | 2 | 3 | 4 | 5 | 6 | 7 | 8 | 9 | 10 | 11 | 12 | 13 | 14 | 15 |
| .025 | 119. | 121. | 124. | 126. | 128. | 130. | 132. | 134. | 136. | 138. | 140. | 143. | 145. | 147. | 149. |
| .050 | 111. | 113. | 115. | 116. | 118. | 120. | 122. | 124. | 126. | 128. | 130. | 132. | 133. | 135. | 137. |
| .075 | 101. | 102. | 104. | 106. | 107. | 109. | 111. | 112. | 114. | 116. | 117. | 119. | 121. | 122. | 124. |
| .100 | 89. | 90. | 92. | 93. | 94. | 96. | 97. | 99. | 100. | 101. | 103. | 104. | 106. | 107. | 108. |
| .125 | 74. | 76. | 77. | 78. | 79. | 80. | 81. | 82. | 83. | 85. | 86. | 87. | 88. | 89. | 90. |
| .150 | 56. | 57. | 58. | 59. | 60. | 61. | 62. | 63. | 63. | 64. | 65. | 66. | 67. | 68. | 69. |

*Winning probability is = 0.300*

| | | | | | | Place pool in tens of thousands | | | | | | | | | |
|---|---|---|---|---|---|---|---|---|---|---|---|---|---|---|---|
| $P_i/P$ | 1 | 2 | 3 | 4 | 5 | 6 | 7 | 8 | 9 | 10 | 11 | 12 | 13 | 14 | 15 |
| .025 | 153. | 155. | 158. | 160. | 163. | 165. | 168. | 171. | 173. | 176. | 178. | 181. | 184. | 186. | 189. |
| .050 | 144. | 147. | 149. | 151. | 154. | 156. | 159. | 161. | 163. | 166. | 168. | 170. | 173. | 175. | 177. |
| .075 | 135. | 137. | 139. | 141. | 144. | 146. | 148. | 150. | 152. | 154. | 156. | 158. | 161. | 163. | 165. |
| .100 | 124. | 126. | 128. | 130. | 132. | 134. | 136. | 138. | 139. | 141. | 143. | 145. | 147. | 149. | 151. |
| .125 | 112. | 114. | 115. | 117. | 118. | 120. | 122. | 123. | 125. | 127. | 128. | 130. | 131. | 133. | 135. |
| .150 | 97. | 99. | 100. | 101. | 103. | 104. | 105. | 107. | 108. | 109. | 111. | 112. | 114. | 115. | 116. |
| .175 | 80. | 81. | 82. | 83. | 84. | 85. | 86. | 87. | 88. | 90. | 91. | 92. | 93. | 94. | 95. |

*Winning probability is = 0.350*

| | | | | | | Place pool in tens of thousands | | | | | | | | | |
|---|---|---|---|---|---|---|---|---|---|---|---|---|---|---|---|
| $P_i/P$ | 1 | 2 | 3 | 4 | 5 | 6 | 7 | 8 | 9 | 10 | 11 | 12 | 13 | 14 | 15 |
| .025 | 188. | 191. | 195. | 198. | 201. | 204. | 207. | 210. | 213. | 216. | 219. | 222. | 225. | 228. | 231. |
| .050 | 181. | 183. | 186. | 189. | 192. | 195. | 198. | 200. | 203. | 206. | 209. | 212. | 215. | 217. | 220. |
| .075 | 172. | 174. | 177. | 179. | 182. | 185. | 187. | 190. | 192. | 195. | 198. | 200. | 203. | 205. | 208. |
| .100 | 162. | 164. | 166. | 169. | 171. | 173. | 176. | 178. | 181. | 183. | 185. | 188. | 190. | 192. | 195. |
| .125 | 150. | 153. | 155. | 157. | 159. | 161. | 163. | 165. | 167. | 169. | 171. | 174. | 176. | 178. | 180. |
| .150 | 137. | 139. | 141. | 143. | 145. | 147. | 149. | 150. | 152. | 154. | 156. | 158. | 160. | 162. | 163. |
| .175 | 123. | 124. | 126. | 127. | 129. | 131. | 132. | 134. | 135. | 137. | 138. | 140. | 142. | 143. | 145. |
| .200 | 105. | 107. | 108. | 109. | 111. | 112. | 113. | 115. | 116. | 117. | 119. | 120. | 121. | 123. | 124. |

*Winning probability is = 0.400*

| | | | | | | Place pool in tens of thousands | | | | | | | | | |
|---|---|---|---|---|---|---|---|---|---|---|---|---|---|---|---|
| $P_i/P$ | 1 | 2 | 3 | 4 | 5 | 6 | 7 | 8 | 9 | 10 | 11 | 12 | 13 | 14 | 15 |
| .025 | 227. | 230. | 234. | 237. | 241. | 245. | 248. | 252. | 255. | 259. | 262. | 266. | 269. | 273. | 276. |
| .050 | 219. | 222. | 226. | 229. | 232. | 236. | 239. | 242. | 246. | 249. | 252. | 256. | 259. | 262. | 265. |
| .075 | 211. | 214. | 217. | 220. | 223. | 226. | 229. | 232. | 235. | 238. | 241. | 244. | 248. | 251. | .254 |
| .100 | 201. | 204. | 207. | 210. | 213. | 215. | 218. | 221. | 224. | 227. | 230. | 232. | 235. | 238. | 241. |
| .125 | 191. | 193. | 196. | 198. | 201. | 204. | 206. | 209. | 211. | 214. | 217. | 219. | 222. | 224. | 227. |
| .150 | 179. | 181. | 184. | 186. | 188. | 191. | 193. | 195. | 198. | 200. | 202. | 205. | 207. | 209. | 212. |
| .175 | 166. | 168. | 170. | 172. | 174. | 176. | 178. | 180. | 182. | 184. | 186. | 188. | 191. | 193. | 195. |
| .200 | 151. | 152. | 154. | 156. | 158. | 160. | 162. | 163. | 165. | 167. | 169. | 171. | 172. | 174. | 176. |
| .225 | 133. | 135. | 137. | 138. | 140. | 141. | 143. | 144. | 146. | 147. | 149. | 151. | 152. | 154. | 155. |
| .250 | 114. | 115. | 116. | 117. | 119. | 120. | 121. | 123. | 124. | 125. | 127. | 128. | 129. | 131. | 132. |

*Winning probability is = 0.450*

Place pool in tens of thousands

| $P_i/P$ | 1 | 2 | 3 | 4 | 5 | 6 | 7 | 8 | 9 | 10 | 11 | 12 | 13 | 14 | 15 |
|---|---|---|---|---|---|---|---|---|---|---|---|---|---|---|---|
| .025 | 268. | 272. | 276. | 280. | 284. | 288. | 292. | 296. | 300. | 304. | 308. | 312. | 316. | 320. | 324. |
| .050 | 260. | 264. | 268. | 272. | 275. | 279. | 283. | 287. | 291. | 294. | 298. | 302. | 306. | 310. | 313. |
| .075 | 252. | 256. | 259. | 263. | 266. | 270. | 273. | 277. | 280. | 284. | 288. | 291. | 295. | 298. | 302. |
| .100 | 243. | 246. | 250. | 253. | 256. | 260. | 263. | 266. | 270. | 273. | 276. | 279. | 283. | 286. | 289. |
| .125 | 233. | 236. | 239. | 242. | 245. | 248. | 251. | 255. | 258. | 261. | 264. | 267. | 270. | 273. | 276. |
| .150 | 222. | 225. | 228. | 231. | 233. | 236. | 239. | 242. | 245. | 247. | 250. | 253. | 256. | 259. | 262. |
| .175 | 210. | 212. | 215. | 218. | 220. | 223. | 225. | 228. | 230. | 233. | 236. | 238. | 241. | 243. | 246. |
| .200 | 196. | 199. | 201. | 203. | 206. | 208. | 210. | 213. | 215. | 217. | 219. | 222. | 224. | 226. | 229. |
| .225 | 181. | 183. | 185. | 187. | 189. | 191. | 194. | 196. | 198. | 200. | 202. | 204. | 206. | 208. | 210. |
| .250 | 164. | 166. | 168. | 170. | 171. | 173. | 175. | 177. | 178. | 180. | 182. | 184. | 186. | 187. | 189. |
| .275 | 145. | 146. | 148. | 149. | 151. | 153. | 154. | 156. | 157. | 159. | 160. | 162. | 163. | 165. | 166. |

*Winning probability is = 0.500*

Place pool in tens of thousands

| $P_i/P$ | 1 | 2 | 3 | 4 | 5 | 6 | 7 | 8 | 9 | 10 | 11 | 12 | 13 | 14 | 15 |
|---|---|---|---|---|---|---|---|---|---|---|---|---|---|---|---|
| .025 | 312. | 316. | 321. | 325. | 330. | 334. | 339. | 343. | 347. | 352. | 356. | 361. | 365. | 370. | 374. |
| .050 | 304. | 308. | 313. | 317. | 321. | 325. | 330. | 334. | 338. | 342. | 347. | 351. | 355. | 359. | 364. |
| .075 | 296. | 300. | 304. | 308. | 312. | 316. | 320. | 324. | 328. | 332. | 336. | 340. | 344. | 348. | 352. |
| .100 | 287. | 291. | 295. | 299. | 302. | 306. | 310. | 314. | 318. | 321. | 325. | 329. | 333. | 337. | 340. |
| .125 | 278. | 281. | 285. | 288. | 292. | 295. | 299. | 303. | 306. | 310. | 313. | 317. | 320. | 324. | 327. |
| .150 | 267. | 271. | 274. | 277. | 281. | 284. | 287. | 290. | 294. | 297. | 300. | 304. | 307. | 310. | 314. |
| .175 | 256. | 259. | 262. | 265. | 268. | 271. | 274. | 277. | 280. | 283. | 287. | 290. | 293. | 296. | 299. |
| .200 | 243. | 246. | 249. | 252. | 255. | 257. | 260. | 263. | 266. | 269. | 271. | 274. | 2.77 | 280. | 283. |
| .225 | 230. | 232. | 235. | 237. | 240. | 242. | 245. | 248. | 250. | 253. | 255. | 258. | 260. | 263. | 265. |
| .250 | 215. | 217. | 219. | 221. | 224. | 226. | 228. | 230. | 233. | 235. | 237. | 240. | 242. | 244. | 246. |
| .275 | 198. | 200. | 202. | 204. | 206. | 208. | 210. | 212. | 214. | 216. | 218. | 220. | 222. | 224. | 226. |
| .300 | 179. | 180. | 182. | 184. | 186. | 187. | 189. | 191. | 193. | 194. | 196. | 198. | 200. | 202. | 203. |

**Table 6-19  Optimal Show Bets**

*Winning probability is = 0.050*

|  |  |  |  |  |  |  | Show pool in tens of thousands |  |  |  |  |  |  |  |  |
|---|---|---|---|---|---|---|---|---|---|---|---|---|---|---|---|
| $S_i/S$ | 1 | 2 | 3 | 4 | 5 | 6 | 7 | 8 | 9 | 10 | 11 | 12 | 13 | 14 | 15 |
| .025 | 11. | 12. | 13. | 14. | 15. | 17. | 18. | 19. | 20. | 21. | 22. | 23. | 24. | 25. | 26. |

*Winning probability is = 0.100*

|  |  |  |  |  |  |  | Show pool in tens of thousands |  |  |  |  |  |  |  |  |
|---|---|---|---|---|---|---|---|---|---|---|---|---|---|---|---|
| $S_i/S$ | 1 | 2 | 3 | 4 | 5 | 6 | 7 | 8 | 9 | 10 | 11 | 12 | 13 | 14 | 15 |
| .025 | 73. | 76. | 80. | 84. | 87. | 91. | 94. | 98. | 102. | 105. | 109. | 112. | 116. | 120. | 123. |
| .050 | 22. | 23. | 25. | 26. | 28. | 29. | 31. | 32. | 34. | 35. | 37. | 38. | 40. | 41. | 43. |

*Winning probability is = 0.150*

|  |  |  |  |  |  |  | Show pool in tens of thousands |  |  |  |  |  |  |  |  |
|---|---|---|---|---|---|---|---|---|---|---|---|---|---|---|---|
| $S_i/S$ | 1 | 2 | 3 | 4 | 5 | 6 | 7 | 8 | 9 | 10 | 11 | 12 | 13 | 14 | 15 |
| .025 | 101. | 106. | 111. | 116. | 121. | 126. | 130. | 135. | 140. | 145. | 150. | 155. | 160. | 165. | 169. |
| .050 | 76. | 80. | 83. | 87. | 90. | 94. | 97. | 101. | 105. | 108. | 112. | 115. | 119. | 122. | 126. |
| .075 | 39. | 41. | 43. | 45. | 47. | 49. | 52. | 54. | 56. | 58. | 60. | 62. | 64. | 67. | 69. |
| .100 |  |  |  |  |  |  |  |  |  |  |  |  |  |  |  |

*Winning probability is = 0.200*

Show pool in tens of thousands

| $S_i/S$ | 1 | 2 | 3 | 4 | 5 | 6 | 7 | 8 | 9 | 10 | 11 | 12 | 13 | 14 | 15 |
|---|---|---|---|---|---|---|---|---|---|---|---|---|---|---|---|
| .025 | 129. | 135. | 141. | 146. | 152. | 158. | 164. | 170. | 176. | 182. | 188. | 194. | 200. | 206. | 212. |
| .050 | 112. | 117. | 122. | 127. | 132. | 137. | 142. | 147. | 152. | 157. | 162. | 167. | 172. | 177. | 182. |
| .075 | 91. | 95. | 99. | 103. | 107. | 111. | 115. | 119. | 123. | 127. | 130. | 134. | 138. | 142. | 146. |
| .100 | 61. | 64. | 67. | 70. | 73. | 76. | 79. | 82. | 84. | 87. | 90. | 93. | 96. | 99. | 102. |
| .125 | 19. | 21. | 23. | 25. | 26. | 28. | 30. | 32. | 34. | 36. | 38. | 40. | 42. | 44. | 46. |

*Winning probability is = 0.250*

Show pool in tens of thousands

| $S_i/S$ | 1 | 2 | 3 | 4 | 5 | 6 | 7 | 8 | 9 | 10 | 11 | 12 | 13 | 14 | 15 |
|---|---|---|---|---|---|---|---|---|---|---|---|---|---|---|---|
| .025 | 159. | 166. | 173. | 179. | 186. | 193. | 200. | 207. | 214. | 221. | 228. | 235. | 242. | 249. | 256. |
| .050 | 146. | 153. | 159. | 165. | 171. | 178. | 184. | 190. | 196. | 203. | 209. | 215. | 222. | 228. | 234. |
| .075 | 131 | 137. | 142. | 148. | 153. | 159. | 164. | 170. | 175. | 181. | 186. | 192. | 197. | 203. | 208. |
| .100 | 113. | 117. | 122. | 126. | 131. | 136. | 140. | 145. | 150. | 154. | 159. | 164. | 168. | 173. | 177. |
| .125 | 88. | 92. | 96. | 100. | 103. | 107. | 111. | 115. | 118. | 122. | 126. | 130. | 134. | 137. | 141. |
| .150 | 56. | 59. | 62. | 65. | 68. | 71. | 74. | 76. | 79. | 82. | 85. | 88. | 91. | 94. | 97. |

*Winning probability is = 0.300*

Show pool in tens of thousands

| $S_i/S$ | 1 | 2 | 3 | 4 | 5 | 6 | 7 | 8 | 9 | 10 | 11 | 12 | 13 | 14 | 15 |
|---|---|---|---|---|---|---|---|---|---|---|---|---|---|---|---|
| .025 | 191. | 199. | 207. | 215. | 223. | 231. | 239. | 247. | 255. | 263. | 271. | 279. | 287. | 295. | 303. |
| .050 | 182. | 189. | 196. | 204. | 211. | 219. | 226. | 233. | 241. | 248. | 256. | 263. | 270. | 278. | 285. |
| .075 | 170. | 177. | 184. | 190. | 197. | 204. | 211. | 218. | 224. | 231. | 238. | 245. | 251. | 258. | 265. |
| .100 | 157. | 163. | 169. | 175. | 181. | 187. | 193. | 199. | 205. | 211. | 217. | 223. | 230. | 236. | 242. |
| .125 | 140. | 145. | 151. | 156. | 161. | 167. | 172. | 178. | 183. | 188. | 194. | 199. | 204. | 210. | 215. |
| .150 | 119. | 124. | 129. | 133. | 138. | 143. | 147. | 152. | 156. | 161. | 166. | 170. | 175. | 180. | 184. |
| .175 | 93. | 97. | 101. | 105. | 109. | 113. | 117. | 121. | 125. | 129. | 133. | 137. | 140. | 144. | 148. |

*Winning probability is = 0.350*

| | | | | | | | Place pool in tens of thousands | | | | | | | | |
|---|---|---|---|---|---|---|---|---|---|---|---|---|---|---|---|
| $S_i/S$ | 1 | 2 | 3 | 4 | 5 | 6 | 7 | 8 | 9 | 10 | 11 | 12 | 13 | 14 | 15 |
| .025 | 227. | 236. | 245. | 254. | 262. | 271. | 280. | 289. | 298. | 307. | 316. | 325. | 334. | 342. | 351. |
| .050 | 219. | 227. | 236. | 244. | 252. | 261. | 269. | 278. | 286. | 294. | 303. | 311. | 320. | 328. | 336. |
| .075 | 210. | 217. | 225. | 233. | 241. | 249. | 257. | 265. | 272. | 280. | 288. | 296. | 304. | 312. | 320. |
| .100 | 199. | 206. | 213. | 221. | 228. | 235. | 243. | 250. | 257. | 265. | 272. | 279. | 286. | 294. | 301. |
| .125 | 186. | 193. | 200. | 206. | 213. | 220. | 227. | 233. | 240. | 247. | 253. | 260. | 267. | 274. | 280. |
| .150 | 171. | 178. | 184. | 190. | 196. | 202. | 208. | 214. | 220. | 226. | 232. | 238. | 245. | 251. | 257. |
| .175 | 154. | 159. | 164. | 170. | 175. | 181. | 186. | 192. | 197. | 203. | 208. | 214. | 219. | 225. | 230. |
| .200 | 131. | 136. | 141. | 146. | 151. | 156. | 161. | 166. | 170. | 175. | 180. | 185. | 190. | 195. | 200. |

*Winning probability is = 0.400*

| | | | | | | | Place pool in tens of thousands | | | | | | | | |
|---|---|---|---|---|---|---|---|---|---|---|---|---|---|---|---|
| $S_i/S$ | 1 | 2 | 3 | 4 | 5 | 6 | 7 | 8 | 9 | 10 | 11 | 12 | 13 | 14 | 15 |
| .025 | 264. | 274. | 284. | 293. | 303. | 313. | 322. | 332. | 342. | 351. | 361. | 371. | 380. | 390. | 400. |
| .050 | 258. | 267. | 276. | 285. | 295. | 304. | 313. | 322. | 331. | 341. | 350. | 359. | 368. | 378. | 387. |
| .075 | 250. | 259. | 267. | 276. | 285. | 294. | 303. | 311. | 320. | 329. | 338. | 346. | 355. | 364. | 373. |
| .100 | 241. | 249. | 258. | 266. | 274. | 283. | 291. | 299. | 307. | 316. | 324. | 332. | 341. | 349. | 357. |
| .125 | 231. | 239. | 247. | 254. | 262. | 270. | 278. | 286. | 293. | 301. | 309. | 317. | 325. | 332. | 340. |
| .150 | 220. | 227. | 234. | 241. | 249. | 256. | 263. | 270. | 278. | 285. | 292. | 299. | 307. | 314. | 321. |
| .175 | 206. | 213. | 220. | 226. | 233. | 240. | 246. | 253. | 260. | 267. | 273. | 280. | 287. | 293. | 300. |
| .200 | 190. | 196. | 203. | 209. | 215. | 221. | 227. | 233. | 240. | 246. | 252. | 258. | 264. | 271. | 277. |
| .225 | 171. | 177. | 182. | 188. | 194. | 199. | 205. | 211. | 216. | 222. | 228. | 233. | 239. | 245. | 250. |
| .250 | 148. | 153. | 158. | 163. | 169. | 174. | 179. | 184. | 189. | 195. | 200. | 205. | 210. | 215. | 221. |

Winning probability is = 0.450

Place pool in tens of thousands

| $S_i/S$ | 1 | 2 | 3 | 4 | 5 | 6 | 7 | 8 | 9 | 10 | 11 | 12 | 13 | 14 | 15 |
|---|---|---|---|---|---|---|---|---|---|---|---|---|---|---|---|
| .025 | 304. | 314. | 324. | 334. | 345. | 355. | 365. | 375. | 385. | 396. | 406. | 416. | 426. | 437. | 447. |
| .050 | 298. | 307. | 317. | 327. | 337. | 347. | 357. | 367. | 376. | 386. | 396. | 406. | 416. | 426. | 436. |
| .075 | 291. | 300. | 310. | 319. | 329. | 338. | 348. | 357. | 367. | 376. | 386. | 395. | 404. | 414. | 423. |
| .100 | 284. | 293. | 302. | 311. | 320. | 329. | 338. | 347. | 356. | 365. | 374. | 383. | 392. | 401. | 410. |
| .125 | 275. | 284. | 292. | 301. | 310. | 318. | 327. | 335. | 344. | 353. | 361. | 370. | 378. | 387. | 396. |
| .150 | 266. | 274. | 282. | 290. | 298. | 307. | 315. | 323. | 331. | 339. | 347. | 355. | 364. | 372. | 380. |
| .175 | 255. | 263. | 271. | 278. | 286. | 294. | 301. | 309. | 317. | 324. | 332. | 340. | 347. | 355. | 363. |
| .200 | 243. | 250. | 257. | 264. | 272. | 279. | 286. | 293. | 300. | 308. | 315. | 322. | 329. | 336. | 344. |
| .225 | 229. | 235. | 242. | 249. | 255. | 262. | 269. | 276. | 282. | 289. | 296. | 302. | 309. | 316. | 323. |
| .250 | 212. | 218. | 224. | 231. | 237. | 243. | 249. | 256. | 262. | 268. | 274. | 280. | 287. | 293. | 299. |
| .275 | 192. | 198. | 203. | 209. | 215. | 221. | 227. | 233. | 238. | 244. | 250. | 256. | 262. | 267. | 273. |

Winning probability is = 0.500

Place pool in tens of thousands

| $S_i/S$ | 1 | 2 | 3 | 4 | 5 | 6 | 7 | 8 | 9 | 10 | 11 | 12 | 13 | 14 | 15 |
|---|---|---|---|---|---|---|---|---|---|---|---|---|---|---|---|
| .025 | 343. | 354. | 365. | 375. | 386. | 396. | 407. | 417. | 428. | 438. | 449. | 460. | 470. | 481. | 491. |
| .050 | 338. | 348. | 359. | 369. | 379. | 389. | 399. | 410. | 420. | 430. | 440. | 451. | 461. | 471. | 481. |
| .075 | 332. | 342. | 352. | 362. | 372. | 382. | 392. | 401. | 411. | 421. | 431. | 441. | 451. | 461. | 470. |
| .100 | 326. | 335. | 345. | 354. | 364. | 373. | 383. | 392. | 402. | 411. | 421. | 430. | 440. | 449. | 459. |
| .125 | 319. | 328. | 337. | 346. | 355. | 364. | 373. | 383. | 392. | 401. | 410. | 419. | 428. | 437. | 446. |
| .150 | 311. | 320. | 328. | 337. | 346. | 354. | 363. | 372. | 381. | 389. | 398. | 407. | 415. | 424. | 433. |
| .175 | 302. | 310. | 319. | 327. | 335. | 344. | 352. | 360. | 368. | 377. | 385. | 393. | 402. | 410. | 418. |
| .200 | 292. | 300. | 308. | 316. | 324. | 331. | 339. | 347. | 355. | 363. | 371. | 379. | 386. | 394. | 402. |
| .225 | 281. | 288. | 296. | 303. | 311. | 318. | 325. | 333. | 340. | 348. | 355. | 363. | 370. | 377. | 385. |
| .250 | 268. | 275. | 282. | 289. | 296. | 303. | 310. | 317. | 324. | 331. | 338. | 345. | 352. | 359. | 366. |
| .275 | 253. | 260. | 266. | 273. | 279. | 286. | 292. | 299. | 306. | 312. | 319. | 325. | 332. | 338. | 345. |
| .300 | 235. | 242. | 248. | 254. | 260. | 266. | 273. | 279. | 285. | 291. | 297. | 303. | 310. | 316. | 322. |

stake on a single race! This feature is a consequence of the Kelly system, which, in effect, says "strike while the iron is hot."

## Statistical Results and Cautionary Remarks

The Ziemba and Hausch system was tested by its inventors at a number of racetracks such as Aqueduct, Santa Anita, Exhibition Park, and so on. The results look quite good. Depending on the track, the percentage of bets won ranged from 55 to 89, with an average of 59, and the rate of return on bets made ranged from 5.5 percent to 42.8 percent, for an average of 11.4 percent. These figures are even better than what we found in our simulations based on the logit predictions. They confirm that inefficiency exists and that some money can be made.

Ziemba and Hausch warn that their system should not be applied unthinkingly. They suggest, for example, that no bets should be made at all when the track is not fast, when some horses are bet so heavily that the payoff to a $2 bet will be $2.10, when the horse is of the Silky Sullivan type, and when the expected return is too low (e.g., less than 1.20). Care is also recommended in betting on horses after long layoffs or on first-time starters. There is also a delicate question of the timing of the bet. Obviously, one should bet as late in the betting period as possible. But this may still mean betting on outdated information. At Monmouth Park, for example, the betting pools are visible from the grandstand but not from the betting windows. It may take two to three minutes from the time you have left the spot where the pool figures are visible to the time that you have actually made a bet. This is quite enough time for the proportions of the place pool on the various horses to change drastically! Thus, you could well be betting on a horse on the basis of information that is no longer true by the time you get to the betting window. Most importantly, one must recognize what we have been saying over and over again: If enough people try to take advantage of any system, the inefficiency will "cure itself," and the differential advantage will disappear.

## A Summing Up

This review of the academic evidence on win, place, and show betting largely bears out what we have been telling you: Horse race betting is a tough game to beat.

The two approaches that seem to offer some hope are the one based on some of our research (Asch-Malkiel-Quandt) and the "Dr. Z" system by Ziemba-Hausch. Although these "systems" are very different, they share one interesting characteristic: Both focus exclusively on place and show betting. This is precisely contrary to most popular advice, which typically says "bet only to win." But one of the points on which academic investigators are clearly agreed is that systems of win betting are sure losers unless you confine yourself to very short favorites (odds of 2 to 5 or less).

We must, however, reiterate our last caution yet again. No system of racetrack betting, no matter how good it is intrinsically—and this includes our own—will work if many people use it.

## Endnotes

1. Combining Formulas 6-1 and 6-3 gives $M_i = (1 - t)/s_i$. Combining this with Formula 6-2 gives $D_i + 1 = (1 - t)/s_i$. Formula 6-6 follows immediately from this.
2. Asch, Malkiel, and Quandt show that the discrepancies between objective and subjective probabilities are large enough for the 1st, 3rd and 9th lowest odds so that these differences are statistically significant—that is to say, if in reality these probabilities were pairwise the same, discrepancies as large as those observed are extremely unlikely to occur.
3. How do we know that this is true? If $B_1$ is bet on horse 1 and a fixed amount $A$ is bet on all other horses, the subjective probability for horse 1, given our earlier definitions, is $B_1/(A + B_1)$. If an extra 2 dollars is bet on horse 1, the (new) subjective probability is $(B_1 + 2)/(A + B_1 + 2)$. Is this always greater than before, no matter what $B_1$ and $A$ were? The answer is yes.
4. In Asch, Malkiel, and Quandt (1984) we also used, as an alternative, the morning line odds and the marginal odds as independent variables. Since the use of this latter set leads to very similar results, we shall concentrate on only one set of independent variables.

# Chapter 7

# The Evidence from "Exotic" Bets

## Preamble

"Exotic" bets are those in which you must pick more than one horse correctly in order to win. In exactas, you pick the winner and the runner-up in a race; in the daily double, it's the winners of two consecutive races. Needless to say, the probabilities of winning exotic bets are very low, even if the individual horses have low odds.

The first step in our examination of whether there is money to be made in exotic betting is to compare the objective and subjective probabilities for each of these bets. If the public's assessment of winning (subjective probabilities) is sufficiently different from what actually happens (objective probabilities), there is a possibility that money can be made. When we compare the two sets of probabilities, we find that there are significant discrepancies. The exacta and daily double betting markets appear not to be efficient. Yet, various strategies that we have tried to exploit this inefficiency do not yield positive profits. We tried to predict winners and runners-up by using our statistical model of Chapter 6, but we come up empty-handed.

The principal reason seems to be the intrinsically low winning probabilities associated with bets of this type. People may have real difficulties in properly assessing what a winning probability of 0.001 or 0.002 means, and the rates of return realized from betting exactas on horses in various odds-classes seem to be very erratic. However, there are two findings that are interesting. The first is that there is (again!) some evidence of the existence of "smart money" (in exacta betting, though not in daily double betting). People who have inside information might like to disguise what they are doing by betting on the exacta (where the betting pools are not displayed at the track) rather than making straight win bets. This will tend to depress exacta payoffs in a particular way, and this is precisely what we observe. Second, daily double betting seems more profitable than betting on the equivalent parlay—that is, betting on a horse in race one and if our choice wins, betting the entire proceeds of the first bet on another horse in race two. So, if you like the fast lane, the daily double may just be your thing. However, in general, if you want to win money or at least break even, we recommend the more conservative strategies for place and show bets as outlined in Chapter 6.


## Introduction

Recall from Chapter 1 the more exotic forms of betting that go under the names of exacta, trifecta, quinella, daily double, and so forth. We now take a more detailed look at the empirical evidence concerning two of these: the exacta and the daily double. Empirical evidence about how exacta and daily double bets fare is not exactly plentiful. Fortunately, our sample of 705 races at the Meadowlands includes 510 races in which exacta betting was permitted and 122 pairs of races in which daily double betting could take place. We will examine the data to attempt to answer our usual questions: (1) is the "market" efficient— that is, does it value alternative investment opportunities so that no above-average profits can be made? (2) Are any existing inefficiencies sufficiently large so that one can actually think of earning a *positive* profit?

These are particularly interesting types of bets to look at because it seems to be pretty hard to win at them. Since exactas and daily doubles require us to pick two, not one, well-performing horses, the probability of winning must be low. Earlier we had suggested that the "overbetting" of longshots may be caused by a special "yen" or "taste" that Peter and others have for betting on low-probability events. If this is true, we would expect most of the exacta and daily double combinations to be "overbet" at least in the sense that it is hard to earn positive profits from them (but even among the exactas and daily doubles there may be some relatively high-probability bets, and these would then tend to be "underbet").

Before we begin, we want to remind you what these two types of bets are. In an exacta bet, you pick the winner and the runner-up; if both your picks are correct, you have won; otherwise you have lost. In a daily double you have to pick the winners in two consecutive races (before the first race begins); if both your picks are correct, you win; otherwise you lose. As we said before, it stands to reason that it is a lot harder to have a winner in exacta or daily double bets than in ordinary bets, since in these exotic bets the outcome depends on the performance of two horses.

## Exacta Betting

When Peter walks up to the betting window to bet on an exacta, he experiences a delicious thrill of anticipation: Payoffs of 50 to 1 dance before his eyes, and being a big spender, he is prepared to wager a full $2. But how is he going to make out in the long run? Is he going to be able to make a positive profit? That is perhaps the most basic question, and we shall postpone our answer. Before we deal with this important question, we will examine the extent to which betting on exactas is efficient—in other words, the extent to which the betting public processes the information available at the track so that, after adjustment for risk, all betting opportunities yield comparable returns.

There are at least two possible ways to proceed. First, we have found before that if people care predominantly about the average return and the variance of the return (the measure that shows how widely individual outcomes are spread out around the average), and if bettors are risk lovers, then the higher the possible average return on a bet, the lower the variance will be. If this is not the case, either bettors are not risk lovers in the aggregate (unlikely, on the whole) or they are not processing information efficiently. We can thus investigate this question by calculating the mean returns and variances for exacta bets.

Second, we can ask the following question. Suppose we told Peter that it is possible to make a particular exacta bet that has a payoff of 50 to 1 and an objective probability of winning of 0.021 (and therefore promises a 5 percent rate of return on the average: expected return = $50 \times 0.021 - 1$). At the same time, there is another horse in the race that by itself has a 0.021 probability of winning and will also pay off 50 to 1. Should Peter care about which of these two opportunities he bets on? We think not—if he is reasonable, he should care only about the array of returns and probabilities. That means that if we can find single-horse bets that are in some genuine sense equivalent to exacta bets, the structure of payoffs on the two types of bets should be very similar, since bettors should evaluate them in the same way. We begin our examination of these issues in reverse order.

## Is There a Single-Bet Equivalent to an Exacta?

We start out by reminding you what our sample of data is: We have complete computer records on 705 races between May 26 and August 11, 1984, at the Meadowlands; 510 of these races were exacta races (and 122 pairs of races were daily double races). Since we know the amounts bet (singly) on each horse in each race, we can compute the subjective probability estimate of each horse's winning chances from Formula (6–3) in Chapter 6. We have computed these subjective probabilities (in 705 races there are a total of 6,729 of them) and arranged them into 20 roughly equal sized groups: Group 1 will contain the 337 horses with the lowest subjective probabilities, group 2 the second lowest 337, and so on (some groups have only 336 horses in them). Then by simply counting up what percentage of horses in the lowest, second lowest, . . . groups actually won, we can obtain an *estimate* of the *objective winning probability* of the horses in that group. At the same time, we can also obtain an estimate of the average *subjective probability of winning* in each group. You will remember that the subjective probability for a given horse, say horse $i$, is just the amount bet on the horse divided by the total win pool. We have these figures for each horse, and by averaging them together within a group, we can obtain a point estimate for the average subjective winning probability in that group.

These objective and subjective probability estimates are displayed in Table 7–1. Notice that even here the usual phenomenon exists: For the low-probability horses, the objective probability is *lower* than the corresponding subjective probability, whereas the reverse is true for the high-probability horses.

We can now use regression analysis to find the "best-fitting" straight line that describes these data; in other words, we are seeking a formula $p_i = a + bs_i$ from which we can "predict" the objective probability once we know the subjective probability. The best-fitting line turns out to be $p_i = -0.0100 + 1.0959s_i$. This is reasonably similar to the corresponding equation we estimated in Chapter 6 on the basis of the Fabricand data. We are not certain, however, that this relation is totally immutable, and thus we are not surprised that the equations for the Fabricand data and the Meadowlands data are not identical. The results are close enough to support the contention that the equations basically express a similar phenomenon. Since we shall analyze Meadowlands data here, we will use the equation derived from these data.

We now construct an artificial single-bet analogue to an exacta.

Table 7-1  Objective ($p_i$) and Subjective ($s_i$) Winning Probability Estimates for
Meadowlands Data

| $p_i$ | $s_i$ |
|-------|-------|
| 0.0030 | 0.0068 |
| 0.0030 | 0.0110 |
| 0.0059 | 0.0151 |
| 0.0119 | 0.0201 |
| 0.0178 | 0.0258 |
| 0.0445 | 0.0323 |
| 0.0297 | 0.0398 |
| 0.0386 | 0.0489 |
| 0.0415 | 0.0581 |
| 0.0804 | 0.0683 |
| 0.0804 | 0.0787 |
| 0.0923 | 0.0908 |
| 0.1310 | 0.1036 |
| 0.1161 | 0.1185 |
| 0.1250 | 0.1368 |
| 0.1637 | 0.1587 |
| 0.1548 | 0.1841 |
| 0.2024 | 0.2220 |
| 0.3006 | 0.2747 |
| 0.4554 | 0.4031 |

Consider a particular exacta race. Assume that this race has eight horses in it; their subjective probabilities are measured by Formula (6-3) in Chapter 6 and we denote these by $s_1$ ($=B_1/B$), $s_2$ ($=B_2/B$), ..., $s_8$ ($=B_8/B$). We can then use our estimated regression equation, which converts subjective to objective probabilities in general, to actually estimate the objective winning probabilities of the eight individual horses. For example, if horse 3 has a subjective probability $s_3 = 0.216$, the corresponding objective probability is $p_3 = -0.0100 + 1.0959 \times 0.216 = 0.227$. But once we have estimates for the objective probabilities for the individual horses, we can use Formulas (6-8) and (6-9) in Chapter 6, the so-called Harville approximations, to estimate the probability *that horse* i *comes in first and horse* j *comes in second—that is, the probability that a particular pair will win the exacta!* We call these estimates $h_{ij}$, that is,

$$h_{ij} = \frac{p_i p_j}{1 - p_i}$$

is the probability that horse $i$ is first *and* horse $j$ is second. In this fashion we can compute the estimate of the winning probability for every possible exacta pair (in every exacta race).

Now comes the key step. In a race with eight horses, there are 56 possible winning exacta combinations (1 and 2, and 1 and 3, . . ., 1 and 8; 2 and 1, 2 and 3, . . ., etc.). If we were simply presented with 56 objective probability estimates and did not know that these represented the winning chances of exacta combinations, we could imagine that we are dealing with a straight-bet race in which 56 horses were running. But this means that we can use exactly the same regression relationship we determined between objective and subjective probabilities to convert back to an estimate of the subjective probability of winning for an exacta combination! An example will make this clearer.

Let us suppose that we are dealing with an exacta bet on horse 3 to win and horse 5 to come in second, with subjective probabilities (given by the ratio of win bets on these horses to the total win pool) of 0.216 and 0.084, respectively. Using our regression equation, the estimates of the objective winning probabilities are

$$p_3 = -0.0100 + 1.0959 \times 0.216 = 0.227$$
$$p_5 = -0.0100 + 1.0959 \times 0.084 = 0.082$$

Using the Harville approximation, the objective winning probability for the *pair* is:

$$h_{35} = \frac{0.227 \times 0.082}{1.0 - 0.227} = 0.024$$

To get the *implied* subjective probability, we write

$$0.024 = -0.0100 + 1.0959s^*$$

where $s^*$ is our notation for the implied or inferred subjective probability. Solving this equation gives

$$s^* = 0.031$$

We can do this exercise for every pair of horses in every exacta race, and in our sample there are 41,246 such pairs altogether. But what good does it do us to compute these numbers?

The answer is that there is an obvious *second* way of calculating the subjective winning probability of every exacta pair: These subjective probabilities are given by the ratio of the amounts bet on each exacta combination to the total amount of the exacta pool—that is, the amount bet on all possible combinations. Just as in the straight win betting case (where the ratio bet on horse $i$ to the total win pool is an estimate of the subjective probability that $i$ wins), the ratio of the amount bet on pair $i$-$j$ to the total amount bet on all pairs is an estimate of the corresponding subjective probability for the $i$-$j$ exacta. We will call the subjective probability computed in this fashion simply $s$. The key observation is this: We have two estimates $s^*$ and $s$ for subjective probabilities that are obtained in different ways and are generally somewhat different numbers; yet *they measure exactly the same thing if the market is efficient. That is to say, if the market evaluates the winning and runner-up chances of individual horses and evaluates the "exacta-winning" chances of pairs of horses in a mathematically consistent fashion, these two sets of estimates of the subjective probabilities must be the same pairwise on the average.*

We say that they must be the same pairwise *on the average* because it would be too much to expect the two sets of numbers to be identical (pairwise) to 15 decimal places. To test the hypothesis that they are the same pairwise on the average, we first compute all the $s$-figures and all the $s^*$-figures for the 41,246 possible exacta pairs. If we plotted all the $s$ numbers on the horizontal axis in a diagram and the $s^*$ numbers along the vertical axis, and *if our hypothesis were correct*, all the dots in the scatter diagram would be very closely bunched along a 45 degree line through the origin (for then the $s^*$ value corresponding to an $s$ of, say, .15 would be approximately .15, the $s^*$ value corresponding to an $s$ of .3 would be about .3, etc.). (See Figure 7–1.)

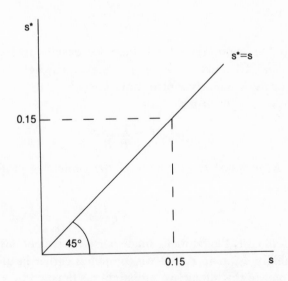

Figure 7-1   Subjective Probability Estimates of
Exacta Combinations.

Another way of saying this is that if we calculate the regression equation

$$s^* = a + bs$$

we should find that $a$ is about 0 and $b$ is about 1.0. The actual regression equation based on the 41,246 exacta pairs has $a = 0.00683$ and $b = 1.10267$. Superficially, $a$ appears quite close to zero and $b$ close to 1. Recall (from Chapter 5), however, the notion of statistical significance. The pertinent question is this: Is the value of $a$ *statistically significantly different* from 0 and that of $b$ from 1? The answer is, it may not surprise you, an emphatic yes. If the "true" $b$ were 1.00000000 and you had a sample of 41,246 dots in your scatter diagram, the probability of obtaining a value of $b$ by regression calculations as high as we did (1.10267) is less than one in a billion. We must therefore *reject* the hypothesis of efficient, mathematically correct processing of the data by the people betting on exactas.

A second comparison of exacta betting with a fictitious single-bet equivalent can also be made by considering the actual payoffs of the exactas with the fictitious payoffs that would be paid in the equivalent race in which each exacta pair is considered to be a single horse. The actual exacta payoffs are easy to obtain: If $B_{ij}$ is the amount bet on the exacta that $i$ wins and $j$ is second, and if $B$ is the sum of all these $B_{ij}$'s in the race, the actual payoff, denoted by $A_{ij}$, is

$$A_{ij} = \frac{(1-t)B}{B_{ij}}$$

where $t$ is the appropriate track take for exactas (0.1918 at the Meadowlands). Of course, in a regular single-horse bet, the payoff is given by exactly the same type of formula (see Formula (6–1) in Chapter 6). We can write this for horse $i$ as

$$\text{payoff} = \frac{1-t}{B_i/B}$$

and since $B_i/B$ is just the estimate of the subjective probability of winning, $s_i$,

$$\text{payoff} = \frac{1-t}{s_i}$$

In the present case, the fictitious single-horse equivalent has a subjective probability estimate $s^*$ that we computed earlier in this section. For horse pair $i$-$j$ this subjective probability is denoted by $s_{ij}$, and the resulting *implied* payoff for pair *i-j*, denoted $P_{ij}$, is

$$P_{ij} = \frac{1 - t}{s_i^o}$$

Having calculated the $A_{ij}$'s and $P_{ij}$'s for all 41,246 possible exacta pairs, we can now ask some questions about them.

First, we would again ask too much if we expected the $A_{ij}$'s and corresponding $P_{ij}$'s to be exactly the same. But what about the *pairwise differences*, $P_{ij} - A_{ij}$? We would certainly expect *randomness* in these differences, that is, no systematic factors, at least when it comes to those pairs that actually won versus those that lost. To view it in a somewhat different way: After we have computed the 41,246 *differences* $P_{ij} - A_{ij}$, we arrange them in two piles. In pile 1 are all those differences that pertain to horse pairs that actually won their exactas; pile 2 will contain those that lost. Of course, pile 1 will be *much* smaller than pile 2: Since (generally) only one pair wins an exacta, pile 1 will contain exactly 510 numbers, whereas pile 2 will contain the rest, 40,736. This allows us to investigate the following "smart-money" hypothesis.

Imagine that some people occasionally have "inside information" about which horses are likely to win. If they simply bet on those horses to win, their bet immediately shows up on the toteboard. The bet, as we have seen, will in itself lower the odds, but perhaps more importantly, their bet will *signal* something to others and may induce others to bet on the horse, thus depressing odds and payoffs even further. Under these circumstances someone with good information might prefer to bet an exacta. (If you "knew" the winner but not the runner-up, you could "wheel"—that is, bet all the exactas involving the predicted winner and the field.) This seems safer from the signaling point of view because exacta pools are *not* generally displayed in readily usable fashion at the track. Such bets, however, would depress actual exacta payoffs *relative* to the payoffs on fictitious single-horse bets for winning combinations. In other words, we would expect that the average value of $P_{ij} - A_{ij}$ would tend to be larger for horses in the

Table 7-2  Means and Variances of $P_{ij} - A_{ij}$ for Winning and Losing Pairs

|  | Winning | Losing |
|---|---|---|
| Number of pairs | -510 | 40736 |
| Mean $P_{ij} - A_{ij}$ | - 33.18 | -261.69 |
| Variance of $P_{ij} - A_{ij}$ | 103.84 | 458.85 |

winning pile 1 than in the nonwinning pile 2. Our actual results are displayed in Table 7–2. The difference between the means is highly significant statistically and goes in the direction predicted by the "smart-money" hypothesis! Although this certainly does not prove that there is such a thing as "smart money," the result is compatible with it. However, if the result had gone the other way — that is, if the mean for the winning group had been substantially lower than for the losers — the hypothesis would have been convincingly rejected. This also illustrates a consequence of the statistical way of thinking: We can resoundingly reject theories, but we can never resoundingly prove them right!

## Mean Returns and the Variance of Returns

We have noted that efficiency can be interpreted to mean that no unusual returns can be made from specific investment opportunities once the differential risks of these opportunities are accounted for. If bettors are risk lovers, as we believe is true on the average, this must mean that a horse pair that has a higher expected return (a desirable feature) must also have a lower variance (an undesirable feature); for if this were not so, the particular combination would *dominate* all other combinations — that is, be preferable to the others *on all counts*. Were that so, nobody would bet on the others. But this latter phenomenon is contradicted by the observation that all exacta combinations typically have some amount bet on them.

The computation of the expected return and variance of return for horse pair $i$-$j$ is easy. The expected return is

$$E_{ij} = (A_{ij})(h_{ij}) - 1$$

where, as before, $A_{ij}$ is the actual payoff if $i$-$j$ wins and $h_{ij}$ is the (Harville approximation to the) probability that $i$-$j$ will actually win the exacta. The variance is

$$v_{ij} = (A_{ij} - 1)^2 h_{ij} + (1 - h_{ij}) - E_{ij}^2$$

We have calculated these expected values and variances for every combination of horses in every exacta race. In not a single race do we find efficiency in the sense that higher $E_{ij}$'s are always accompanied by lower $v_{ij}$'s. It would have been fairly surprising if we had found strong support for efficiency here, given that, as we define the term, we did not even find it in win betting. In win betting, however, there was at least a broadly reasonable pattern: On the whole it was true (if not for every single horse) that horses with high returns *tended* to have low variances. In exacta betting even this broad pattern seems to be missing. The reason seems obvious: Since exacta bettors' actions are not readily observable by other bettors, it is difficult for "market forces" to correct erroneous estimates made by bettors. Moreover, all the exacta bets are low-probability bets, and Peter may really be a little confused when it comes to calculating and assessing the significance of very low probabilities. Finally, since in the variance formula the payoffs are (in effect) squared, even a small error in the estimated winning probabilities or in the intrinsic goodness of the Harville approximation is likely to have a big effect on the variance. Thus, again, we find the result suggestive but not entirely conclusive.

## Are There Winning Exacta Strategies?

Just how well can one do if one bets on exactas? The first thing we do is to compute the average rate of return we might obtain by betting on every exacta combination in some particular "payoff class." In Chapter 6 we examined rates of return for straight win bets, and we categorized them by the "odds class" that the particular horse fell into. Here we characterize combinations of horses by payoff class—that is, by the payoff that they would pay if those combinations actually won.

Tables 7-3 and 7-4 present the results of these tabulations. The difference between the two is that the ranges of payoffs that define a "class" are defined differently. In Table 7-3, the upper boundary of each range is double the upper boundary of the previous one, and so we get 0-4, 4-8, 8-16, 16-32, and so on as the ranges. In Table 7-4, each range has exactly the same "width." For each table we counted how many of the combinations of horses had payoffs that classified

Table 7-3   Rates of Return on Exacta Bets: Proportional Class Intervals

| Payoff Range | Number of Pairs in Sample | Number of Winners in Category | Rate of Return |
|---|---|---|---|
| 0. to 4.00 | 25 | 9 | 0.25 |
| 4.01 to 8.00 | 326 | 45 | −0.08 |
| 8.01 to 16.00 | 1545 | 108 | −0.12 |
| 16.01 to 32.00 | 3653 | 110 | −0.30 |
| 32.01 to 64.00 | 5815 | 106 | −0.19 |
| 64.01 to 128.00 | 7409 | 80 | −0.07 |
| 128.01 to 256.00 | 7874 | 34 | −0.21 |
| 256.01 to infinity | 14599 | 18 | −0.56 |

Table 7-4   Rates of Return on Exacta Bets: Constant Class Intervals

| Payoff Range | Number of Pairs in Sample | Number of Winners in Category | Rate of Return |
|---|---|---|---|
| 0. to 16.00 | 1896 | 162 | −0.11 |
| 16.01 to 32.00 | 3653 | 110 | −0.30 |
| 32.01 to 48.00 | 3139 | 68 | −0.13 |
| 48.01 to 64.00 | 2676 | 38 | −0.26 |
| 64.01 to 80.00 | 2317 | 34 | 0.05 |
| 80.01 to 96.00 | 1866 | 18 | −0.13 |
| 96.01 to 112.00 | 1757 | 17 | −0.04 |
| 112.01 to 128.00 | 1469 | 11 | −0.24 |
| 128.01 to 144.00 | 1347 | 5 | −0.54 |
| 144.01 to 160.00 | 1188 | 8 | 0.10 |
| 160.01 to infinity | 19938 | 39 | −0.46 |

them into one or another of the intervals; we then counted up how many of these were winners and, finally, how much money we would win per dollar bet if we bet on all the exacta combinations in the first range, . . ., etc. The results are quite interesting, if only because they are so erratic and inconclusive. Looking at Table 7-3 we would conclude that low-payoff combinations are profitable (a 25 percent return if we bet on combinations with a payoff of less than 4), but this finding rests on very few cases: Among all 41,246 possible combinations only 25 had potential payoffs less than 4! As the payoff level rises, the return deteriorates but for a while is still better than the 19 percent take. Finally, for a payoff range of 16 to 32, the rate of return is −0.30. But then, somewhat inexplicably, things get quite a bit better, and for a payoff range of 64 to 128 the rate of return is only minus 7 percent! Finally, for very high potential payoffs, the rate of return is terrible. Table 7-4 tells a story that is, if anything, even more erratic, with positive returns in the 64 to 80 range and 144 to 160 range (though the latter is based on only eight winners in the group). In general, it seems doubtful that money can be made consistently by betting on low-payoff or extremely high-payoff combinations. But it seems possible that one can do better than the track take by betting on combinations that have low to medium potential payoffs. In all this it remains unfortunately the case that the figures are erratic and do not provide clear signposts for the eager bettor.

Next we can examine whether a simple adaptation of the strategies used in Chapter 6 can be used to devise consistently winning strategies for exactas. Our logit model predicts the winning probability of every horse in every race. In each exacta race, then, we determine the horses that our logit model predicts have the highest and second highest winning probabilities and pick these two horses as the predicted winners of the exacta. We bet $2 on our pick; debit our wealth with $2 in every event and credit it with whatever payoff we receive if our pick wins. Does this strategy earn us a positive return? Alas, no. If we use our best logit model for picking, we achieve an average rate of return of −0.232; somewhat worse than what can be attributed to the track's take. This result seems quite in line with our earlier result that suggests that winners of exactas have unusually depressed payoffs: Being able to predict winners with a slight edge just isn't good enough if the payoffs take a big beating!

We also have tried more complicated betting strategies. For example, we used our best logit model to predict the likely winner and then wheeled it—that is, bet every possible exacta combination with our selected horse picked first. That yields a disappointing rate of return of −0.228. If we further complicate the strategy by not only betting the above exactas but also all possible exactas in which the most-likely-to-win-horse is picked to come in second—that is, wheel it both ways—the average rate of return declines to −0.314!

Why is it so hard to win at exactas, and why in particular does it not seem to be a smart thing to do to bet on horses that have a relatively high probability of winning? After all, in Chapter 6 we argued strongly that favorites are relatively good bets; why, then, is it not more profitable to bet on relative favorites here? The reason seems to be that favorites are *not* underbet in exactas relative to the very small probability of winning an exacta at all! (If you look at the top few categories in Tables 7–3 and 7–4, you will note that negative returns are achieved consistently with a single exception that is based on so few observations that we do not wholly trust the calculated rate of return figure.) Using the Harville approximation, it is easy to calculate that if you bet an exacta on two horses with odds of 2 to 1 and 3 to 1, respectively, the probability of their winning the exacta is only about 0.074 (provided we assume that their subjective probabilities of winning are approximately the same as their objective probabilities). For two horses with odds of 3 to 1 and 4 to 1, respective!·, this probability drops to 0.042!

We conjecture that when Peter bets on exactas, he (erroneously) reasons thusly: "I want to win big, so I shall bet an exacta. But I don't have a ghost of a chance of winning if I bet on longshots, so I shall show them! I shall bet on (relative) favorites." The trouble is that although either of these two horses might be quite likely to come in first or second, it is extremely unlikely that both will come in, and in a specified order.

This seems to suggest that one might make out better (even earn positive profits on the average) by betting on relative longshots in exactas. But there are two difficulties with that strategy. First, Tables 7-3 and 7-4 show that extreme longshot combinations are not profitable. Second, even though it is possible that, relative to the winning probability, the payoffs to some longshot combinations are very high, the winning probabilities are so low that you will almost never win! Of course, if you win (or should we say, *when* you win), you will win big and it may yield positive average profits in the long run. Alas, the long run can be very long. If you bet on a pair of horses with odds of 10 to 1 and 12 to 1, respectively, the exacta winning probability is 0.005, which means you will have to wager 200 times on the average to achieve a single win. If you bet on two horses with odds of 20 to 1, your winning probability is 0.0016 — that is, you will have to bet an average of 666 times to win once! Since the "average result" tends not to occur *regularly*, you might perfectly well find that you have not won a single bet after a 1,000 wagers.

Rita, ever ready to wield the rolling pin on Peter's back when he comes home a loser, is not likely to be impressed by a learned discourse about how everything will be mathematically all right if she is just willing to wait a few more years! Finally, even to judge the statistical reliability of such a strategy is hard, and we would need data series much, much longer than we actually have since successful outcomes can be observed only very infrequently. The upshot of all this is that exacta wagering is a most uncertain enterprise. Betting on strongly favored combinations seems not to work. Betting on relative longshots may work, but you'll have to be patient (and Peter, in particular, must overcome his fear of Rita's rolling pin, since most of the time he will come home empty-handed). Nevertheless, our conjecture is that relative longshots — for example, an exacta combination that pairs a short-odds horse with a long-odds horse — might be an interesting strategy, particularly if you have a big bankroll and like to brag. If you get high utility from telling your friends about spectacular wins, this could be the thing to do: How else can you tell your friends that you won $500 on a $2 bet? (And you don't have to tell them that you waited 10 years for it to happen.)

Ziemba and Hausch have recently (in *Betting at the Racetrack* [1986]) extended the "Dr. Z" system (described in Chapter 6) to exotic bets. In the case of exactas, their procedure is: First get a reasonably efficient estimate of the winning probabilities of the exacta combinations by referring to the win odds on the individual horses in each pair; then look for combinations that are substantially underbet in the exacta pool. Such combinations offer prospective payoffs higher than what appears to be justified by their winning chances. Ziemba and Hausch report that a good exacta bet often involved a strong favorite in the *second* position (i.e., bet to come in number 2), paired with various horses at various odds in the first position. As before, we suspect that the Dr. Z system makes good sense—provided, of course, that not too many people follow it! And we are reasonably confident of one thing: The exacta is sufficiently difficult to beat that some sort of selective approach, under which you make only occasional bets, probably offers the best hope.

## Daily Double Betting

Unlike the case of exactas where we had to find an indirect way of constructing a hypothetical single-horse bet equivalent, the analogous bet to a daily double is fairly straightforward. Imagine the following strategy. You decide which horse will win race 1 and bet $2 on it. If the horse loses, you are done (and for record keeping purposes you debit your account with $2). If you win, you receive a payoff of $P_1$ dollars. You now choose the probable winner in race 2 and bet the entire $P_1$ payoff on your predicted winner. If this second pick loses, you are still out your original investment of $2, and you debit your account accordingly. However, if your second pick also wins, with a payoff of $P_2$ dollars for a $2 ticket, your total return is $P_1P_2/2$ dollars and your net return is $P_1P_2/2 - 2$ dollars, with which you now credit yourself.[1]

This strategy, as you know, is called a parlay. If the market is efficient, it should make no difference to bettors whether they bet their favorite combination as a daily double or as a parlay. If either horse loses, you have lost your stake whichever route you choose; if both win, both types of bets win. Under these circumstances it would make no sense for one of the two types, say for the daily double, consistently to pay more. For if it did, people would notice it sooner or later and would increase the amount of money bet on the daily double. That would lower the daily double payoff (and to the extent that some wagers are *diverted* from the parlay to the daily double, it would raise the payoffs to the former). A persistent difference in either direction therefore is not sustainable if racetrack participants are reasonably observant.

One of the most interesting comparisons is that between two sets of figures for winning combinations. In each daily double pair, we denote the payoff to the winning daily double bet by $D$ and the payoff to the equivalent parlay by $L$. It is interesting to look at the frequency distributions of the $D$- and $L$-type payoffs in Table 7–5. (For the moment neglect the column labeled "Adjusted $L$.")

In general, it seems that the $L$ figures show some concentrations in the low-payoff range (69 out of 122 have payoffs less than or equal to 30, and only 58 $D$ figures are in that range), whereas the $D$ figures seem to show some concentration in the high ranges (33 payoffs are larger than 70 compared to only 17 $L$ figures in that range). This is confirmed by comparing the average $D$ and average $L$: These are 52.54 and 41.38, respectively. This seems to suggest that it is more profitable to bet on the daily double than on the "equivalent" parlay, thus suggesting the presence of a definite inefficiency.

How sizable is this inefficiency? Notice an interesting distinction: Parlay bettors must pay *two takes* (of 0.1797 on the average) compared to daily double bettors, who pay only one take (of 0.1909 on the average). Let us now adjust all the parlay returns *as if* they were assessed only one take of 0.1909. This is accomplished by multiplying all $L$ numbers by 0.8091 and dividing each by $(0.8203)^2$. The new mean of the adjusted $L$'s is 49.75, much closer to the mean of the $D$ figures, and the frequency distribution of the adjusted $L$'s is rather

Table 7–5   Frequency Distribution of Daily Double and Parlay Payoffs

| Payoff Range | D | L | Adjusted L |
|---|---|---|---|
| 0 to   10.0 | 14 | 19 | 13 |
| 10.1 to   20.0 | 24 | 28 | 28 |
| 20.1 to   30.0 | 20 | 22 | 19 |
| 30.1 to   40.0 | 11 | 11 | 11 |
| 40.1 to   50.0 | 7 | 8 | 9 |
| 50.1 to   60.0 | 11 | 7 | 8 |
| 60.1 to   70.0 | 2 | 10 | 6 |
| 70.1 to   80.0 | 9 | 2 | 8 |
| 80.1 to   90.0 | 2 | 1 | 5 |
| 90.1 to 100.0 | 2 | 1 | 1 |
| 100.1 & greater | 20 | 13 | 14 |
|  | 122 | 122 | 122 |

more similar to that of the $D$'s than was the frequency distribution of unadjusted $L$'s (the number of adjusted $L$'s less than or equal to 30.0 is 60, and the number greater than 70's is 28).[2] This pinpoints the source of the inefficiency: Peter apparently does not take account of the fact that he has to pay more "take" if he makes the two trips to the betting window that the parlay entails. Other than this defect, the payoffs are remarkably similar; as it is, if your choice is between the daily double and the parlay, bet on the former!

As we did with the exacta, we ask whether there is any evidence of "smart money" in daily double betting. For every possible daily double bet, we compute the difference $D - L$ and divide all these differences into two piles: one pile corresponding to the (122) winning pairs and a very much larger pile of $D - L$ numbers for losing pairs. If there are smart money bettors who wish to disguise their actions, they will tend to bet on winning daily doubles pairs, thus reducing the daily double payoffs relative to the parlay payoffs on the winning pairs. This is, again, because the pattern of daily double betting is not displayed by the racetracks in a readily usable form. The most that is usually shown is a series of prospective payoffs—called "will pays" —on the various doubles combinations. This information is extremely difficult to compare with equivalent parlays; moreover, some tracks show the "will pays" only after the first race is completed, at which point it is useless for doubles betting. For this reason, a bettor with superior information could bet the double quite heavily without leaving any "tracks" for others to follow.

What happens is the reverse of what we would expect from extrapolating our exacta findings. Winning daily doubles are underbet as we showed before, but losing daily doubles are *overbet* in comparison with the equivalent parlay. That is to say, the daily double payoff that would have been earned by a losing pair if it had won is much lower than the corresponding parlay would have paid. This is a strange result, particularly in view of the reverse finding for exactas. It may be due to the fact that our sample of daily doubles is much smaller (122 versus 510 exactas) and we are correspondingly less certain of the results. It is also possible that it is much harder to have useful inside information about daily doubles since that, in effect, requires the bettor to have such information about *two* races rather than just one. In any event, we do not find any confirmation of the "smart money" hypothesis in the case of daily doubles; if anything, the reverse is true.

The last question we examine is whether simple strategies exist with which one can make above-average returns on daily doubles. Our most straightforward strategy is this: We use our logit model to predict the likely winners in the two races of each daily double and bet on that combination in every double. The average rate of return from this exercise is $-0.059$, which is much better than the track take (about $-0.19$) but clearly not enough to get rich. Although the sample of daily doubles we have studied is much smaller that the sample of exactas, and we are correspondingly less certain statistically that our results are meaningful, the picture here is broadly consistent with what we have found elsewhere: The "betting market" is far from completely efficient, and there do not seem to be simple strategies that allow one to earn unusually large positive returns.

## A Summing Up

The behavior of exotic betting is quite interesting from the viewpoint of a market analyst. These betting "markets," at least in the two instances we have examined, show some real inefficiency. Such patterns are not surprising, for the exotic bettors have relatively poor information—not about the horses themselves, but about the actions of the betting crowd as a whole. For this reason, unless the inefficiencies are very glaring (and perhaps even then), there are no self-correcting tendencies in the market.

From the standpoint of profit and loss, however, the exotics do not look very promising. The inefficiencies that exist are exploitable only in the sense that one can improve on the average performance of the crowd (equivalent to the track take); but the chances for positive profits are slim, in part because the take is itself higher in exotic than in straight betting. (Indeed, the take in exotic bets involving *more than two horses* at times borders on the scandalous—New York State is currently considering a "pick six" that would permit its race tracks to retain 25 to 36 percent of the betting pools!)[3]

If you must make these kinds of bets, good luck, and have fun! The best we can suggest is to take a real ride and go with *relative* longshot combinations—not the most extreme longshots, but those exacta pairs that include a short-odds and a longer-odds horse. You will, however, need substantial funds, and probably a strong stomach, to pursue this course for long.

# Endnotes

1. Note that there is an approximation in all this, since tickets can be bought only in $2 increments. If the payoff on the first horse were $3.60, you could theoretically buy 1.8 tickets for the second race. If the amount bet originally is large enough, the rounding due to this will not be too serious.
2. As a matter of fact, the difference between the two means is not statistically significant.
3. The exotic take, however, is a bargain relative to many of the analogous parlays or other compound single-horse bets.

*Chapter 8*

# Can You Win at the Racetrack?

We come now to the bottom line. Given the large mass of popular theorizing and academic data analysis extant, can you beat the races? A careful reading of the previous seven chapters will have suggested the answer already, but even so, a summary of where we stand should prove useful.

## Fundamental Analysis: Handicapping

We have discussed at length (especially in Chapter 3) popular approaches to handicapping. By and large, these involve fundamental analysis, an attempt to find the real underlying factors that predict how horses will perform, and more specifically, whether they are likely to win any given race. The answer to the question "Can you make money by handicapping?" is: in principle, yes. That's the good news.

The bad news — and you should be ready for this by now — is that in practice, as opposed to principle, winning money is a very difficult task. In fact, there are only two circumstances under which profitable handicapping is likely to occur. The first is if you are really a first-rate handicapper, one of the elite who simply knows how to pick winners better than most. As we have pointed out, perhaps *ad nauseam*, there is roughly an 18 percent disadvantage to be overcome in order to make money betting the horses (a bit more if your tastes run to the exotic bets). In a certain sense, then, it is necessary to devise a method that earns better than an 18 percent rate of return; you need the 18 percent simply to pay the track take and break even.

Although it is certainly not logically impossible to do this, it is mighty hard to do it consistently. The evidence we presented earlier

(in Chapter 4) on the money-losing propensities of the expert handicappers in the *Daily Racing Form* testifies eloquently to this point.
Furthermore, as we have mentioned, the kind of handicapping advice
that you can buy at the bookstore is, for the most part, not very
specific and therefore cannot be tested carefully. From our point of
view, this is a shortcoming; but we must concede that, for some, it is
also a source of continuing hope. If handicapping advice cannot be
proved successful, neither can failure be persuasively demonstrated.
When old Joe Tout tells you that his book will, for a mere $24.95,
bring you gambling fortune, we don't believe him but we cannot really
prove him a liar.[1]

The second circumstance under which you could turn a profit handicapping is if you have access to inside information. This is also something we have discussed before. It is likely that in quite a few races
there is pertinent information—something that bears on winning
probabilities—that does not find its way into the public record available to the crowd. This might have to do with the physical condition of
a particular horse; upon occasion, it could involve outright hanky-
panky. There is, however, no useful advice to offer here. Inside information is something you either have or you don't, and if you could get
it from time to time, we do not believe that there are enough instances
in which inside information would make a difference.[2]

The only lesson, then, is this: Be alert. If you come across a "hot"
tip, as many of us do upon occasion, (1) it may be wrong; (2) if it's
right and others also know about it, as they well may, it won't help
much. Even those with good information may lose money consistently
(although they ought to do a good deal better than the crowd as a
whole).

## Technical Analysis: Systems

What about systems, the completely (or largely) mechanical formulas
whose solutions tell you how and when, and perhaps how much, to
bet? This, as you know, is a big area of study. In fact, the number of
conceivable betting systems is virtually limitless—perhaps not what a
mathematician would call infinite but larger than anyone could reasonably attempt to test. About all we can do here is to summarize
some of the existing evidence, which comes largely from the academic
literature.

## Betting to Win

Systems of win betting based on market data—that is, odds—are a losing proposition. You will lose more slowly betting favorites than longshots, and heavy favorites are especially good, but lose eventually you will.[3] We cannot rule out the possibility that someone has or will come up with a profitable system of win betting, but the existing evidence argues strongly against this.

## Exotic Betting

Our earlier analysis of daily doubles and exactas (Chapter 7) suggests that there is no market-based strategy that will yield positive returns. We did point out that nonextreme exacta bets—for example, those that pair a short-odds horse with a long-odds horse—look *relatively* good. This may only mean, however, that you will go broke relatively slowly following that route. For suggestions about a more selective approach, see Ziemba and Hausch (1986).

We have not examined exotics that involve more than two horses (trifectas), because the number of combinations that would require analysis is unmanageable. But there is no reason to suspect that these bets offer better profit opportunities than the others. If anything, they may be worse because the track take is typically larger on these types of bets.

## Betting to Place and Show

This is clearly the most interesting area of systems betting that has been revealed to date. There seem to be some pretty substantial inefficiencies in the place and show "markets," and there are at least two approaches to such bets that offer some hope of profits (we'll review them shortly). At the same time, however, the very fact that we (and others) are saying this may encourage some of you to search out these inefficiencies and seek to exploit them, If enough of you do this, both the inefficiencies and the profit possibilities will disappear.

## "Fundamental" Systems

Betting systems, as you know, need not be based on technical analysis of market data (the betting odds). They can be, and often are, based on "fundamentals." For example: Bet any recently claimed horse that is dropping down following a "bad" race, provided that the horse has not picked up weight and has run no more than twice in the past 3 weeks.

This is the area of numberless possible variations. It includes such simplicities as "don't bet horses that sweat a lot," and also embraces the complex computer and calculator programs that we reported on in Chapter 3. (It is not, incidentally, very easy to figure out precisely how the latter systems work; you do, however, know what variables are being considered, and some trial and error may give you a feel for how heavily the different items are weighted.)

We cannot test every conceivable fundamental system (we cannot even think of them all). The existing evidence, however, including our own results with the computer and calculator programs, indicates that most such systems don't work; they may pick a seemingly reasonable proportion of winners, but the bottom line is almost always a negative rate of return. There are a very few systems that do seem to work (we'll mention them again shortly), but even these are subject to familiar *caveats* and should be employed with caution.[4]

At this point, you may feel that we are being overly pessimistic. Perhaps on your visits to the track you have observed some interesting and potentially profitable "regularities." And it may seem that we are trying to discourage you from exploring these empirical patterns and putting them into practice if something useful emerges. Nothing could be further from the truth! Search for "patterns" and use your ingenuity, and you may find relationships that others have missed. But even here, there is one stern warning. *Do not bet heavily on patterns you have discovered until you have tested your theory on new data* (recall our discussion of "out of sample forecasting" in Chapter 5).

You might discover, for example, that whenever the odds on a horse drop by more than a factor of two in the last 2 minutes of betting, the horse is a sure winner *provided that* its jockey wears green and the horse's name has three syllables. This discovery may be based on your careful study of hundreds or thousands of races. We advise, however, that you not risk too much on this finding until you test it on a brand new set of races. The reason is simple: You will always be able to find *some* pattern in a sample of data if you look for one long enough and hard enough. The relevant question is whether the pattern also appears within new data *that were not used to establish the presence of the pattern*. Does your discovery, in other words, have predictive power?

## The Best Available Betting Strategies

After all that has been said, you are on your way to the racetrack. Which betting system gives you the best chance of turning a profit? Our answer to this critical question will be qualified—you should be used to that by now—but here, based on the available evidence, are your three best bets.

### Asch-Malkiel-Quandt

Modesty does not prevent us from mentioning our own approach, which we have told about in detail (Chapter 6). Briefly stated, we suggest that you look primarily at two factors: (1) horses' early or morning line odds and (2) the "marginal" odds implied by betting in the last few minutes before the race goes off. Very roughly, horses with relatively low odds that also attract late money tend to be good *place and show* bets. To follow our methods carefully, however, requires that you utilize our regression equations, which in turn means that you will need a computer or programmed calculator.

Here are the strong and weak points of our approach (you will note, both here and below, that certain characteristics show up as both good *and* bad points, which is not as silly as you might think).

PRO:

1. The approach is legitimate—that is, it actually does work. You needn't take our word for this. We have described things completely and specifically enough for you to try it out yourself.
2. The approach is sufficiently complicated that it may not become popular, in which case it should *continue* to work.

CON:

1. It *is* complicated and therefore not easy to use. You will, in fact, need to invest time, effort, and money—although in very modest amounts—to follow our suggestions.
2. It works best when utilizing final betting odds at the time of the race; but for practical purposes, one must use earlier odds (there simply isn't enough time to see the final odds, do the necessary computations, and then bet).
3. The approach is relatively stodgy. You wind up betting on quite a few short-odds horses to place and show. This does, however, provide some safety (which you may regard as good or bad);

future results are of course uncertain, but you are unlikely to lose money at a rapid clip by following our suggestions.

4. The fact that a betting system works for certain samples of races does not assure that it will continue to work as well for new samples.

## "Dr. Z"

We have also told you about the Dr. Z system, which involves place and show bets on horses that are underbet to place (or show) relative to win—that is, you look for animals that have substantially smaller percentages of the place or show pools than of the win pool. Dr. Z's methods tell you not only which horses to bet on, but how much. The good and bad points of this system are as follows.

PRO:

1. The system works and yields positive rates of return.
2. Though complex, the system is manageable, especially if you buy Dr. Z's module for use in certain programmable calculators (the Hewlett-Packard 41 series).

CON:

1. The Dr. Z system does not recommend bets in most races; thus, to follow the system you must sit out much of the action, which requires some discipline.
2. It is a fairly stodgy system that involves frequent place and show bets on low-odds horses.
3. The system has now been popularized by Ziemba and Hausch's 1984 book, *Beat the Racetrack*. This may reduce or destroy its usefulness, an unhappy event that could show up in two ways: (a) fewer and fewer bets will be recommended by the system; and/or (b) some apparently good system bets will be wiped out by late money. You might, for example, make a place bet with positive expected value a minute or two before a race, only to find that others have done the same thing, driving down the implicit place odds on your horse to the point at which the bet is no longer a good one. As we point out with regard to every recommended betting approach, the fact that a method has worked at particular times and places is not a guarantee that it will continue to do so.

## Quirin's "Fundamental Systems"

William Quirin, in his fine analysis of racetrack data (*Winning at the Races* [1979]), provides a number of computer-generated systems that produce simulated profits when applied to large samples of races. The simpler variety of systems, which he terms "spot plays," requires that you look for horses with particular combinations of qualities in their recent records. When these horses appear, and they tend to appear only occasionally, you bet them to win.

Quirin's more complex systems utilize multiple regression equations that also have turned a profit when applied to samples of several hundred races. These are "optimal" equations in the sense that they did the best job among numerous possibilities. We regard Quirin's work as quite impressive, and you should by now be able to anticipate what we regard as the strong and weak aspects of his approach.

PRO:

1. The systems work, and Quirin has specified what he did in such a way that anyone can follow his methods (you must, however, buy his book to get the relevant instructions!).
2. The multiple regression technique (which we have described before—see Chapter 5) is sufficiently complex that it may never become truly popular; the simpler spot play systems are easier to follow, but since they produce only an occasional recommendation for betting, they may not appeal to bettors who like continual action.

CON:

1. Quirin's regression-based systems *are* complex and time consuming, thus relatively costly to employ.
2. Despite these costs, the increased popularity of microcomputers may mean that Quirin's methods will be followed more widely by others, thereby reducing their value.
3. The fact that a system works for particular samples of races does not necessarily mean it will continue to work for others. (Pardon the repetition, but the warning is an important one.) Quirin himself points this out explicitly, an example of honesty that is all too rare in the handicapping literature.

## Summary of the "Best"

Each of the above approaches to betting offers some hope of a profit. Notice, though, how similar are the advantages and disadvantages of these disparate methods—no mere coincidence. *Complexity* is generally present, as it must be, for simple systems/methods would be quickly destroyed as people get wind of them and try to follow them. This makes the recommended approaches harder to use, both for you (bad) and for others (good).

*Conservatism* (or "stodginess") is also present in each of these betting systems, though in varying degrees. Recall that this is really a consequence of the risk-loving character of the betting crowd. People seem to like high-risk gambles and take them. But in the parimutuel betting market, such behavior drives down the odds on such choices, thereby making them generally unprofitable types of bets. It is not absolutely impossible that one could design a profitable strategy that incurs relatively high risks; but the opportunities are plainly better where the crowd does *not* overbet. This suggests precisely what we have seen: The most successful betting strategies focus on low-risk bets, which is exactly what we mean by "stodgy."

## A Suggestion

We have described what are, on the basis of objective and verifiable facts, the most promising current approaches to racetrack betting. Here is a suggestion that we regard as quite intriguing but one that we have not yet tested systematically: Try betting on the *intersections* of the various approaches—that is those horses that are recommended by *more than one* of the systems discussed above.

For example: The Asch-Malkiel-Quandt (AMQ) approach tells you roughly to look both at the betting odds and at late changes in the odds. Horses that are *not* real longshots and whose odds are *falling* during the last few minutes of the betting period tend to be good place and show bets. The Dr. Z system tells you, again roughly, to look for horses that have a substantially smaller percentage of the place or show pool bet on them than of the win pool—that is, they are *underbet* to place or show relative to win. These horses tend to be good bets in the pool (place or show) in which they are underbet.

Our suggestion is that you identify horses that look like good bets under *both* betting approaches. Find a horse that satisfies Dr. Z's criterion (underbet to place or show), and if it also satisfies our conditions (not a longshot and with late odds falling), back it to place or show.

There is one obvious shortcoming to this suggestion. In most races, no horse will meet the standards of both Dr. Z and AMQ, so the recommended bets will be relatively infrequent—perhaps as few as one or two per day. Our suspicion, however, is that the horses that do satisfy both criteria will, on average, do quite well for you. You will need some ambition and patience to pursue this suggestion, but the resulting rate of return could prove to be very interesting indeed.

# Epilogue

We are just about at the finish line, if you'll pardon a metaphor, so herewith a few final bits of advice and caution. Many people go to the track for fun and profit. By all means do so—but don't count on the profit. Follow our suggested approaches. They will give you the best possible chance to win money and should at the very least enable you to avoid disastrous losses.

If the suggested approaches don't seem to provide enough action, you will no doubt invest more heavily in the longshots and exotics. Fine. You are a free agent, and we wouldn't really presume to tell you where to find your fun. Be aware, however, that by pursuing high-risk bets, you enter an area of high average losses. Fun is costly, which is something economists have known for centuries!

*Payoffs and Taxes.* Gambling income, like your paycheck, is fully taxable. Gambling losses, on the other hand, *cannot* be deducted from "regular" income in calculating tax liability but can be used to offset gambling winnings. In other words, you must pay taxes only on *net* gambling gains.

For most bettors, this poses no problem—they don't have net gains. If you hit some big payoffs, however, beware. The racetrack may take your social security number and report such payoffs to the IRS; and if you receive a payoff of more than $1,000 where the betting odds were 300 to 1 or greater, the track will actually withold 20 percent of your money (in practice, this occurs only in the longer-shot exotic bets). Should you find yourself in this lucky position, it would be a good idea to have a reasonably detailed record of all your gambling winnings and losses. This is especially important if you are going to deduct losses from your big payoffs. Uncle Sam may well ask for verification, and a careful diary showing the dates of your visits to the racetrack and amounts wagered and collected will make life a lot easier (you also may find such records interesting to keep as you try out different betting strategies). Losing tickets, incidentally, are not likely to satisfy your friendly IRS agent—it's too easy to pick up tickets that others have discarded (for obvious reasons, tickets with footprints on them are a real no-no!).

*Fun versus Profit.* As we have just pointed out, the best profit opportunities at racetracks are in the area of low-risk gambles, that is, high-probability–low-payoff bets. The most profitable strategies tend to be rather conservative, even stodgy, whereas the most exciting may lose you a bundle in a hurry. Our advice, as you know, is to go against the crowd and improve your rate of return. We regard the risk-loving behavior of bettors as an opportunity to be exploited, but if this doesn't fit your idea of a good time, we are not about to convince you otherwise.

*A cautionary note (yet again).* Picking winners isn't enough. If you still don't believe this, we remind you that we have devised a few show-betting strategies (see Chapter 6) that will enable you to cash two out of every three tickets you buy; these strategies do *not* consistently show a profit (although they do beat the typical bettor's rate of return by a wide margin). What you must do to make money is, with some consistency, to pick winners that are *undervalued by the crowd.* You must, in other words, bet on horses whose objective chances of winning are *greater* than the subjective probabilities assigned by the betting public. This is truly the name of the game.

*A cautionary note (one more time).* Betting systems work only if "no one" uses them. This is not literally true, but it's close enough. Some extremely clever handicapping methods and betting strategies have been devised over the years. Indeed, lots of bright people have devoted a great deal of time to such efforts, with occasionally impressive results. None of these will work—that is, yield a positive rate of return—if many people use them. Profitable systems cannot be popular. Popular systems are sure losers. Beware of all purveyors of such, including us!

*A few last words.* Most racetrack bettors lose consistently. Are there winning methods and systems? Yes (probably). Some of these may result from inside information, which does most of us no good at all. Others may result from intelligent analysis, either of fundamental factors or market data. The value of these systems is in most instances likely to be transitory, lasting only until they become visible to others— at which point new systems must be developed. It is true that if a successful betting strategy is complex and not obvious, it may take a while for even a relatively efficient market to "catch up" with it. Nevertheless, it is unlikely that becoming wedded to any particular betting method or system—even a "very good" one—will remain forever profitable.

Forewarned is forearmed.

## Endnotes

1. Actually, we probably could do so, but the effect required would be disproportionate to the value of the demonstration.
2. This raises the whole issue of what *is* valuable inside information. Is it truly valuable to know that a horse has just recovered from equine dysentry? Probably yes. Is it valuable to know that the trainer's or jockey's wife (husband) left him (her) a week ago? We suspect not, but others might disagree.
3. There is, in fact, some evidence that extreme favorites—horses that go off at odds of 3 to 10 or lower—are profitable bets on average. Such bets, however, come along so infrequently that you could grow old waiting for them.
4. For some interesting suggestions that are best put to use with the aid of a microcomputer, see Mitchell (1984).

# GLOSSARY OF TERMS

**bid, ... hung.** A racing pattern in which a horse first improves its position, passing other horses and moving closer to the leader ("bid"), but then fails to improve further in the last part of the race ("hung").

**breakage.** The rounding down of track payoffs, usually to the nearest $0.10 or $0.20 on a $2 bet.

**claiming race.** A race in which the entered horses may be bought ("claimed") at a specified price (the "claiming price").

**class.** A term used in two distinct senses: (1) the quality of a race, usually measured by the size of the purse; (2) the quality of a horse; appropriate measurement is a matter of controversy.

**daily double.** A bet in which the winners of two consecutive races are specified; a type of exotic bet.

**Daily Racing Form.** A newspaper sold at all thoroughbred race tracks and many news stands that contains detailed information about the past performances of all horses entered at various tracks. Sometimes known as the racetrack bettor's bible.

**entry.** Two horses coupled in a race in the sense that a bet on the entry to win (place, show) is successful if either horse wins (places, shows).

**exacta.** A bet in which the first and second finishers in a race are specified in order; a type of exotic bet.

**exotic bet.** A "compound" bet on two or more horses. *See* daily double, exacta, quinella, trifecta.

**expected value.** As applied to risky situations, the sum of the value of each possible outcome multiplied by the probability of its occurrence. The expected value of a win ticket is thus: The payoff if the horse wins times the probability that it will win; plus the loss (i.e., the amount bet) if it loses—a *negative* number—times the probability that it will lose. If a particular risk is undertaken many times, the average outcome or return to that risk will tend toward its expected value.

**fast track.** A dry, hard racing surface, conducive to fast racing.

**furlong.** One eighth of a mile.

**handicap.** A category of race in which weights are assigned to the entered horses in order to equalize their winning chances.

**jockey.** A horse's rider.

**length.** A horse's body length. Used to describe how far behind or ahead are the contestants in a race.

**maiden.** A horse that has never won a race.

**maiden race.** A race confined to maidens.

**morning line odds.** A handicapper's estimate of the probable odds on the entrants in a race.

**mudder.** A horse that runs well on poor or muddy tracks.

**odds** (or betting odds). A statement of the payoff ratio to a particular bet. Odds of 3 to 1, for example, would imply that each dollar bet will retrieve $3 if the bet wins. In addition, the bettor's initial "investment" is returned; thus a $2 bet at 3 to 1 odds will receive $8 if successful—the $6 indicated by the odds plus the original wager.

**overlay.** A horse whose objective winning probability is sufficiently under-estimated by the betting crowd so that it has positive expected value; a "good" bet. (Sometimes defined as the opposite of an underlay, that is, a horse that goes off at higher odds than the early or morning line.)

**payoff.** The dollar amount returned to a successful bet.

**place bet.** A bet that a horse will finish first or second.

**place pool.** The amount of money bet to place on all horses in a given race.

**purse.** The prize money in a race; the purse is usually divided (unequally) among the owners of the first four finishing horses.

**quinella.** A bet on the first two finishers in a race, with order not specified; a type of exotic bet.

**show bet.** A bet that a horse will finish first, second, or third.

**show pool.** The amount of money bet on all horses to show in a given race.

**speed rating.** An index of a horse's speed in a given race. The track record for the distance of the race is assigned a value of 100, and 1 is subtracted from 100 for each fifth of a second by which the horse's running time falls short of the record. A speed rating of 90 thus indicates that the horse ran the race in a time two seconds (10 fifths of a second) slower than the record.

**stretch** (or **homestretch**). The last part of a race; usually the last furlong.

**system.** A largely or purely mechanical method of selecting horses to bet; a "formula" method.

**time.**   Usually refers to the time in which a horse runs a race.

**track take.**   The amount that the track subtracts from a betting pool to cover taxes and other expenses, including profit. Usually expressed as a percentage, track takes in the United States currently average a bit over 18 percent of win, place, and show pools; and a bit over 22 percent of exotic bet pools.

**track variant.**   An index of the average speed of winning horses on a given day (or night) of racing. One point is added for each fifth of a second by which the winning times fall short of the track records. A track variant of 15 thus indicates that the winning horses ran, on average, three seconds (15 fifths of a second) slower than the track records on the day in question.

**trifecta** (or **triple** or **triactor**).   A bet on the first three finishers in a race, with order specified.

**underlay.**   A horse whose odds fall during the betting period, so that its final odds are less than its early or morning line odds.

**weight.**   The weight carried by a horse in a race; consists of the weight of the jockey, equipment, and any "dead weight" added for handicapping purposes.

**win bet.**   A bet that a particular horse will win a race.

**win pool.**   The total amount bet to win on all horses in a race.

**workouts.**   Usually refers to the running times of a horse's practice runs (the runs themselves are "workouts").

# REFERENCES

## I. POPULAR

Ainslie, Tom, *Ainslie's Complete Guide to Harness Racing* (New York: Simon & Schuster, 1970).

Ainslie, Tom, *Ainslie's Complete Guide to Thoroughbred Racing* (New York: Simon & Schuster, 1979).

Bauman, William, *Smart Handicapping Made Easy* (Secaucus, N.J.: Citadel Press, 1960, 1972).

Bernstein, Aaron, *Beating the Harness Races* (New York: Arco, 1976).

Beyer, Andrew, *Picking Winners* (Boston: Houghton Mifflin, 1975).

Beyer, Andrew, *My $50,000 Year at the Races* (New York: Harcourt Brace Jovanovich, 1978).

Beyer, Andrew, *The Winning Horseplayer* (Boston: Houghton Mifflin, 1983).

Bolus, Jim, *The Insider's Pocket Guide to Horse Racing* (Dallas: Taylor Publishing Co., 1990).

Christopher, David L., *Winning at the Track* (Cockeysville, MD: Liberty Publishing Co., 1987).

Cohen, Ira S., and George D. Stephens, *Scientific Handicapping* (Englewood Cliffs, N.J.: Prentice-Hall, 1963).

Conklin, Les, *Betting Hor$e$ to Win* (Secaucus, N.J.: Citadel Press, 1954).

Da Silva, E.R., and Roy M. Dorcus, *Science in Betting* (Garden City, N.Y.: Doubleday, 1961).

Davidowitz, Steven, *Betting Thoroughbreds* (New York: E.P. Dutton, 1977, 1983).

Fabricand, Burton P., *Horse Sense* (New York: McKay, 1965).

Fabricand, Burton P., *The Science of Winning* (New York: Whitlock Press, 1979).

Feldman, David, *Woulda, Coulda, Shoulda: Handicapping tips for anyone who ever bet on a horse race or wanted to* (Chicago: Bonus Books, 1989).

Illich, Albert George, *Al Illich's How to Pick Winners* (New York: Arco, 1971, 1983).

Mitchell, Dick, *Winning Thoroughbred Strategies* (New York: Morrow, 1989).

Olmsted, Bill, *The Thoroughbred Speculator's Best and Worst Product Guide* (Edgewater, MD: TBS Publishing, 1991).

Perlmutter, Nate, *How to Win Money at the Races* (New York: Collier, 1964).

Quinn, James, *The Best of Thoroughbred Handicapping* (New York: Casino Press, 1984).

Quirin, William L., *Winning at the Races: Computer Discoveries in Thoroughbred Handicapping* (New York: Morrow, 1979).

Silberstang, Edwin, *How to Gamble and Win* (New York: Simon & Schuster, 1979, 1981).

Scarne, John, *Scarne's New Complete Guide to Gambling* (New York: Simon & Schuster, 1974).

Ziemba, William T., and Donald B. Hausch, *Beat the Racetrack* (New York: Harcourt Brace Jovanovich, 1984).

Ziemba, William T., and Donald B. Hausch, *Betting at the Racetrack* (New York: Norris M. Strauss, 1986).

## II. ACADEMIC

Ali, M., "Probability and Utility Estimates for Racetrack Betting," *Journal of Political Economy*, 85 (1977): 803–815.

Asch, P., B.G. Malkiel, R.E. Quandt, "Market Efficiency in Racetrack Betting," *Journal of Business*, 57 (1984): 165–175.

_____, "Racetrack Betting and Informed Behavior," *Journal of Financial Economics*, 10 (1982): 187–194.

Gruen, Arthur, "An Inquiry into the Economics of Race-Track Betting," *Journal of Political Economy*, 84 (February 1976): 169–177.

Harville, D.A., "Assigning Probabilities to the Outcomes of Multi-Entry Competitions," *Journal of the American Statistical Association*, 68 (1973): 312–316.

Hausch, Donald B., and William T. Ziemba, "Transactions Costs, Extent of Inefficiencies, Entries, and Multiple Wagers in a Racetrack Betting Model," *Management Science*, 31 (April 1985): 381–394.

Hausch, D.B., W.T. Ziemba, and M. Rubinstein, "Efficiency of the Market for Racetrack Betting," *Management Science*, 27 (1981): 1435–1452.

Henery, R.J., "An Extreme-Value Model for Predicting the Results of Horse Races," *Applied Statistics*, 33 (1984): 125–133.

Hoerl, A.E., and H.K. Fallin, "Reliability of Subjective Evaluations in a High Incentive Situation," *Journal of the Royal Statistical Society*, Series A, 137 Part 2, (1974): 227–230.

McCulloch, B., and T. van Zijl, "A Direct Test of a Multientry Competitions Probability Model," Victoria University, Wellington, 1984.

McGlothlin, W.H., "Stability of Choices Among Uncertain Alternatives," *American Journal of Psychology*, 69 (1956): 604–615.

Mitzak, O., I. Kusyszyn, and M.M. Starr, "The Development of a Computer Method for Detecting Profitable Smart Money Harness Horses," paper presented at the 5th National Conference on Gambling and Risk Taking, South Lake Tahoe, Nevada, October 1981.

Quandt, R.E., "Betting and Equilibrium," *Quarterly Journal of Economics*, CI (1986), 201–207.

Snyder, W.W., "Horse Racing: Testing the Efficient Markets Model," *Journal of Finance*, 33 (1978): 1109–1118.

Starr, M.W., and S.H. Kleinman, "The Under/Over Bettor Bias: An Artifact of Subjective Probability Estimation," paper presented at the 6th National Conference on Gambling and Risk Taking, Atlantic City, N.J., December 1984.

Suits, Daniel B., "The Elasticity of Demand for Gambling," *Quarterly Journal of Economics*, 93 (February 1979): 155–162.

Tversky, A., and D. Kahneman, "Judgment Under Uncertainty: Heuristics and Biases," *Science* 185 (1974): 1124–1131.

Ziemba, W.T., and D.B. Hausch, *Beat the Racetrack* (New York: Hartcourt Brace Jovanovich, 1984).

# INDEX